Dear Paula,
I hope this brings you the best of luck and fortune.
Enjoy,
[illegible]

P.S. I look forward to our continued partnerships and friendship.

FENG SHUI FOR BETTER LIVING

Published by
Mervera Publications, Inc.
3rd floor, Maripola Bldg., 109 Perea St.,
Legaspi Village, Makati City, 1200 Philippines.
P.O. Box 9249 MCS Mailing Centre
Makati City, 1231 Philippines.

Tel: (632) 8124743 & 8134703 fax: (632) 8934793
ISBN: 971-8932-003

Printed in the Philippines.
First edition printed in October, 1993
Second printing (second edition) in October, 1994
Third printing (in Malaysia) November, 1995
Fourth printing in October, 1997
Fith printing (third edition) printed in January, 1999
Sixth printing in August, 2000

FENG SHUI FOR BETTER LIVING

Third Edition

Merlina Merton

About the Author

The author, who is professionally known as Merlina Merton, has a lifetime background in metaphysical studies. Apart from conducting lectures and seminars on *feng shui,* she also writes and lectures on *hermetic science, tantric yoga,* and *hand analysis with chirotherapy.*

When she began her professional practice in the Philippines, it lead to the co-founding of the country's first, registered *feng shui* consultancy company. She is now the president of three thriving corporations *Better Living Feng Shui Services, Inc. Mervera Publications,Inc. and Feng Shui World Inc.*

Merlina writes columns and articles about *feng shui* and related topics for leading newspapers and magazines. Her writings, seminars, lectures and numerous T.V. appearances have undoubtedly made a major contribution, not only to the popularity enjoyed by *feng shui* and its practitioners today, but also to the public acceptance of *feng shui* as a valid means to the attainment of a better life.

This book is an expession of the author's desire to provide an easy-to-understand *feng shui* primer and reliable reference manual, so that everyone will be able to enjoy the benefits of good *feng shui* in the home. These benefits include:

*a more positive mental attitude; *clearer decision making;
*better health; * improved concentration and performance;
*increased earning capacity; *happier personal relationships; and,
*harmony within the family.

Acknowledgements

This book is the culmination of my efforts to heighten public awareness of the art of *feng shui*. Its contents are culled from my columns, lectures, T.V. and radio interviews. I am indebted to my editors and other friends in media for their encouragement and support.

A big thankyou to Thelma San Juan, former lifestyle editor of *'The Manila Chronicle'*, for inviting me to write the first *feng shui* column in the Philippines for that publication

My gratitude goes to Jullie Yap Daza who invited me, on so many occasions, to guest on her popular T.V. talk shows '*Tell the People*' and ''*Jullie*' and to write a *feng shui* column for the magazine *'Lifestyle Asia'*.

My thanks to Marita Nuque of *'Astroscope'* magazine, for whom I wrote the column *'Orientations'*; to Feli Tan of *'Business World'*; Pinky Colmenares of *'Manila Bulletin'*; Lita Logarta of *'Philippine Daily Inquirer'*; Winsome Lane of *'Hong Kong Standard'* and the other 'ladies of the press' who published my articles or wrote about me and my work. To Johnny Litton for the invitations to guest on his T.V.show, *'Oh No,It's Johnny!* and to all the other hosts who were kind enough to to invite me to guest on their T.V. and radio shows. To Maria Ressa and Rene Santiago of *CNN.*, and to Tatsuyuki Takaoka and Henry Sacramento of *Nippon T.V.* for their features.

It is interesting to note that, with the exception of a few males, all the media people who helped me make the public aware of the natural science and art of *feng shui* were female. This is not just coincidental as, according to *feng shui* computations, we are now in the 'seventh cycle' which is a twenty-year period begining in 1984 and ending in the year 2003. The seventh cycle represents female energy, the lungs, the West and finance. In this cycle, female energy not only makes its presence felt in media, but also in politics, business, banking and sexual issues.

All this aside, there is still one male that I would like to acknowledge for his tireless research and our endless hours of productive debate and shared insights: I refer to my colleague and former associate, Victor Dy.

My appreciation also goes to the institutions, organizations, universities, clubs, associations, national and multi-national companies, banking and financial institutions, medical associations, real estate and architects' associations, and to the many Rotary clubs and women's groups for their kind invitations to speak at their meetings and special events. These invitations provided me with the opportunity to acquaint the professional, corporate and academic communities, as well as the general public, with the concept of *feng shui* as a means of environmental management and enhancement. It also afforded me the opportunity to dispel the misconception, held by many, that *feng shui* is some oblique Chinese, quasi-religious, superstitious practise.

My thanks also go to our clients and to the participants of our seminars for their appreciation of our services and their support in our aim to propagate *feng shui* as a national as well as a personal asset.

I wish to thank my staff, past and present, for the initial typing of the text and the illustrations in this book. My gratitude also goes to Jason Dy for the beautiful animal drawings, to Jose Icabandi for the initial layout, and to Victoria Ortigas for the proofreading and compilation of the index.

And lastly, a special thank you to *Feng Shui Master* George K.C. Lau for his advice and encouragement.

Preface

What is Feng Shui? What can it do for you?

Feng shui or *Chinese geomancy* is presently enjoying a surge of interest in the Western world. Books, magazines and newspaper articles have been written in English and other European languages extolling the virtues of this ancient art. Yet, despite all the information now available, *feng shui* is still a mystery to most Westerners, and many Chinese are only vaguely familiar with its concepts and practical applications.

Feng shui has been described as 'the art of living in harmony with nature'– this is an apt but inadequate description of this natural science. The study of *feng shui* not only gives you an understanding of the laws and processes of nature, it also provides a methodology that enables you to position yourself so as to take advantage of the beneficial energy around you, and to adjust your surroundings to eliminate or disperse negative or injurious energy – I call this '*environmental management.*'

You will find in the chapters of this book many ways to 'manage' the environment of your own home. You will learn how to create the balanced and harmonious energy of *good feng shui* through spatial arrangements, the use of lighting, colour, plants, and simple analysis of directional influences. With *good feng shui* in your home, you and your family can prosper in health, peace and harmony.

Feng Shui and Environmental Restoration

When literally translated, *feng shui* means 'wind and water' and even though the study of this life-enhancing natural science takes us far beyond this literal interpretation, at the basic level, these two elements are essential to the maintenance of life as we know it. Nature has provided us with everything we need to live comfortably on our beautiful planet. When we follow natural laws, we can make a good life for ourselves and our families. When instead, we prefer to conquer nature, the result is the deterioration of our environment, and with it our health, our future, and the future of our children.

Enough sunlight and fresh air, a clean and adequate water supply and good drainage are the basic requirements of *good feng shui*. The pollution of our air by vehicular and industrial gases, and the befouling of our water with industrial and human wastes are destroying the *feng shui* of our cities. There are many environmental groups working on this problem and they deserve our support.

We can also help individually by caring for the environment of our own home and workplace. When we become conscious of *feng shui* principles and learn how to apply them to our personal space, we not only improve our own lives, we also contribute to the collective environmental restoration.

Feng Shui and the Western Mind

People with a Western education and upbringing may find it difficult to reconcile some of the information in this book with their training and their thought processes. The Western mind likes to ask "Why is this so?" and "How does it work?" It is not enough to know that if 'this' is done, 'that' will be the result. The Western mind says, "I want to know how this phenomenon occurs before I can accept its validity." Because of this kind of thinking, many people in the West lose the chance to benefit from the arts and natural sciences of the East.

The Eastern mind has an entirely different approach. It is not so concerned with 'how' and with 'why,' it says; "If I can see that 'this' (cause) consistently results in 'that' (effect) I will accept my observation as valid and will use this knowledge to my advantage." *Feng shui*, acupuncture and Chinese medicine are some of the natural sciences that evolved from thousands of years of observing the processes or laws of nature. The Chinese have successfully applied these laws to every human condition and endeavour.

In the following chapters I have attempted to explain *feng shui* in a way that can be appreciated by the western mind, especially when it comes to the psychological correspondences of certain spatial arrangements. I have also touched on the metaphysical aspects of *feng shui.*

This book contains valuable information, not only for homemakers, but also for builders, property developers, real estate brokers and investors. The advice given here is based on the '*form school*' of *feng shui* and certain aspects of the '*compass school*' as these methods can be safely and easily applied by the layman. The technical and professional methods will be addressed in a forthcoming book on office, commercial and industrial *feng shui*.

TABLE OF CONTENTS

Part One

Background and Principles of Feng Shui

CHAPTER ONE

FENG SHUI – PAST AND PRESENT

Ancient and Modern Feng Shui
National Feng Shui
Government Buildings
Urban Feng Shui
The Feng Shui of Hong Kong

ANCIENT FENG SHUI

The practice of *feng shui* began more than three thousand years ago in China. It was intended to ensure that the Emperor (who was Heaven's representative on Earth) would be well-located and protected, particularly when he performed the rituals that were meant to enhance the well-being of the nation. The terrain, the seasons, the directional aspects and the celestial constellations were studied, so that their good influences could be harnessed by the positioning and layout of the palace buildings. The Emperor's tomb was also located and constructed so that his spirit could impart the 'blessings of Heaven' to his descendants.

In ancient China, scholars received large stipends from the palace so they could spend their time studying the intricate laws of nature and learning how to apply these laws to improve the fate of the Emperor and his court. This '*royal feng shui*' eventually filtered down to the Mandarins and landowners, and ultimately to the entire Chinese nation.

Feng shui masters instructed the people how to maximize the potential of their land without abusing it, and how to build their houses so as to benefit from the topographic and geodetic features of the terrain.

An intricate calendar/almanac was used to guide the people when to plant, when to reap, when to build, when to tear down, when to marry and when to be buried. Everyone in those days knew what to do and when to do it so that the laws of nature would not be violated.

Today, this knowledge is still available to us through books on *feng shui*, the advice of practicing *feng shui consultants*, and the *Tong Shu* (Chinese Almanac). The *Tong Shu* (*Tong Sing)* could well be the world's most popular book. It is published in several versions, of which more than one million copies are sold annually in Hong Kong alone.

MODERN FENG SHUI

The principles of *feng shui* have remained unchanged since their inception, but have been adapted to meet the needs of modern architecture. They are now being successfully applied, not only to homes, but also to high-rise buildings with controlled internal environment systems (centralized air-conditioning and/or heating), elevators, escalators, sophisticated electrical and plumbing layouts.

The application of these principles is not restricted by the size or type of project, be it national, urban or personal.

NATIONAL FENG SHUI

On a national scale, *feng shui* principles should be applied in the location and orientation of new cities, towns, or large government projects, such as: dams; power generating plants; defense installations; national highways; bridges and others. The locations of these projects are bound by engineering constraints, political interests, national security, etc., but, working within that framework, the application of *feng shui* concepts can minimize problems during the construction period, and maximize the success of the project when it is operational.

GOVERNMENT BUILDINGS

The performance of government officials is affected by the location, orientation and design of the buildings in which they hold office.

A well-located building with *good feng shui,* provides the envigorating and balanced energy that can enhance the officials' capacity to perform their duties with maximum efficiency, confidence and decisiveness. Good top-level decision making, and effective implementation of those decisions down the line, lead to a peaceful and prosperous citizenry.

URBAN FENG SHUI

Zoning is of major importance when assessing and planning the layout of a city. Industrial, commercial, residential and government sectors should be located in areas where the natural terrain has *feng shui* aspects suited to their specific, as well as their integrated functions.

Air and seaports are the doors or 'mouths' of a city. They bring in sustenance in the form of trade, commerce, goods and people. Roads, railways, rivers, canals, etc. are the 'arteries' and 'veins' that distribute this sustenance or 'life's blood' throughout the city. Consequently, traffic flow is given special consideration in '*urban feng shui.*'

When *feng shui consultants* (*geomancers*) and urban planners cooperate on a project they often arrive at the same conclusions, as both consider the terrain, exposure to natural light, ventilation, water availability, drainage, orientation, topography, and the engineering feasibility of the project. Both aim to build a stable, functional, and expandable city, but, the geomancer's assessment gives prominence to those aspects that foster good health and good fortune.

Urban energy fields:

A city creates around itself an *energy field.* An active high-rise city such as New York, generates energy that stretches for miles beyond the city limits. In any place where people converge, there is a field of energy that is both horizontal and vertical, the strongest force being where there are densely populated high-rise residential and commercial areas.

Roads, railways, rivers and canals have a sharp penetrating action that divides or sectionalizes the city by cutting through its *energy field.* Elevated highways, flyovers and railways also cut through the field, but on a higher level. Buildings that are adjacent or close to a flyover are often adversely affected by this cutting action.

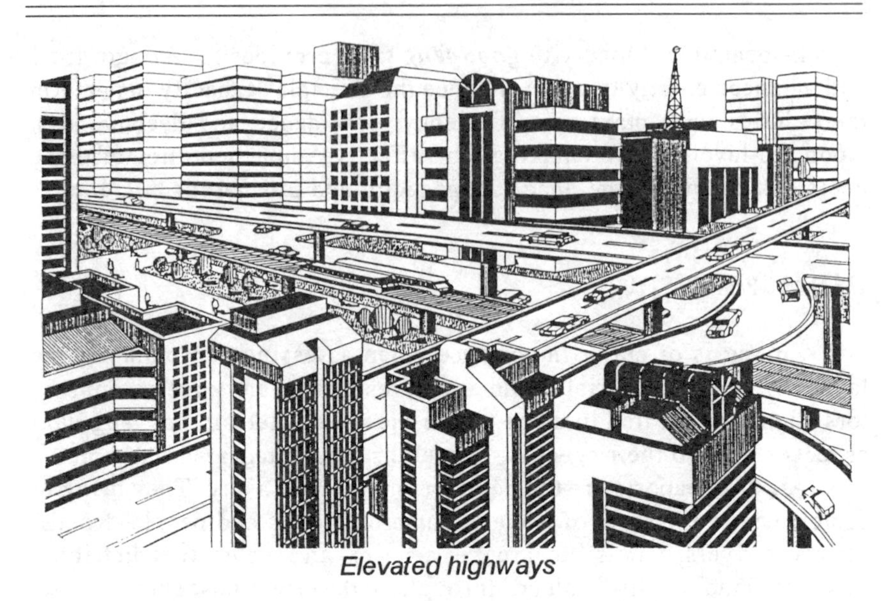

Elevated highways

Whenever an elevated road or rail system is built, there is a change in the *feng shui* of the area and many of the buildings that are 'cut' have to adjust their entrances and use '*defensive feng shui*' techniques.

The many ways that the city's environment affects the health and performance of its citizens is only beginning to be understood in the West. The Chinese have been using the natural science of *feng shui* to manage the environmental impact on their lives for thousands of years. The principles of *feng shui* have been proven again and again over this long history. If these principles are deeply understood and applied with skill, there is always a good result.

A city that enjoys the benefits of *good feng shui,* co-ordinated with modern technology, will undoubtedly prosper. A prime example is the city of Hong Kong, prospering regardless of its political uncertainties.

THE FENG SHUI OF HONG KONG

The city of Hong Kong is generally well laidout. The natural terrain of the main island has two basic conditions of *good feng shui*, i.e., high ground at the rear, and a clear view or a body of water in front.

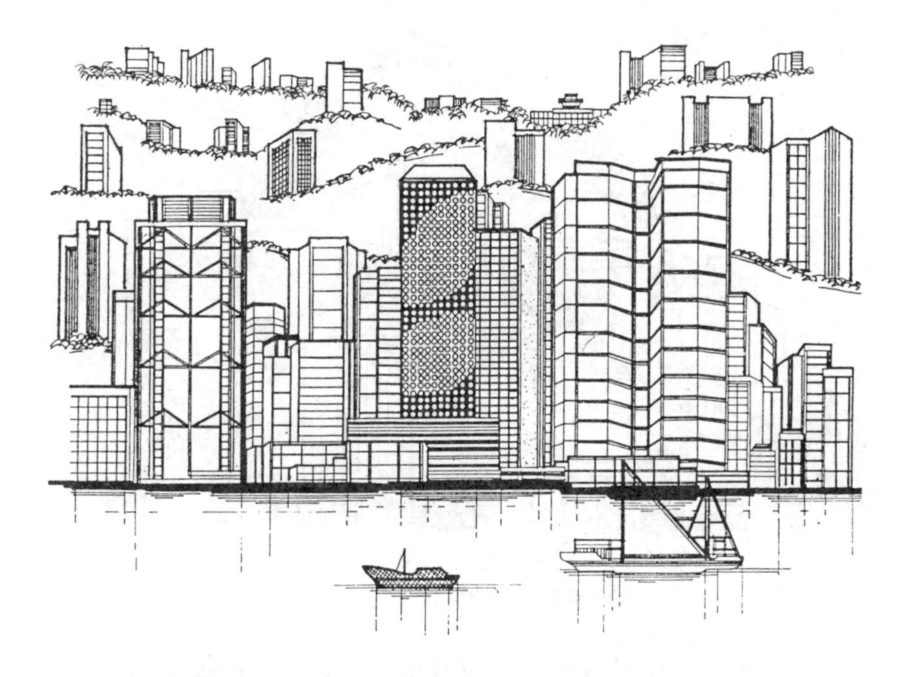

Hong Kong

Hong Kong's famous 'Central' financial district has mountains behind it, and the beautiful Hong Kong harbour providing an unobstructed view in front. These topographical conditions give confidence and inspiration to the business community.

The decision makers of Hong Kong's executive world live halfway up the mountainside, aptly named 'Mid Levels.' This is ideal *feng shui* as they have higher ground behind them and they overlook most of the city, including the harbour.

Contrary to popular belief, it is not considered fortunate to live on the highest point of a mountain or hill, because of over-exposure to wind and storms – a site that is too windy does not accumulate *chi* (energy). A hilltop home also does not have higher ground, in any direction, to give it 'backing.' The occupants need to be financially substantial, physically fit and emotionally stable to be unaffected by such total exposure.

Living on the top of a mountain

'The Peak', an elite district of Hong Kong, is a prime example of mountain-top living. Needless to say, it is home only to the rich and powerful, most of whom are British expatriates who return to the United Kingdom after a few years. Some, not entirely unscathed by their 'Peak' experience.

CHAPTER TWO

PRINCIPLES OF FENG SHUI

Yin and Yang: The Law of Polarity
Chi – The Life Force
The Five Elements
Creative and Destructive Cycles

YIN AND YANG: THE LAW OF POLARITY

The sub-atomic particles that compose the visible and invisible life of this universe are without form, they are simply energy particles or waves moving at tremendous speed. These particles/waves form the myriad things we experience as real – *On the sub-atomic level, the only reality is energy*.

The ancient Chinese sages knew this truth thousands of years ago. They studied nature's processes and, through their observations, realized that in order for life to manifest there must be two poles of energy – positive and negative. They named these poles '*yin*' and '*yang*,' *yin* being magnetic, *yang* being electric; *yin* being darkness, *yang* being light; *yin* yielding, *yang* firm; *yin* female, *yang* male. The interaction of *yin* and *yang* provides the energy of life or '*chi*.' The understanding of *chi* is the cornerstone of all Chinese esoteric teachings.

CHI – THE LIFE FORCE

In China the intrinsic energy is called '*chi*.' Other cultures have named it 'life force,' 'cosmic breath' or '*prana*.' *Chi* can be strong or weak, beneficial or harmful; it pervades all things in the universe.

YIN ATTRIBUTES	YANG ATTRIBUTES
DARK	LIGHT
MOON	SUN
COLD	HOT
NIGHT	DAY
WATER	FIRE
FEMALE	MALE
NEGATIVE	POSITIVE
MAGNETIC	ELECTRIC

The symbol of yin and yang

When we grasp the concept of *chi,* we become aware of the subtle energy within and around us. The *chi* of the house we live in; the *chi* of the people we interact with; the *chi* of the food we eat and the air we breath influences our health, our mental attitudes, our personal relationships and our fortune.

TERRESTRIAL CHI

Geomancers see the Earth as a living entity. *Chi* runs beneath the ground in lines of force that are similar to the human nervous system, or more appropriately, to the Chinese system of *meridians* (energy channels) within the human body. Just as the Chinese doctor reads the *chi* of a patient through his pulse, and examines the external features of his body to discover his condition, so too, the *geomancer* reads the *chi* of a site, and examines its features to determine the *feng shui* of the terrain. The Chinese doctor has cures that can restore the balance of *chi* in his patient. The *geomancer*, who is considered a 'Doctor of the Earth,' likewise has cures that can balance the *chi* of a site.

CELESTIAL CHI

Geomancers study the planets, their correspondences with the *five elements,* and other astrological aspects, to assess the heavenly influences that affect the Earth. Beneficial *chi* from the Earth combined with benign aspects from Heaven create excellent *feng shui*.

Some geomancers use the *'moving star'* method of calculation to know the past, present and future potential of a property and its effects on the occupants. *Energy grids* are made, based on the orientation of the site and the time cycles. We call these calculations *'charting the chi.'*

The 'moving star' a.k.a. 'flying star' method of feng shui is an advanced form of geomancy that will be explained in a future book.

THE FIVE ELEMENTS

All Chinese esoteric teachings, such as traditional Chinese medicine, *feng shui* and martial arts, use the principles of *yin* and *yang* and the *five elements*. The *elements* could more aptly be described as the 'five qualities or functions of *chi*,' they correspond to the frequencies of *metal*, *water*, *wood*, *fire* and *earth*.

During the year the *elements* wax and wane with the seasons, following a pattern of growth and depletion in a continuous cycle. *Yin* reaches its apex in winter, which is cold, dark and damp. *Yang* reaches its apex in summer, which is hot, bright and dry.

CREATIVE AND DESTRUCTIVE CYCLES OF THE ELEMENTS

Nature could be described as '*the continuing process of change that perpetuates life in all its forms*.' The tides of nature ebb and flow in a rythmic, biological dance. Nothing ever really dies, or is ever lost, it just undergoes a process of integration and disintegration – the natural law of change.

The *elements*, which are intrinsic to all creation, follow nature's law. They act as agents of change by constantly creating and destroying each other in a balanced and continuous cycle. When this cycle is disturbed or becomes imbalanced, the results are disease, pain, misfortune, and premature death (disintegration).

The principle of the creative and destructive cycles of the *elements* is used by Chinese doctors in curing their patients. It is also employed by *geomancers* to balance the *chi* of a property and to affect *'feng shui cures*,' some of which are given in this book.

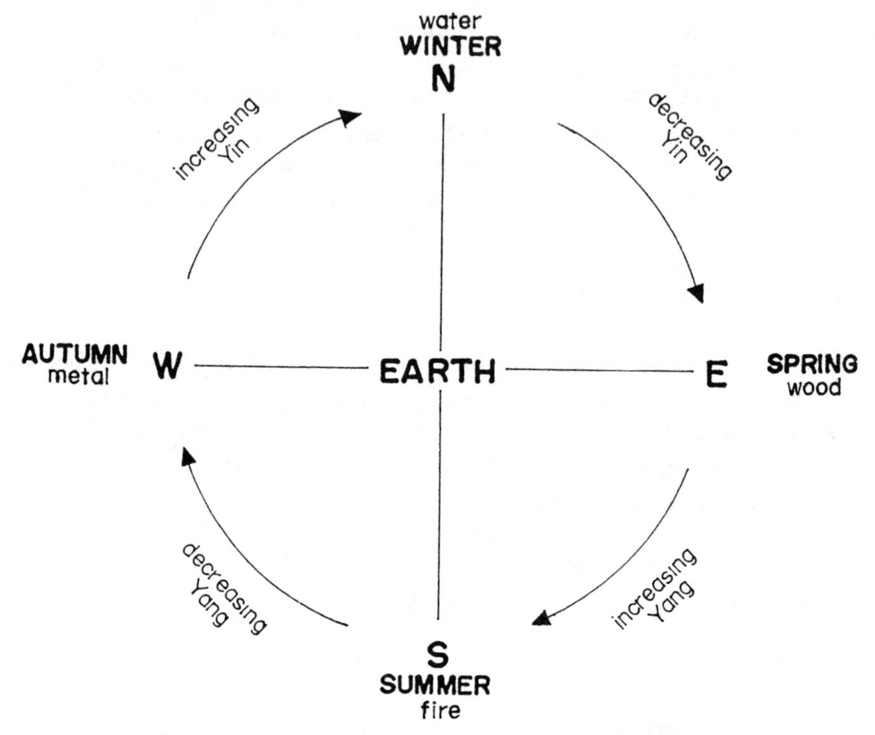

The seasonal waxing and waning of yin and yang

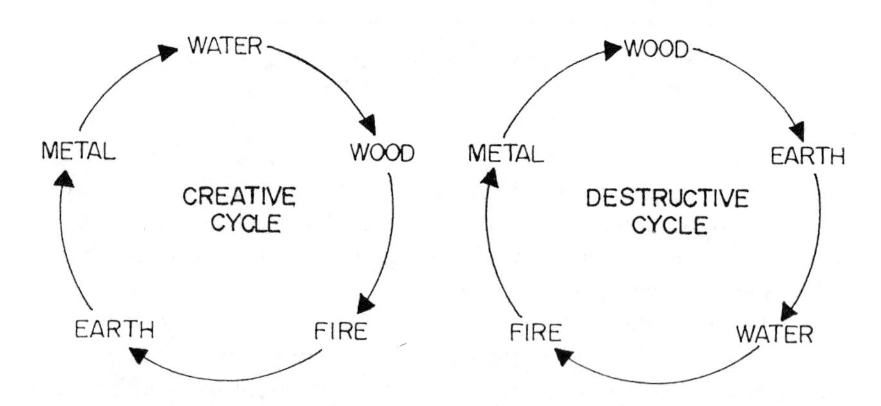

The creative & destructive cycles of the elements

THE CREATIVE CYCLE OF THE ELEMENTS:

Earth creates *metal* – earth provides the substance of metal.
Metal creates *water* – metal can be liquified.
Water creates *wood* – water is required to nurture wood/vegetation.
Wood creates *fire* – wood provides fuel for fire.
Fire creates *earth* – the ashes of fire is the primal substance of earth.

THE DESTRUCTIVE CYCLE OF THE ELEMENTS:

Wood destroys *earth* – by depleting it and covering it.
Earth destroys *water* – by blocking its flow and absorbing it.
Water destroys *fire* – by putting it out.
Fire destroys *metal* – by melting it.
Metal destroys *wood* – by chopping it.

CHAPTER THREE

THE BA-GUA

The Latter-Day Ba-gua

The Primordial Ba-gua

The Elements and Their Corresponding Colours

THE LATTER-DAY BA-GUA

The *latter-day (later-heaven) ba-gua* is the *geomancer's* guide in analyzing a property. Each of its eight sectors (*guas*) occupies 45 degrees of the compass and has the following correspondences.

a) one of the eight directions
b) one of the *five elements*
c) a season
d) a planetary influence
e) a colour
f) a family member

Each *gua* also corresponds to one of the basic eight trigrams. These eight trigrams, when combined, become the 64 hexagrams of the Chinese classic book of divination, the *'I-ching.'*

Note: *In Chinese books, the North is always placed at the bottom and the South at the top. Throughout this book, I have placed the North at the top, in order to adjust to the western perspective.*

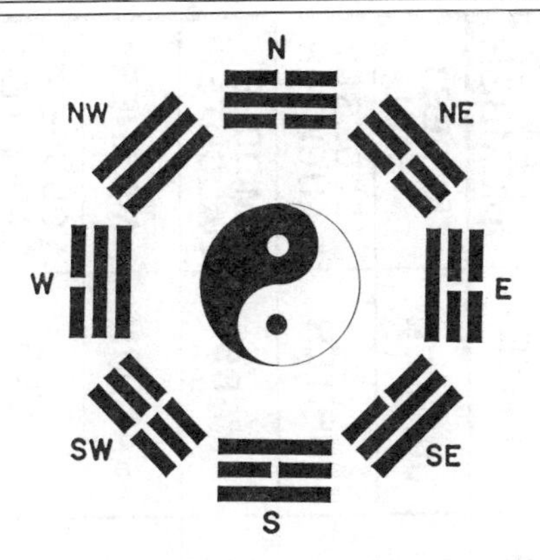

The trigrams of the latter-day ba-gua

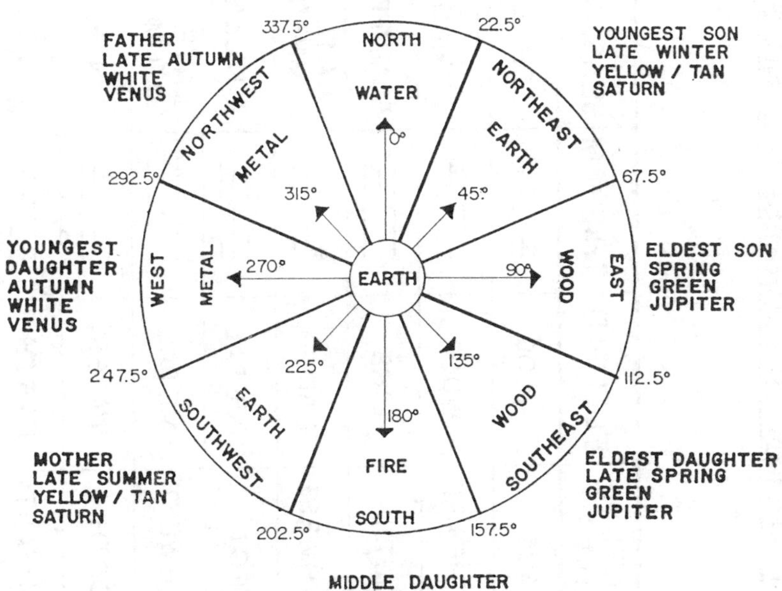

Correspondences of the latter-day ba-gua
Each gua occupies 45 degrees on the compass

CHART OF THE CORRESPONDENCES OF THE LATTER-DAY BA-GUA

DIRECTION/ GUA	ELEMENT	TRIGRAM	SEASON	COLOUR	PLANET	FAMILY MEMBER
EAST	WOOD	☳	SPRING	GREEN	JUPITER	ELDEST SON
SOUTHEAST	WOOD	☴	LATE SPRING	GREEN	JUPITER	ELDEST DAUGHTER
SOUTH	FIRE	☲	SUMMER	RED	MARS	MIDDLE DAUGHTER
SOUTHWEST	EARTH	☷	LATE SUMMER	YELLOW / TAN	SATURN	MOTHER
WEST	METAL	☱	AUTUMN	WHITE	VENUS	YOUNGEST DAUGHTER
NORTHWEST	METAL	☰	LATE AUTUMN	WHITE	VENUS	FATHER
NORTH	WATER	☵	WINTER	BLUE / BLACK	MERCURY	MIDDLE SON
NORTHEAST	EARTH	☶	LATE WINTER	YELLOW / TAN	SATURN	YOUNGEST SON

THE PRIMORDIAL BA-GUA

The *primordial (early-heaven) ba-gua* was revealed by the legendary Emperor Fu Hsi who ruled China over 5,000 years ago. The ancient arrangement of the *yin* (broken) and *yang* (unbroken) lines of the trigrams charted the seasons and the movements of the moon and the sun.

This early version of the *ba-gua* is still used today in the analysis of *feng shui* and the divination of past and future events. Chinese people hang it over their doors, (and sometimes over their windows) knowing that the harmony of its design will neutralize inauspicious *chi* which might otherwise enter their premises. When and how to use this *ba-gua* and other *feng shui* tools will be discussed in the following chapters of this book.

The primordial ba-gua

The primordial ba-gua over a door

THE ELEMENTS AND THEIR CORRESPONDING COLOURS

Colours are rays or frequencies of energy. Each colour ray has a different quality. Colours that corresponds to an *element* have the qualities of that *element*: e.g., red corresponds to the *fire element* – the frequency of the red ray is warm. Blue and black correspond to the *water element* – these colours are cool; yellow and tan (*earth*) are dense; green (*wood*) is lively; and white (*metal*) is bright and sharp.

Participants in our *feng shui* seminars often ask us why black corresponds to water – The deeper the water, the darker it appears.

Below is a diagram of the colours that are productive or complimentary to each other, and those that are destructive or conflicting. You can refer to this diagram when selecting colour schemes for your home, clothing, bedding, and everything else that affects your immediate environment. The color compatibilities are also used in *feng shui cures*.

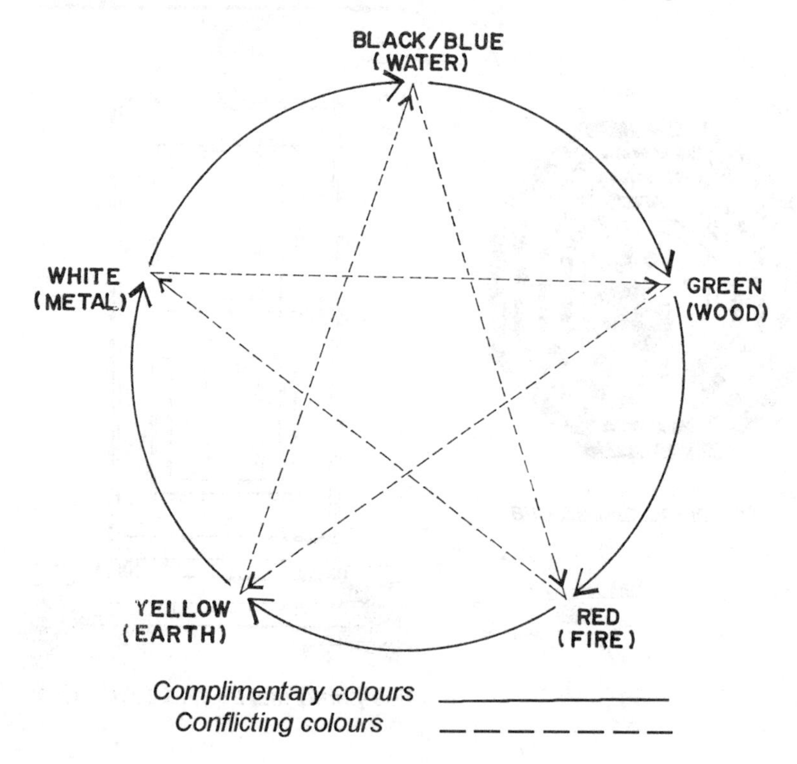

CHAPTER FOUR

PERSONALIZED FENG SHUI

How Feng Shui Affects Your Fortune
What About Karma?
How to Choose a Geomancer
Feng Shui Services and How to Use Them
Being Your Own Geomancer

We call *feng shui* 'personalized' when the *geomancer* adjusts his assessment of your home and/or workplace to your birth data. *Geomancers* use your year of birth to calculate if you need easterly or westerly directions. Guided by this information, they place the rooms, the stove, the beds, and the main doors of your house to your best advantage. This is known as the '*four east – four west*' method, and is based on the *latter-day ba-gua* and the nine stars (numbers) of the *lo-shu diagram*. Additional methods are used by the '*three harmony*,' '*three yuen*,' '*moving star*' and '*shien kong moving star*' schools.

The top *geomancers* of Hong Kong often combine these methods depending on what they need to achieve, e.g., better health, more money etc. Some supplement this with a complete natal chart called the '*four pillars of fate*' which is derived from your year, month, day and hour of birth. They use this information to more finely tune the *feng shui* to your individual needs.

Another method of fate calculation is known as '*tzu wei*.' This form of Chinese astrology is very popular in Taiwan and Hong Kong. It can provide a detailed fortune analysis from your birth data. These calculations help your *geomancer* to know many of the high and low points of your past, present and future life.

HOW FENG SHUI AFFECTS YOUR FORTUNE

Your personal fortune or energy cycle is the predominant factor that governs the events in your life. The *feng shui* of your home and workplace can temper the negative aspects of your fortune cycle and enhance the positive aspects, for example:

If your fortune or energy cycle is strong:

Good feng shui can give you the boost that will bring you to the peak of your endeavours.

Bad feng shui can hinder you from attaining your goals.

If your fortune or energy cycle is neutral:

Good feng shui can make you prosper, by providing an environment that supports your energy needs and enhances your capacity to think clearly and make correct decisions.

Bad feng shui will cause you to make errors in judgement that will strain your physical and financial resources.

If your fortune or energy cycle is weak:

Good feng shui can provide the environment that will prevent you from making faulty decisions and taking wrong actions.

Bad feng shui will deplete you further. Accidents and illness, financial losses, marital and family problems will be the result.

WHAT ABOUT KARMA?

So where does *karma* come into all this? *Karma*, (the law of cause and effect) simply states –"*You sow what you reap.*" Misdeeds, misjudgements and wrongdoing will result in negative repercussions. If you can avoid these repercussions by surrounding yourself, in your home and office, with the protective atmosphere of *good feng shui*, what happens to your *karma*?

It is not in the scope of this book to go into the complexities of *karma*, but you can safely accept that *karmic effects* can be delayed by *good feng shui* and balanced by positive actions.

If, through the application of *feng shui*, you are the recipient of good fortune that you have not yet earned; you should be generous and help others who are in need. Giving back to the universe some of the good luck you have received will generate good *karma*, and can transmute or diffuse those negative *karmic events* that are just waiting to happen.

When you have your home or workplace designed or adjusted to conform to *feng shui* concepts, your negative *karma* will sometimes be absorbed by the *feng shui consultant* because he has interfered with the *karmic effects* of your life. Consequently, *geomancers* who do not have adequate spiritual training, and even some who do, will often suffer from sickness and misfortune. To avoid absorbing *karmic effects* the *geomancer* must practice certain meditations and do good deeds.

Occasionally, the fortune cycle of a prospective client can be so negative and his *karma* so strong, that even though we are consulted to design or adjust the *feng shui* of his property, we are prevented from doing so.

In one case I recall, the first appointment with our client had to be cancelled due to a traffic accident that blocked his access to our office. When the appointment was re-set, there was a torrential rainstorm and we thought it would be wiser to postpone again. On the next occasion there was a mix-up in our appointment book, which was most unusual as my secretary is very efficient. As this was the third time we had to cancel, I decided not to proceed with the case because there seemed to be *karmic implications*. Some weeks later, our prospective client was involved in a shooting incident.

HOW TO CHOOSE A GEOMANCER

Because of the increasing demand for *feng shui consultants*, many under-trained people are now in professional practice. Some of them are integrating Western and Chinese methods – this '*hybrid feng shui*' is usually ineffective.

The principles of *feng shui* are part of a philosophy and methodology that is the foundation of all Chinese natural sciences; it is a whole and complete system in itself. An inadequate knowledge of this system can dilute its effectiveness. Incorporating other methodologies into the system can have harmful results.

The criteria for selecting a geomancer are:

By results, by recommendation, and by his written works. You should also bear in mind that *feng shui* is a natural science, and in its pure form has nothing to do with religion. Modern *geomancers* are not necessarily connected with a temple, nor do they wear fancy robes, or use titles such as, 'Doctor,' 'Reverend,' or 'Professor.' Although there are some excellent *geomancers* who use some of the above, it is generally better to be wary of too much window dressing.

Most of the better-known *geomancers* in Asia dress normally, they look and behave like any other person, and speak knowledgeably and logically about their profession. When they accept you as a client, they not only make a thorough inspection of your property, they also require your birth data, the family and property history, the architectural plans and correct bearings.

Well-trained *geomancers* should know how to read and assess area and topographical maps, floor plans and architectural drawings, and how to plot the orientation of a site from the surveyors bearings. They should have at least one architect or draftsman on their staff or on call, and maintain confidential files and records for future follow-up assessments. The *geomancer's* files enable him to update the aspects of *feng shui* that are based on the annual and cyclical moving star charts.

FENG SHUI SERVICES AND HOW TO USE THEM

Feng shui assessments must consider many aspects of a property, these include: orientation; topography; the influence of nearby road and waterway configurations; other constructions in the vicinity; the shape and design of the building; the building's ability to attract and retain good *chi* within its walls; the use for which the property is intended; and the compatibility of its energy to that of the owner/occupant.

Feng shui consultants offer a menu of services, which include: selecting and assessing a site; designing, laying out, or adjusting houses, offices, stores, factories, subdivisions and industrial estates.

They also provide auspicious dates, times and procedures for a vast variety of events, the most common of these being; opening a new business; moving into a house or office; signing important contracts; groundbreaking; tree-cutting; tearing down walls; digging wells; and dates for weddings, funeral rites and burials.

The *geomancer* is often asked to check the suitability of a name for a new baby or a new business enterprise. Even the colours and plate numbers of the family cars are studied for their fortunate or unfortunate aspects – see, *Chapter 34*.

Chinese families retain a *geomancer* to ensure that the *feng shui* of their homes, offices, stores and factories will consistently maximize their potential to attract good fortune, and minimize or neutralize the negative features of their environment.The *geomancer* usually becomes the advisor and confidant of the family and his advice is sought for all family events.

After his initial *feng shui* services, the *geomancer* makes annual minor recommendations to offset the negative aspects of the current year. Any changes in the internal or external aspects of the premises, such as an extra room added to the building, or a construction site or new road nearby can affect the *feng shui* and must also be calculated and assessed. If the *geomancer's* advice is not meticulously followed, good results cannot always be expected.

Many aspects of *feng shui* are interdependent, for instance: Beneficial *chi* must be channelled into the premises and guided throughout the building. Therefore; the gate must be correctly placed to bring in the good *chi*; the main door must, among other considerations, be harmonious with the gate; rear and side doors, and certain other internal placements must then harmonize with the main door; and toilets, septic tanks, and other unsanitary elements must be placed so as not to negate the positive energy flow, or pollute the good areas of the *chi-grid.*

Good feng shui requires that all the major components of a house, office or factory should be in harmony with each other, and in accordance with the *chi-grid.* Components that are 'out of sync' can minimize or negate the *feng shui.*

If you are not prepared to carry out all the advice of your *feng shui* consultant, perhaps because of cost or convenience factors then, in fairness to him and to yourself, you should ask which are the most essential points of the *feng shui* assessment. You should then ensure that these are correctly implemented.

DO-IT-YOURSELF FENG SHUI

When you are not sure of the qualifications of your *geomancer* or you cannot locate one in your vicinity, this book can be used as your primer for basic do-it-yourself *feng shui*. It is also a reliable guide to simple, effective and safe *feng shui* 'cures'.

Part Two

Creating Good Feng Shui in Your Home

CHAPTER FIVE

LUCKY AND UNLUCKY HOUSE

How to Know if Your Home Has Good or Bad Feng Shui

There are Chinese communities in almost every country in Asia and in most Western countries as well. Wherever the Chinese go, they prosper. Usually they do not flaunt their prosperity by ostentatious living, but remain in the small house, office or store where they quietly built their fortune. The first home of the family is almost never sold or discarded. If and when the family outgrows it and has to move to larger premises, the original house is used as an office or a warehouse, or is occupied by the married children. This is because the Chinese believe in 'lucky houses.'

Just as there are 'lucky houses,' there are also 'unlucky houses.' If the family suffers financial losses, sickness or disunity they will immediately call a *feng shui consultant* to look at the premises and cure the problems. Sometimes the *consultant* will advise them to move out and will help them select a property more suited to their personal *feng shui* needs. But whether through cure or change, once the family finds a house that provides them with an environment within which they can prosper, they rarely relinquish their hold on it.

People who are unaware of the powerful influence that the home environment has on themselves and their families, will often move out of a lucky house when they have made enough money to buy a bigger and better one. They may also invest in other businesses in which they are unfamiliar. If their personal fortune cycle is strong, they will be attracted to properties with the balanced vibrations of *good feng shui,* as well as businesses for which they have an affinity. Usually they will continue to prosper in the new premises. But, if their personal cycle of fortune is weak, they will be attracted to premises with *bad feng shui* – when they move in, their business and health will deteriorate.

HOW TO KNOW IF YOUR HOME HAS GOOD OR BAD FENG SHUI

Why is it you feel relaxed and comfortable in one place and tense and apprehensive in another? The reason is usually related to *feng shui*.

If your home or building has its shape, exposure, spatial arrangements and colours in harmony, then it has *good feng shui*, and you will respond positively to its environment. When these components are discordant or clashing, the *feng shui* is bad, and your response to it will be negative.

Effects of good feng shui:

When you live and work in an environment of *good feng shui*: you will be capable of performing your duties with ease; your health will improve; your relationships with others will be smoother; your mental attitude will become more positive, and your productivity will be enhanced. The end result will be increased wealth, health and happiness.

Effects of bad feng shui:

When your house and/or workplace has *bad feng shui*: you will become nervous and irritable; prone to minor illnesses, and incapable of performing your duties well. Your relationships with others will deteriorate, and your productivity will decrease. The end result will be poor health, misery, and depleted resources

If any effects of *bad feng shui* are manifesting in your home, you don't have to just cope, you can do something about it – you can opt for *good feng shui*. What do you have to lose? The Chinese have been applying *feng shui* principles for thousands of years, if it didn't work for them would they still be using it today? Surely not, so read on....

CHAPTER SIX

DIRECTION AND SHAPE

Direction, Shape, and the Elements
Hollows and Protrusions
Forecasting the Family Fortune
U & L Shaped Houses
Feng Shui Cures

DIRECTION AND THE ELEMENTS

The *chi* that emanates from a compass direction is affected by the position of the sun and other celestial bodies versus the Earth. It is also imbued with the qualities of its corresponding *element*. The following are the qualities of the *directional chi,* and how they influence us:

East and Southeast chi; is like the morning sun. It has a stimulating and invigorating influence on our metabolism – the *element* of these directions is *wood*

West and Northwest chi; is like the setting sun, it helps us to relax and to release our stress and our inhibitions – the *element* of these directions is *metal*

North chi; is cooling and mentally stimulating – its *element* is *water*

South chi; can inspire us to action. Fame or notoriety are also associated with the South – its *element* is *fire*

Northeast, Southwest, (and Centre) chi; these directions have positive and negative qualities (see, *overleaf, and page 187)* – Their corresponding *element* is *earth.*

The influence the *directional chi* has on us depends, in part, on our gender. The Northwest, North, Northeast and East, mainly affect males. The Southeast, South, Southwest and West, mainly affect females.

SHAPE AND THE ELEMENTS

Guidelines:

1. A house confines *chi* within its walls.
2. The occupants are affected by the *chi* within the house.
3. Every shape is governed by an *element*.
4. The *chi* assumes the qualities of the *element* of the house shape. e.g., if the house is square, the *chi* within it assumes the qualities of the *earth element* – because the *earth element* governs square shapes.

Note: *In a feng shui analysis, the element of a property is based on its orientation but, the element of its shape is always factored in.*

Shapes, Elements and Indications:

a) *Square:*
A favourable shape; it belongs to the *earth element* and indicates solid strength.

b) *Rectangular – (short):*
This shape also belongs to the *earth element*; it is favourable if the narrower side faces the street, as it indicates a long future; unfavourable if the wider side faces the street, as this indicates a short future.

c) *Trapezoidal:*
This relates to the *earth element.* It is favourable if the wider side is at the rear.The front represents the present and the rear represents the future. A house or lot that is wider at the rear indicates growth and expansion. If the rear is narrower, it indicates a diminishing future.

d) *Square, with a semi-circle in front:*
This is a combination of the *earth* and *metal elements*. It is said to bring protection and wealth to the occupants as *earth* produces *metal* (the *metal element* is also interpreted as silver or gold).

e) *Circular:*
This shape relates to the *metal element*; it is interpreted as movement and silver or gold. It lacks stability for houses, but can be good for financial institutions.

f) *Triangular:*
This shape relates to the *fire element* and is unsuitable for houses, rooms or buildings. The sharp corners of a triangle also emit harmful '*arrows of chi*' to the neighbouring areas.

g) *Irregular:*
This relates to the *water element*; it is problematic due to its many hollows and protrusions.

h) *Rectangular – (long & narrow):*
This relates to the *wood element;* it is favourable if the narrow side faces the street and unfavourable if the long side faces the street.

For more about shapes, see – '*Feng Shui Tips for Property Buyers*' – *Chapter 27.*

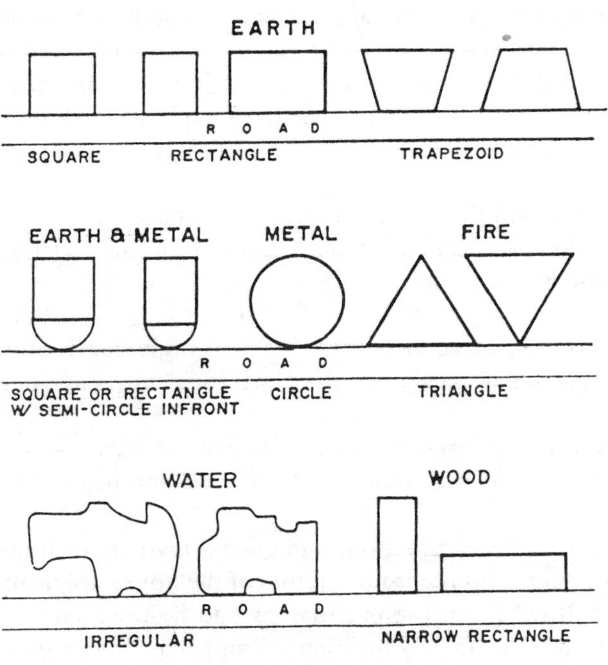

Shape and the elements

HOLLOWS AND PROTRUSIONS

Houses that have protruded or hollow areas exert specific effects on the occupants.

If there is a protrusion in the shape of the house, the *directional chi* that corresponds to the protruded area (*gua*) will be strong and will affect the family member or occupant who is subject to that *gua*.

If there is less mass, i.e., a hollow or missing *gua* in the shape of the house, the lack of the corresponding *directional chi* will affect the family member or occupant who is subject to that *gua*.

How to locate the eight guas of your house:

Step I – When you assess the *feng shui* of your house or apartment, first obtain an accurately scaled floor plan. Then, excluding open areas such as car ports and balconies, calculate the centre of mass, i.e., the centre of the house. This centre point is considered to be the 'heart'or the 'nucleus' of the home, it is from here that the *chi* organizes itself and radiates throughout the house.

Step II – Ascertain the exact North from the house plans, or by using a compass, and draw the North/South line passing through the centre point of the plan.

Step III – With a protractor or a 45°/90° triangle, mark in the other directional axes using the North/South line as your guide.

Step IV – Mark in the *guas* midway between the axes – exact degrees of the *guas* are shown in the drawing on page 41.

With the compass directions and *guas* drawn on the house plan, it can easily be seen which *guas* or sectors of the house are protruded and which are hollow. From the protrusions and hollows you can predict certain tendencies of family members. Remember that a *gua* occupies 45° of the compass, i.e., 22.5° each side of the directional axes.

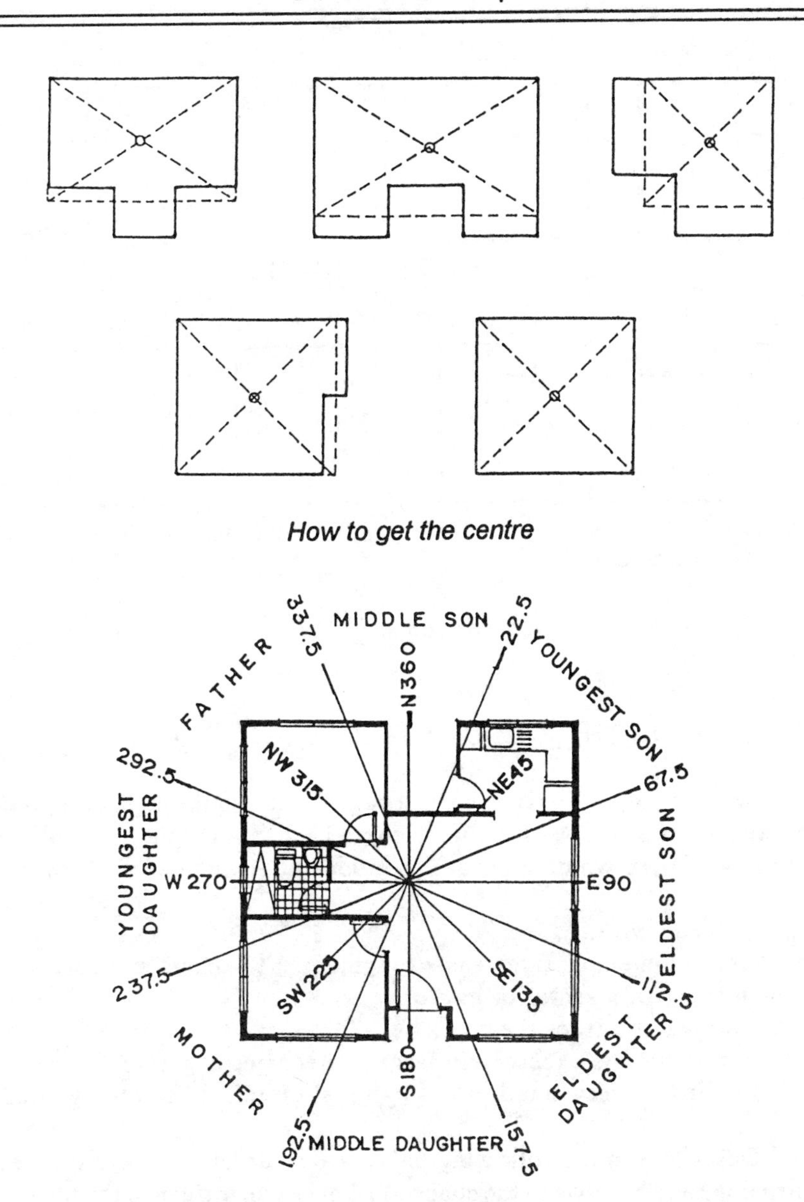

How to get the centre

The guas and corresponding family members marked on the house plan
**The north gua in this plan is hollow*

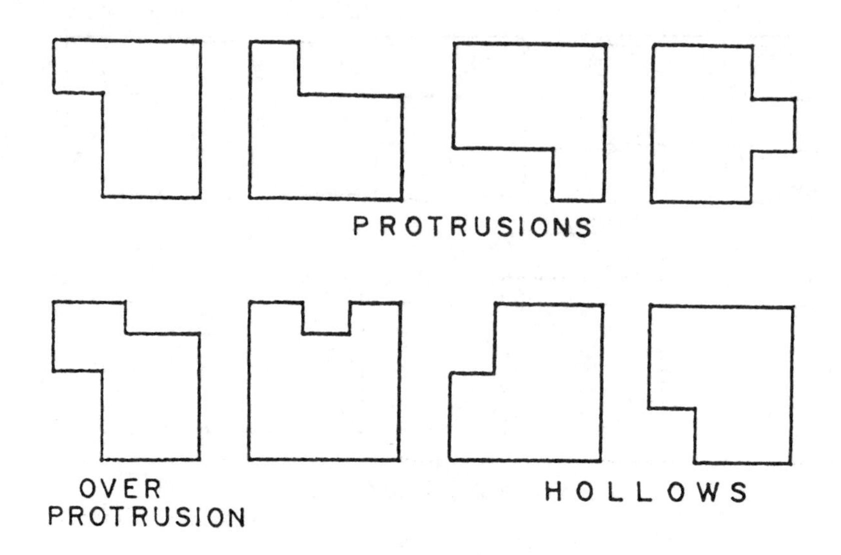

Examples of house shapes with hollows & protrusions

FORECASTING THE FAMILY FORTUNE

Refer to page 41 or the chart on page 24 to find the direction (*gua*) that corresponds to each family member. Then, follow the instructions on page 40 to see which *guas* are protruded and which are hollow.

Some general rules:

a) A protrusion emphasizes and strengthens the aspects and correspondences of a sector or *gua*.
b) A hollow diminishes them.
c) If a protrusion is excessively large, it becomes negative.
d) If a hollow is very small, it has minimal effect and can be ignored.

Described in the following pages are some of the ways that the protrusions and hollows in the shape of a house can influence the fortune of family members.

EAST

Protruded:
a) The eldest son will excel in most of his endeavours.
b) Good business growth.

Hollow or over-protruded:
a) The eldest son may be rebellious or leave the family.
b) Business will suffer setbacks.

SOUTHEAST

Protruded:
a) Daughters of the household will marry well or have a successful career.
b) Business can be extended to far places – this is good for overseas trade.

Hollow or over-protruded:
a) Daughters of the household may have difficulty in finding a suitable husband.
b) Social and business setbacks.

SOUTH

Protruded:
a) Daughters may excel in the arts.
b) The family will be respected.

Hollow or over-protruded:
a) Daughters may be temperamental and sexually indulgent.
b) Loss of family honour.

SOUTHWEST

Protruded:

a) The wife, or older females of the household, will control the family.
b) If the Southwest protrusion is combined with a hollow in the Northwest, and/or, if there is a stairwell or a toilet in the *Northwest gua,* the husband may abandon the family or seldom be at home.

Hollow or over-protruded:

a) The wife, or older females of the household, may neglect family obligations.
b) A large hollow could cause sickness or death to the older females of the household.
c) Problems with real estate.

WEST

Protruded:

a) The young women will contribute joy and wealth to the family.
b) The family will have financial success.

Hollow or over-protruded:

a) The young women will be wayward and extravagant.
b) If the West is over-protruded and has a water placement such as, a toilet, a pool or a water tank, the young women of the household may become promiscuous.

NORTHWEST

Protruded:

a) The eldest male will guide the family well.
b) Co-operation among all family members.

Hollow or over-protruded:

a) The family head may be weak, or have a selfish, dictatorial attitude.

b) The family may revolt against the authority of the father, leading to the loss of family fortune.

NORTH

Protruded:
a) Sons will be helpful to the family.
b) The house will be relatively safe from burglary.

Hollow or over-protruded:
a) Sons may be willful and insubordinate.
b) The house will be prone to accidents or burglary.

NORTHEAST

Protruded:
a) The sons will have good health.
b) Financial stability is indicated.

Hollow or over-protruded:
a) The family will have no heir, or the sons will be unproductive.
b) Financial losses can occur.

If there are only one or two children in the family, the sectors or *guas* of the house will affect them according to their age. For instance:

A daughter will be mainly affected by the *West gua* until her late teens. She will feel the influence of the *South gua* from her teens to her late twenties. The *Southeast gua* will be the dominant influence thereafter, until she herself becomes a wife and mother, then the *chi* of the *Southwest gua* will become her dominant directional influence.

A son will be mainly affected by the *Northeast gua* up to his teen years and by the *North gua* through his twenties. He will be influenced by the *East gua* thereafter, until he himself becomes a husband and the master of the house: then the *chi* of the *Northwest gua* will become his dominant directional influence.

Although the hollows and protrusions of a house contribute greatly to the fortune of the occupants, they can be interpreted in many ways, depending on other aspects of the house and the family circumstances.

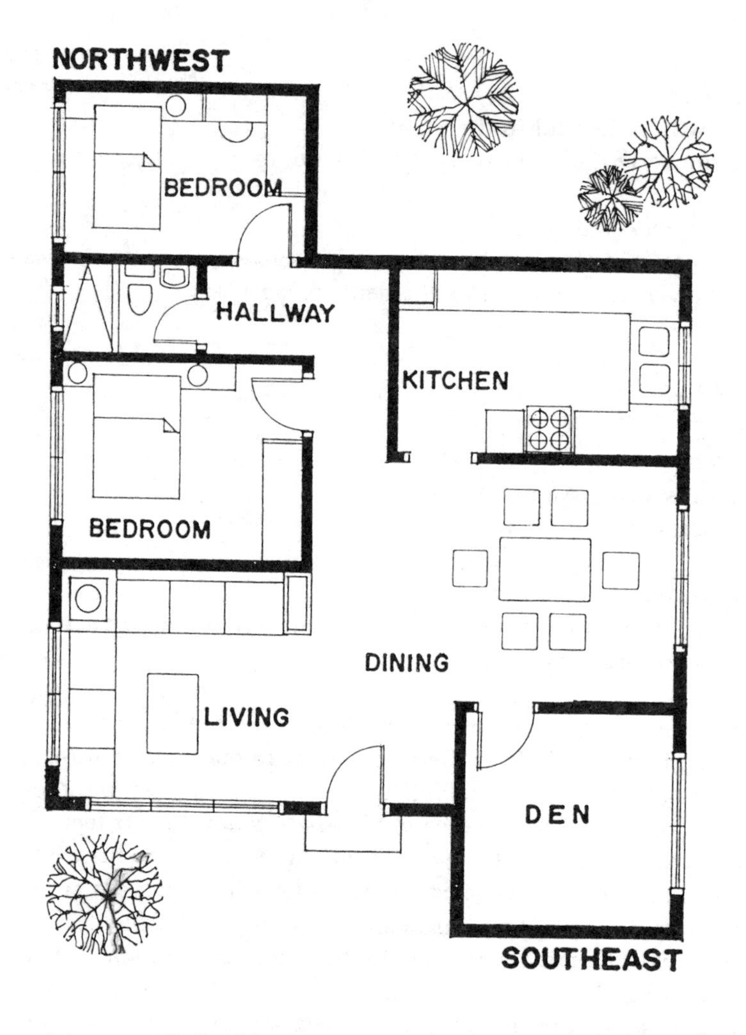

A house with the Northwest gua and Southeast gua protruded
** A well-governed family * Overseas business will be gainful*
** Daughters can have good marriages and/or careers*

THE HEART OF THE MATTER – 'U' AND 'L' SHAPED HOUSES

Many architects, particularly those in tropical regions, are fond of designing houses and buildings that are '*L*' shaped or '*U*' shaped. These designs are meant to maximize the cross ventilation that is so essential in hot and humid climates. If the '*L*' or '*U*' is not too exaggerated, and the protrusions and hollows caused by the shape are in the appropriate areas, these houses could have the *feng shui* that is suitable for a family; but more often than not, they have *feng shui* problems.

The centre of the house is its 'heart':

One major problem is when the centre or 'heart' (which should be calculated from the floor plan) is outside the walls of the house, this is usually the case when the '*U*' or '*L*' shape is exaggerated. The heart of the house functions as its centre of gravity. It sustains the cohesive energy that keeps the family united. If the centre is outside, then the house is 'heartless.' The marriages of persons living in heartless homes are adversely affected and sometimes end in divorce. The children react to the lack of unifying energy by leaving the family home, as soon as they are old enough to support themselves.

'*U*' and '*L*' shaped houses often have a swimming pool in the hollow of the '*U*' or the '*L*' – this takes a disastrous toll on the health of some family members, because the humid *water chi* permeates all areas of the house. Those members who do not need the *water element* will get sick, feel debilitated, or be unproductive, lazy and depressed.

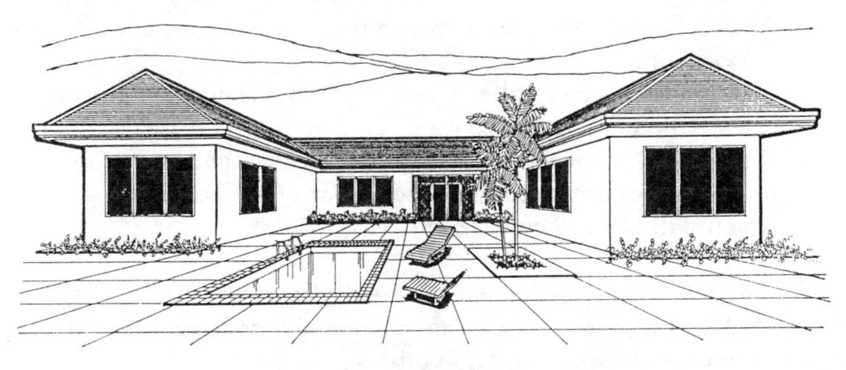

'U' shaped house

'L' shaped house

YOUR FENG SHUI CURES:

1] To correct hollows created by *'U'* and *'L'* shaped houses:
   a) Extend a roofed terrace over the hollow section and enclose it with screen, glass, or any other light material.
   b) Square off the house with spotlights, a large rock and/or garden pathways.

Note: *cure (b) is considerably less effective than cure (a).*

2] If you have a pool, and some members of the family are showing any of the preceding reactions, use the following remedies:
   a) Let them sleep in the bedrooms that are furthest from the pool.
   b) Landscape the garden so that grass covered mounds of earth (artificial mountains) are between the pool and the house. If you cannot do this, then;
   c) grow plants or place potted plants between the pool and the house – plants will help absorb the *water chi*.
   d) If the windows of the bedroom overlook the pool, use yellow blinds or curtains. Yellow is the colour of the *earth element*, which will block the *water chi*.

Remember that in *feng shui* we are dealing with subtle energies. The varied frequencies of *chi* within a home will be beneficial to some family members and detrimental to others.

'U' shaped house – corrected by a roofed & enclosed terrace (The terrace need not necessarily fill the entire hollow)

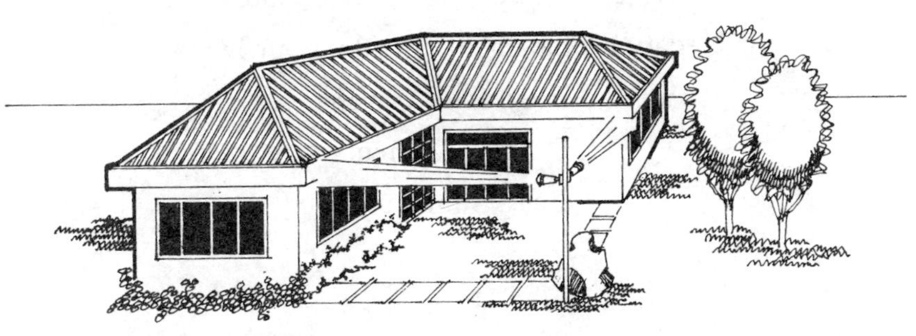

'L' shaped house – squared off with spotlights, a large rock & pathways

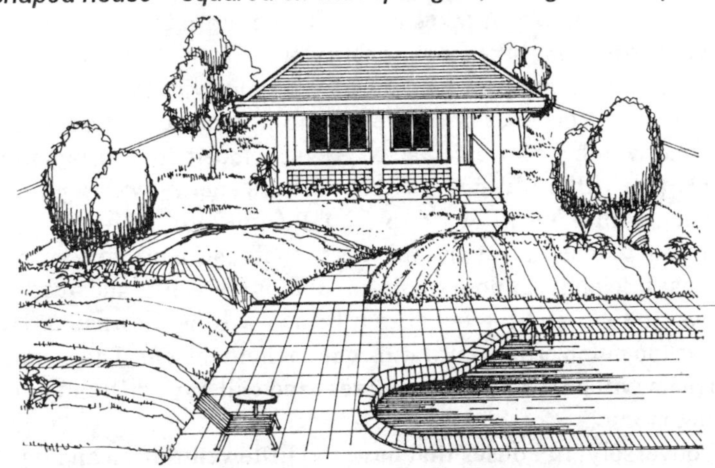

Corrective landscaping between the house and the pool

CHAPTER SEVEN

YOUR FRONT DOOR

The front door is considered to be the 'mouth' of your home. Just like your own mouth that takes in food to maintain the strength of your body, your front door takes in the energy or *chi* from the outside and then distributes it to all areas of the house. The quality of energy that enters your door mainly depends on where the door is located on the grid of your house, and which direction it faces. A well-placed door brings in beneficial *chi* that will build-up a field of positive energy within your home – the door should open inward to draw the *chi* into the house.

If your house has many openings, such as: doors to terraces and balconies; side and rear doors; atriums and/or air-wells, and overly large windows, the *chi* and the benefits it brings will be dissipated. Houses that have too much cross ventilation cannot hold the *chi*. The people who live in them will be susceptible to illness and will have difficulty in accumulating money.

Conversely, in houses that have too little ventilation and light, the *chi* becomes stagnant and *yin*; this causes sickness and other problems.

In order to maintain a good energy level in your house, the rooms should not have more than two walls with windows and/or terrace doors, and these should not be facing each other.

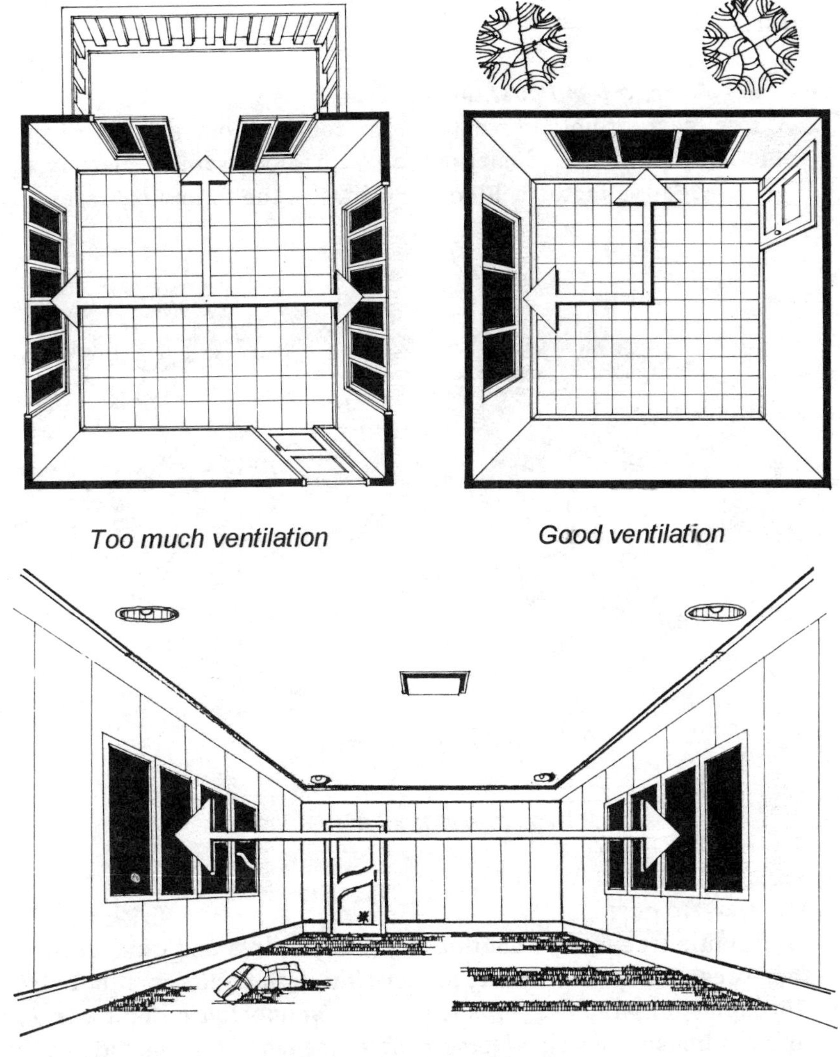

Too much ventilation

Good ventilation

Windows facing each other

NEGATIVE PLACEMENTS OUTSIDE YOUR DOOR

Bearing in mind that your front door draws the *chi* into your house, then what is outside your door becomes very important. The following external factors should NOT be within a range of 45° from the centre of your front door or gate.

a) *A large tree, a lamp post, or a pole:*
A tree, post, or pole in front of your door will block the *chi* from entering your house. Sometimes a tree can be useful if there is a worse negative factor behind it, such as in the following cases.

A large tree in front of the door

b) *An electric post:*
The subtle frequencies emitted by electric wires and transformer boxes can enter your house, not only through your doors, but also through your windows. This will create an imbalance in the energy of your house and will adversely affect the temperament and health of the occupants.

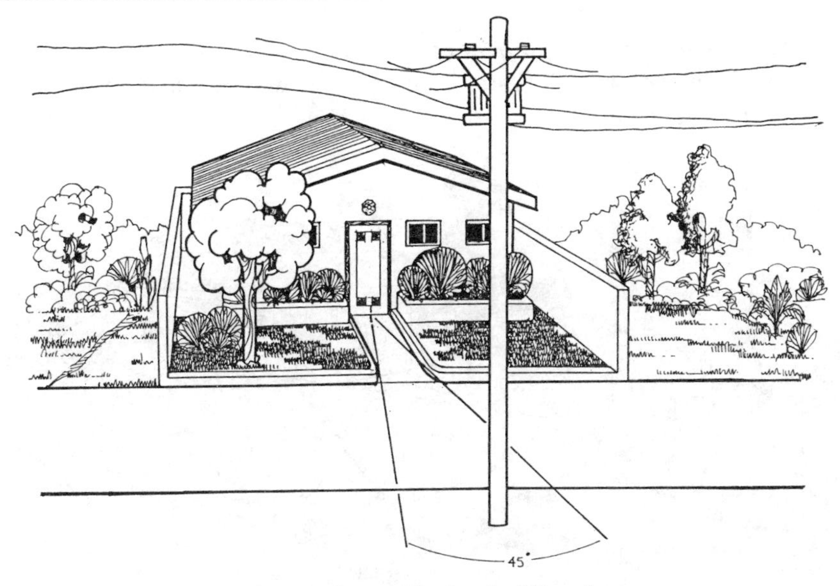

An electric post in front of the door

c) *A gable or a sharp corner of a building:*
Sharp corners of buildings or ridge lines of roofs can direct '*arrows of chi*' into your house through your doors or windows.

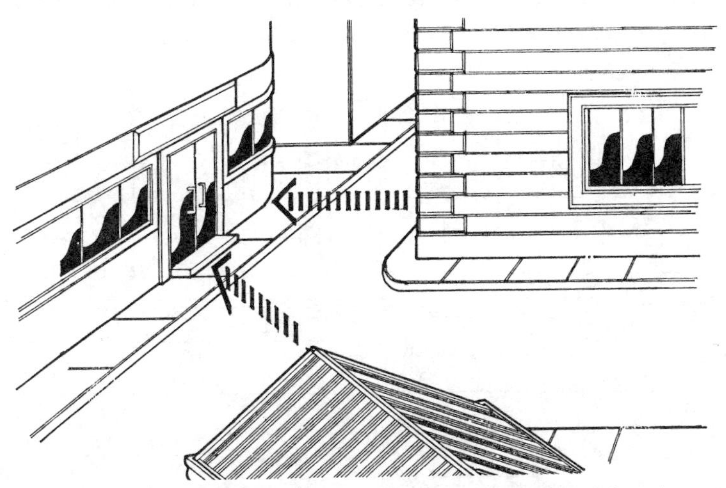

A sharp corner and a roof ridge line pointed toward the door

d) *A water tank facing your door:*
The frequency of still water is too *yin* – it will diminish the energy level of your house.

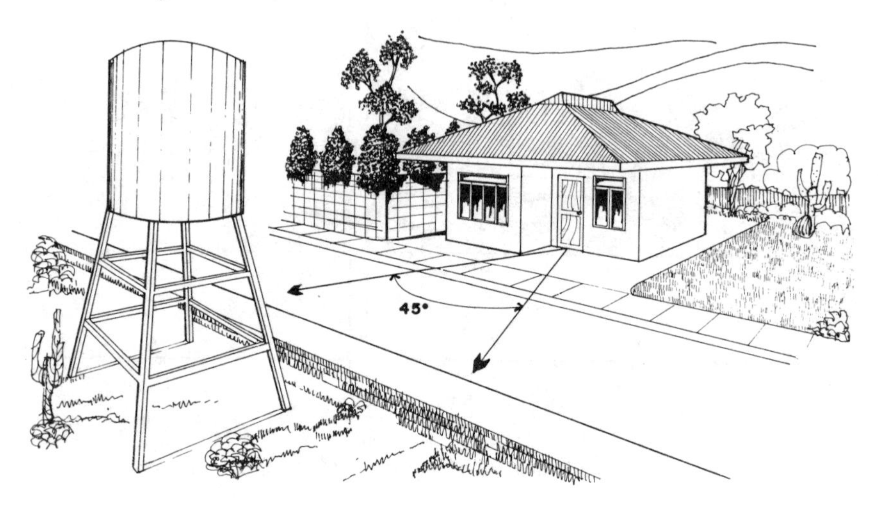

e) *A chimney stack or exhaust flue facing your door:*
Chimney stacks have a very negative effect, not only on the environment, but also on the *feng shui* of your house – *the special effects of chimney stacks are discussed in Chapter 27.*

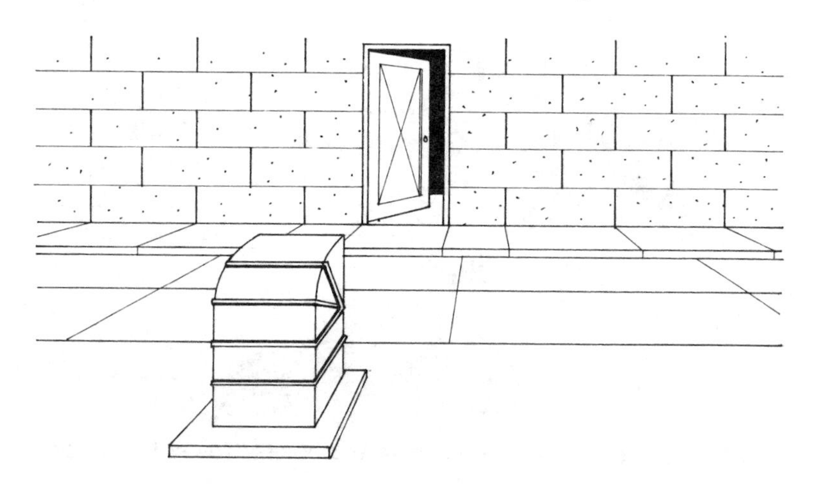

f) *A tall building facing your front door:*
This placement will not only block the *chi*, it will also oppress the energy of your house.

g) *A church or temple facing your door:*
A house is a home for living people, who are *yang*. A church or a temple is the home of deities, who are *yin*. *Yin* energy should be confined to your altar; it should not enter through your front door.

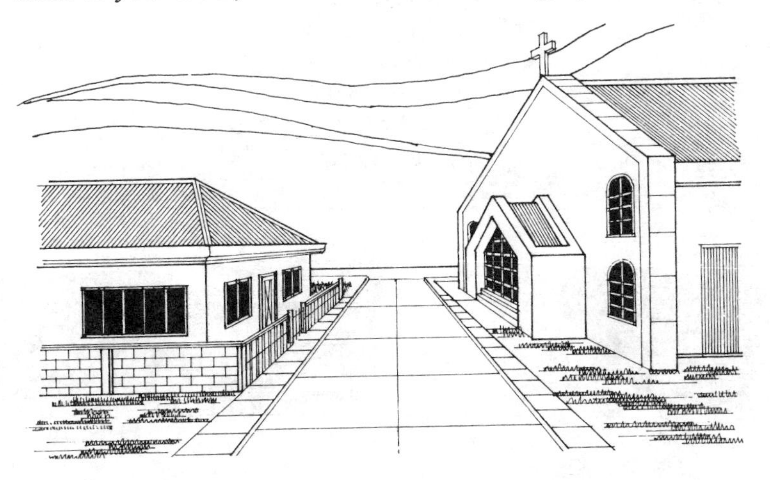

h) *A neighbour's gate, door or driveway facing your door:*
A neighbour's gate or door opposite yours can create conflict. If the opposing gate or door is bigger than yours, it will absorb some of the *chi* that should be coming to you.
A driveway will send *'sha'* (negative *chi*) to your door.

i) *A road directly facing your door:*
This will send strong, damaging *chi* into your house.

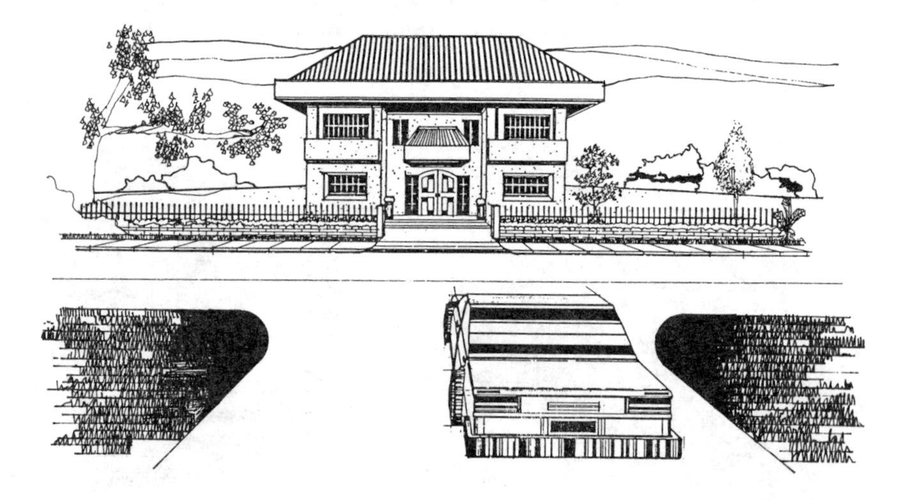

j) *A house with two gates or two doors on the same wall:*
This, like having two masters, leads to quarrels or insubordination.

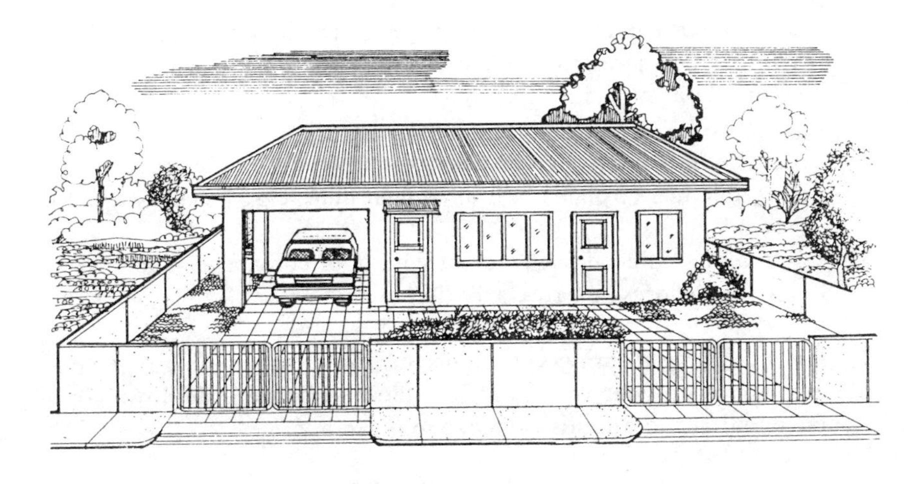

k) *A driveway or road curved toward your door:*
A curve is like a blade, it will 'cut' the house.

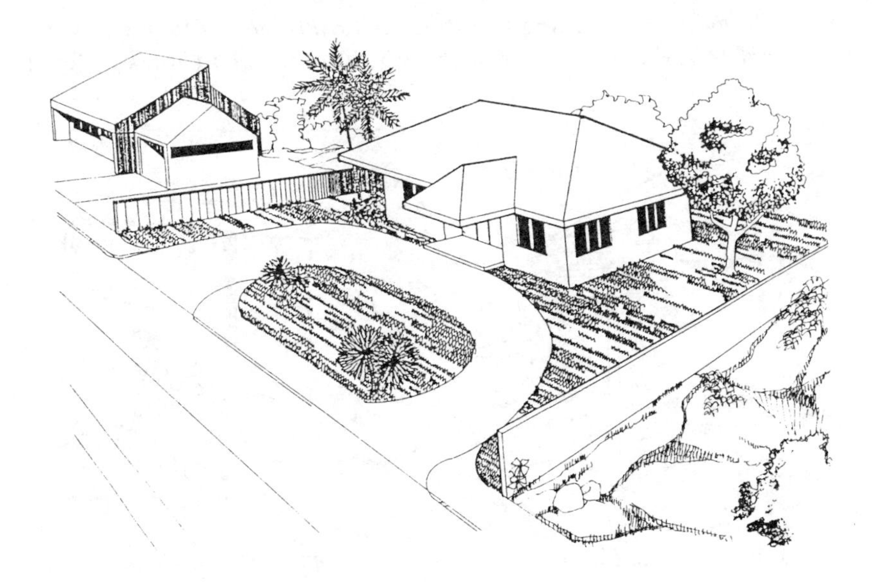

YOUR FENG SHUI CURES:

1] You can install an awning over your door to block the view of (and the *chi* that emanates from) negative factors that are on a higher level than your door; e.g., items a) to g)

2] Negative *chi* from ground or near ground levels can be diffused by placing a divider or plants in front of your door; e.g., items h), i) & k)

3] A potted plant placed each side of your door can absorb some types of negative energy, particularly that of the *water chi*; e.g., item d)

4] A tall building fronting your house can be offset by placing a concave mirror on your roof to reflect the building upside down, or a convex mirror to diminish its size; e.g., item f)

5] A *primordial ba-gua* is considered to be the 'aspirin' of *feng shui*. place one over your door and/or on your gatepost as a defence against any kind of *feng shui* violation – *see bagua cutout on page 269.*

Note: *windows overlooking negative views should be fitted with vertical or horizontal blinds, with the slats adjusted to block the view.*

An awning over the door

plants shielding the door

GUIDELINES FOR FENCES AND GATES:

1. The fence or boundary wall on either side of the gate should be of the same height.
2. A boundary wall should not be inset with see-through designs.
3. Iron security fences should not have spikes pointing toward the house.
4. Designs should not have; (a) crosses, (b) arrows pointed downward or (c) triangles.
5. Gates should open inward to draw in the *chi*.

Note: *rule 4. also applies to designs of doors, facades and interiors.*

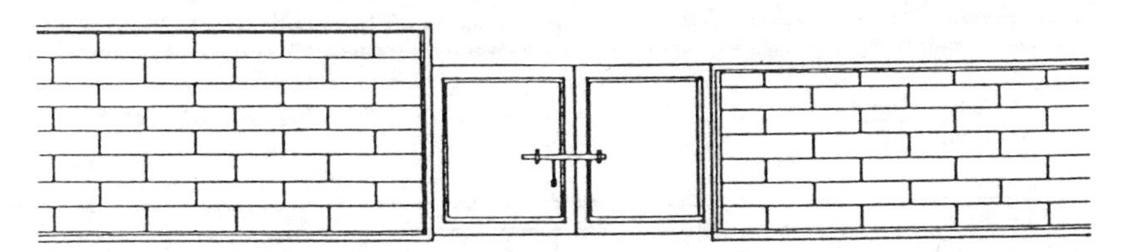

1. Bad: a wall or fence of different heights on either side of the gate

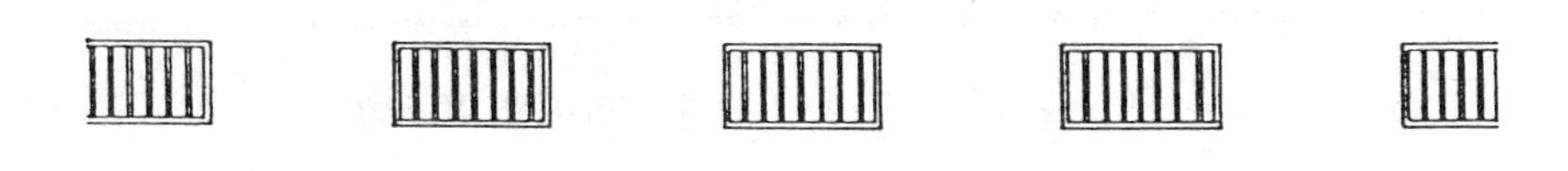

2. Bad: a wall with see-through designs

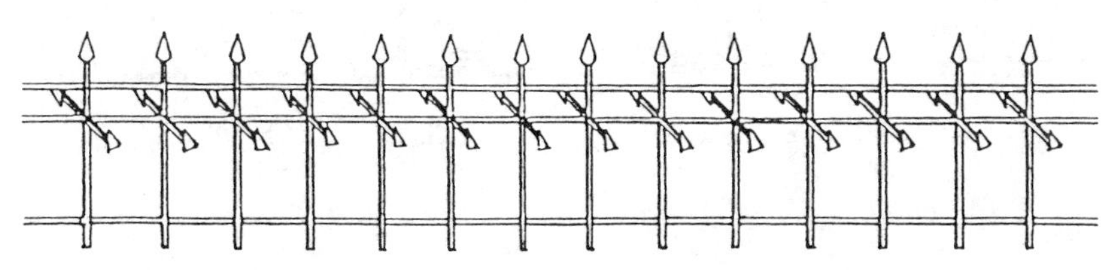

3. Bad: a security fence with spikes pointed toward the house

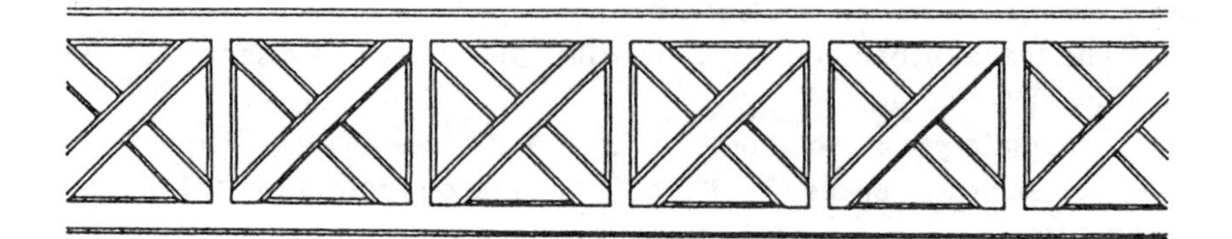

4a. Bad: fence design with crosses

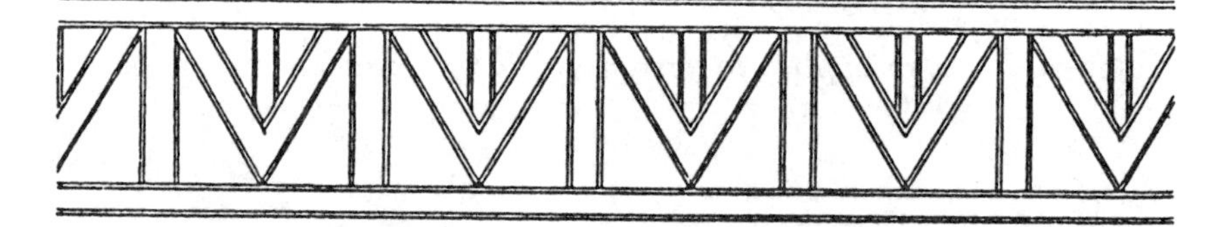

4b. Bad: fence design with arrows pointed downward

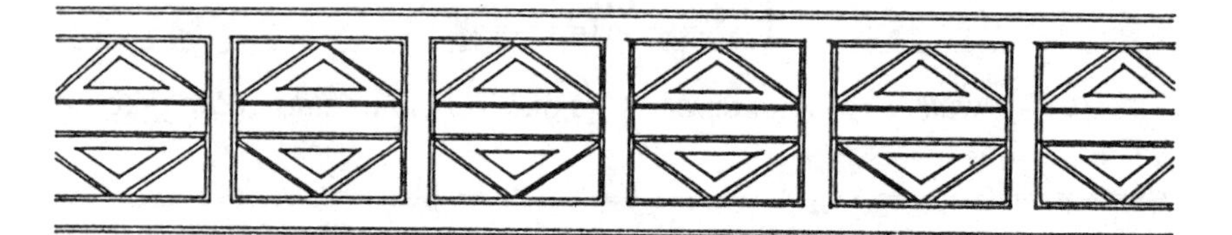

4c. Bad: fence with triangular design

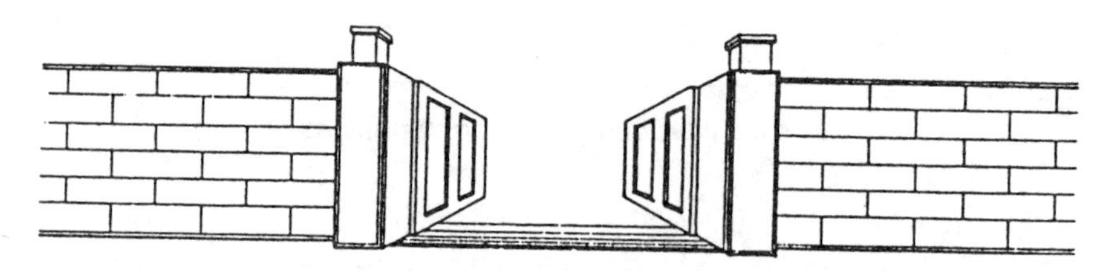

5. Good: gates opening inward

You have just learned about *external placements* that give '*sha*' (*negative chi*) to your door, and what cures you can use to minimize or eliminate the negativity.

Now, let's take a look at those *internal placements* that prevent good *chi* from entering the door, and circulating throughout your house.

NEGATIVE PLACEMENTS INSIDE YOUR DOOR

a) *A toilet of an upper floor over your door:*

Toilets are very negative factors in *feng shui*. *Water chi* flows downward, permeating whatever is beneath it. The dirty *water chi* of a toilet pervading the 'mouth' of your house will not augur well for your health and prosperity.

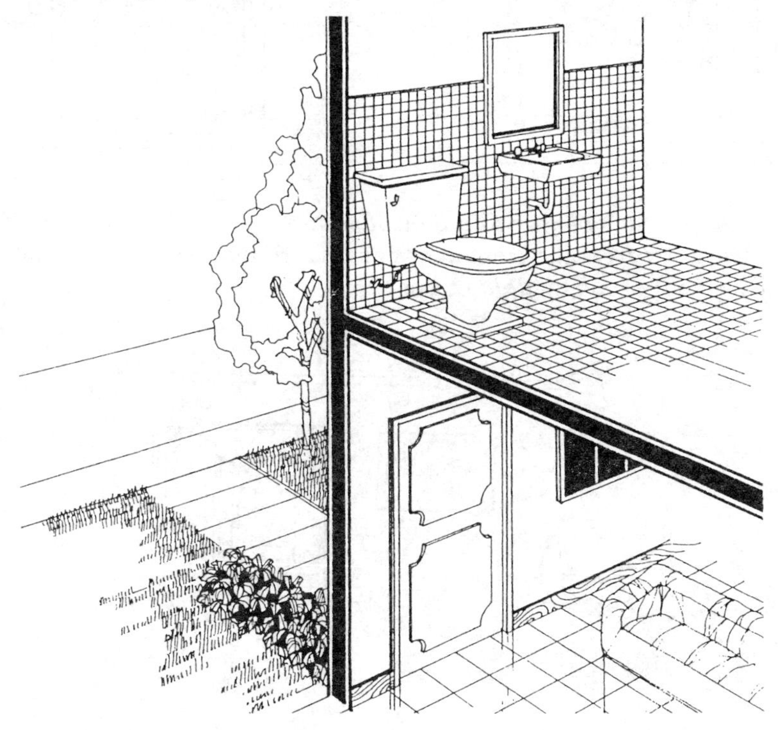

b) *A door opening to a corner:*
This placement sends sharp *chi* to the door.

c) *A door opening to a mirror:*
This is a definite negative in *feng shui* – see, *Chapter 16.*

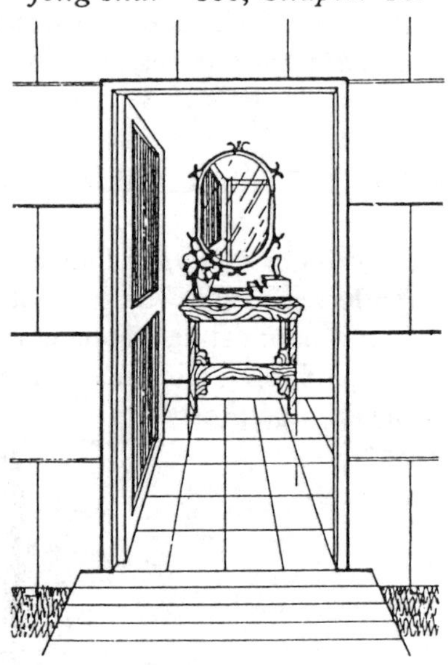

d) *A front door opening to a bedroom door:*
Strong *chi* from the front door can disturb the bedroom *chi* and disperse the *energy field* of the bed.

e) *A front door facing the stairs:*
This will lead to the loss of fortune. For the cure – see, *'Stairs – Conveyors of Chi'– Chapter 14.*

f) *A front door opening to a toilet door:*
The *yin chi* from the toilet will neutralize the good *chi* entering through your door.

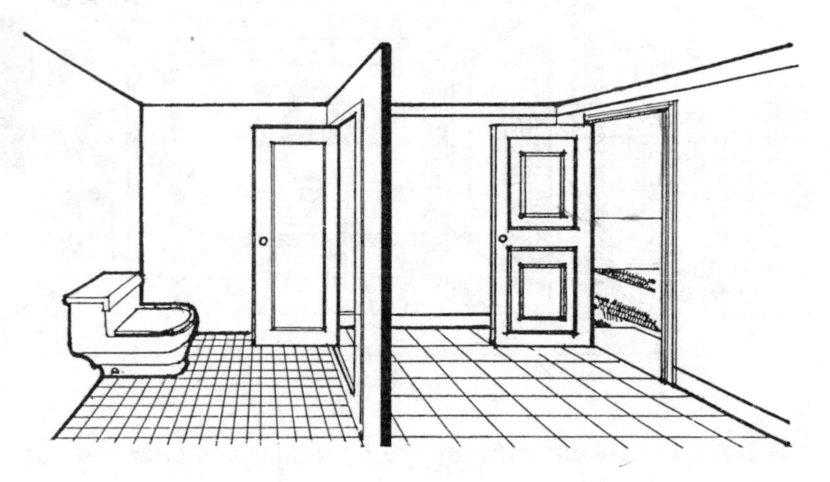

g) *front door opening to a pillar:*
This blocks the *chi* from entering the house. It will be even worse if the corner of the pillar faces the door, as it will send its arrow-like *chi* to the door 24 hours a day.

h) *A front door opening to a wall:*
This is only bad if the wall is close to the door, which will again block the *chi* from entering the house.

YOUR FENG SHUI CURES:

1] If a toilet is over a front door, there is no suitable cure. You must decide if the toilet is essential. If you think you can live without it, remove the w.c. and seal-off the soil pipe. Otherwise you will have to move your door.

2] If a front door opens to a toilet door, you can;
a) fit the door with an automatic closer and/or
b) place a screen, curtain or plants between the two doors.

A screen or divider between the front door and the toilet door

3] If your front door opens to a bedroom door, you should;
   a) place a screen or divider between the two doors or inside your bedroom door.
   b) If you do not have sufficient space for a screen, hang a curtain outside the bedroom door and/or,
   c) fit the bedroom door with an automatic closer.

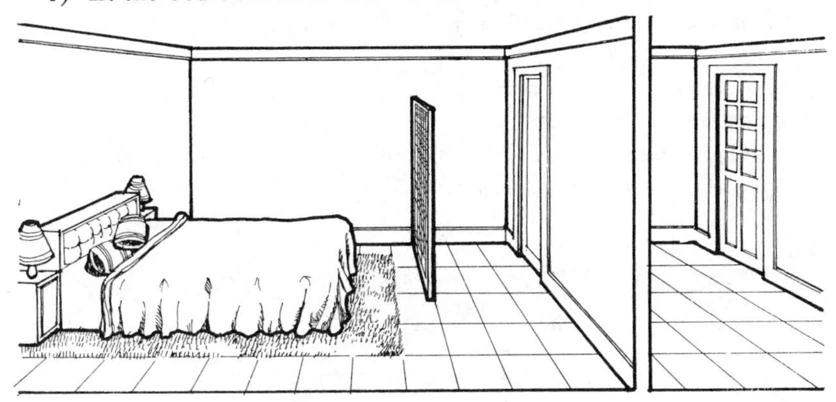

A screen or divider inside your bedroom door

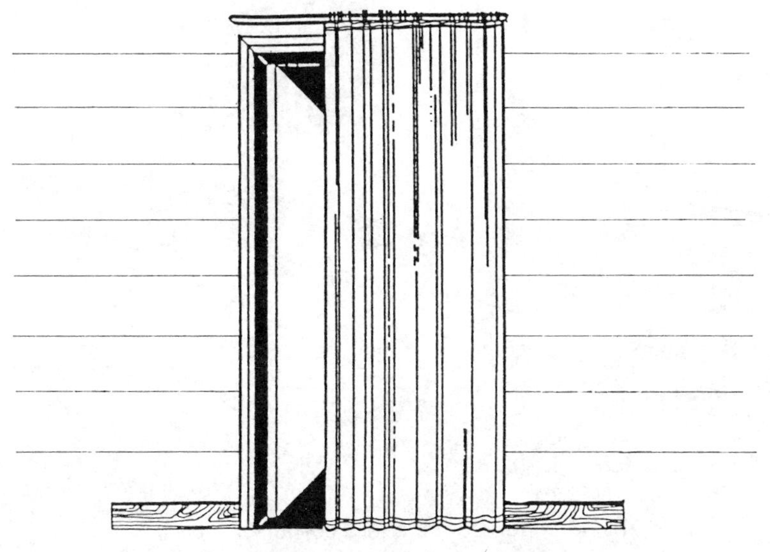

A curtain covering a door

4] If a front door opens to a wall, you should hang a painting (not a mirror) on the wall so that it directly faces the door. The painting should have depth, to draw in the *chi*. It can be a landscape but, it should not depict high mountains as these symbolically block the *chi*. If the painting depicts water, be sure that the water is not flowing toward the door. For more advice about paintings and where to place them – see, *'The Art of Feng Shui' – Chapter 17*

5] If a corner points to a door, you can;
   a) round it off, at least enough to blunt the sharp edge, or;
   b) place plants in front of it. Plants can also be used to disguise or soften the sharp corners of a pillar.

A vine softening the sharp corner of a pillar

DOOR ALIGNMENTS

Chi in – *Chi* out:

If you can see your rear door or a large rear window from your front door, you could lose your fortune in that house, especially if these two openings are aligned. The *chi* will flow in the front door and right out the rear, without circulating in the house at all.

Aligned doors and gates:

A front door that is directly aligned with a gate to the street does not provide an auspicious pathway for the *chi* to enter your house.

Two or more doors in a row create *chi* that is too strong and sharp. Just as a dam blocks the flow of water, a wall blocks the flow of *chi*. When a door is opened, the *chi* is sucked through in a rush. If the door of another room is directly in the path of this rush of *chi*, it will accumulate energy outside it. When this second door is opened the energy will rush into the room with double strength. This creates chaotic *chi* in the room which will negatively affect the people who occupy it. If there are three or more doors aligned, the sharpness and strength of the *chi* and its negative affect on the occupants will increase accordingly.

Partially aligned doors:

These are often worse than fully aligned doors because, they prevent the *chi* from flowing smoothly.

Doors that create conflicting energy:

Three doors that face each other from three different directions, particularly if they are in close proximity, create a clash of energy. This is known as a 'quarrel configuration.'

YOUR FENG SHUI CURES:

1] When you live in an apartment and your door faces a door of another unit – place a *primordial ba-gua* over your door.

2] For two doors that face each other, or a three-door quarrel configuration – hang a windchime or install a ceiling light between the doors.

3] For two doors that are partially aligned – hang a curtain over the confronting portion of one of the doors.

4] If your front and rear doors are aligned – place a divider, a screen or a bookcase between the two doors.

5] If your front door faces your gate, do any or all of the following;
   a) create a winding or curved path from the gate to the door and block the *chiong* (confrontation) with plants or lattice;
   b) place a *ba-gua* over your door, or;
   c) hang a *windchime* on your porch or directly on your door.

The *primordial ba-gua* is the most used *feng shui cure*. The harmonious energy pattern radiated by the trigrams of the *ba-gua* can neutralize or disperse *sha* or 'hidden arrows.' It should only be used on the outside of your house or unit.

The *windchime* is another effective cure. It can neutralize *sharp chi* or disperse *stagnant chi* by the soundwave it emits. *Windchimes* should be made of metal tubing of different lengths. Those made of glass, shells or other materials do not qualify as a *feng shui cure*. *Windchimes* can be used inside the house or on terraces and balconies – we rarely use them in the garden. If a *windchime* is hung where there is no breeze, it should be struck from time to time. A silent *windchime* is ineffective.

Primordial ba-gua

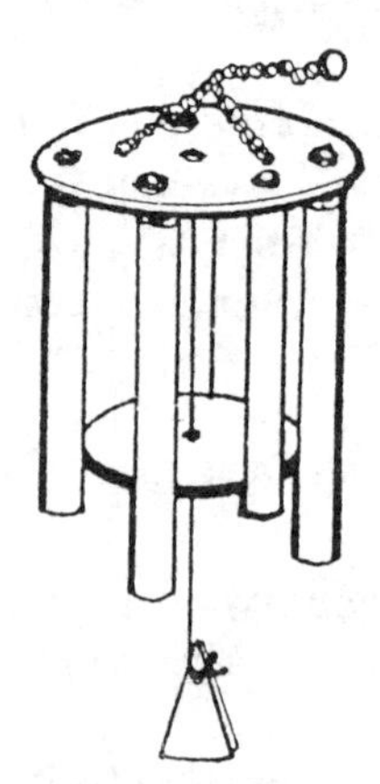

Windchimes

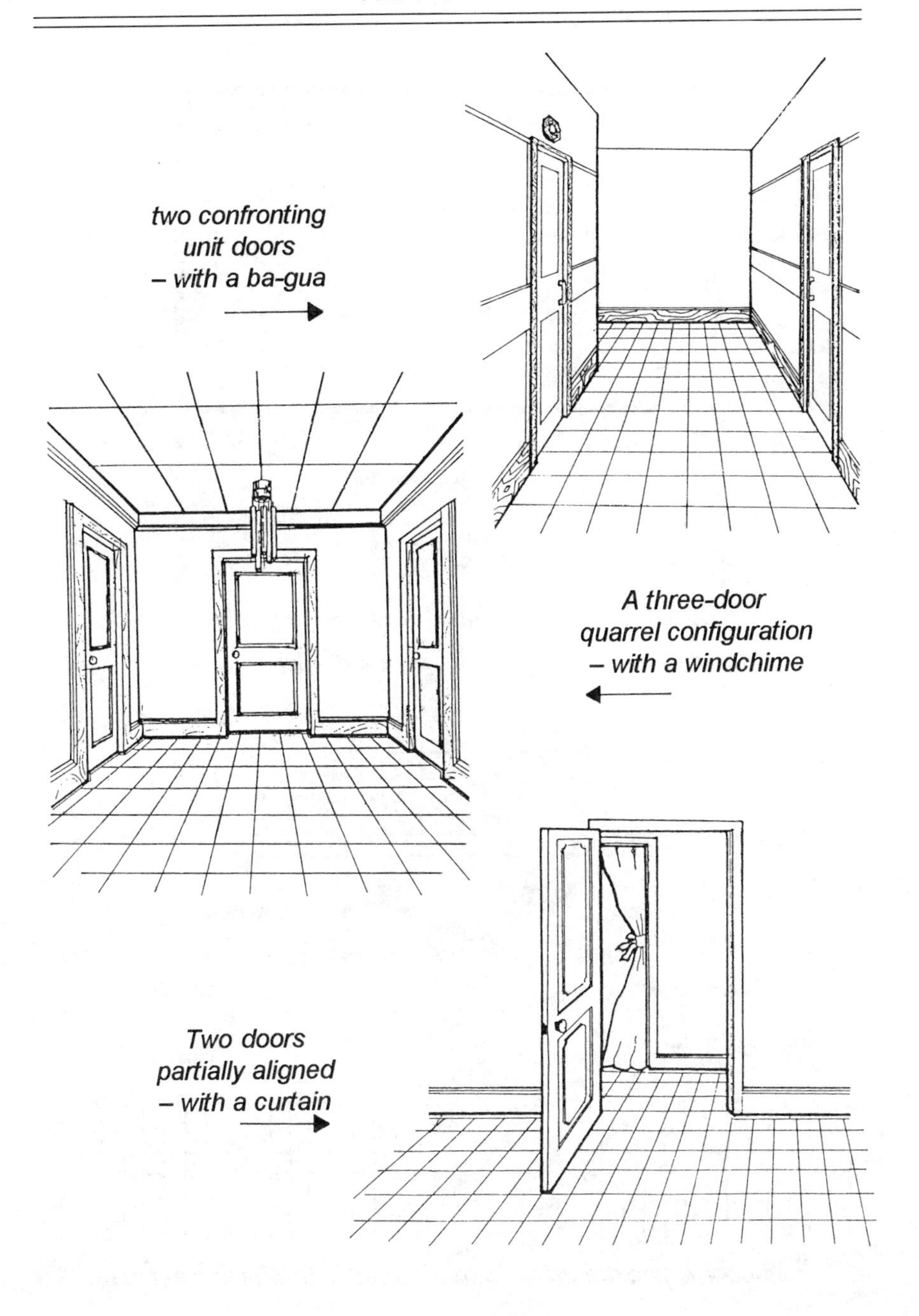
two confronting
unit doors
– with a ba-gua
A three-door
quarrel configuration
– with a windchime
Two doors
partially aligned
– with a curtain

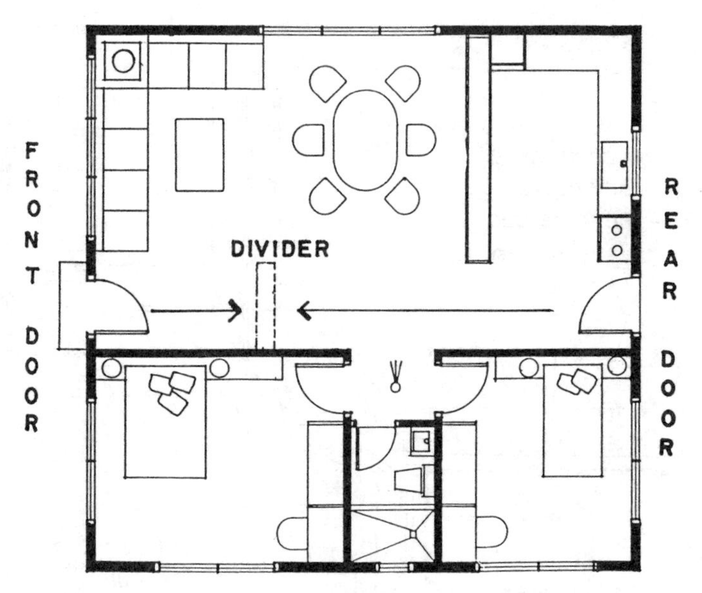

Front & rear doors aligned – with a divider between

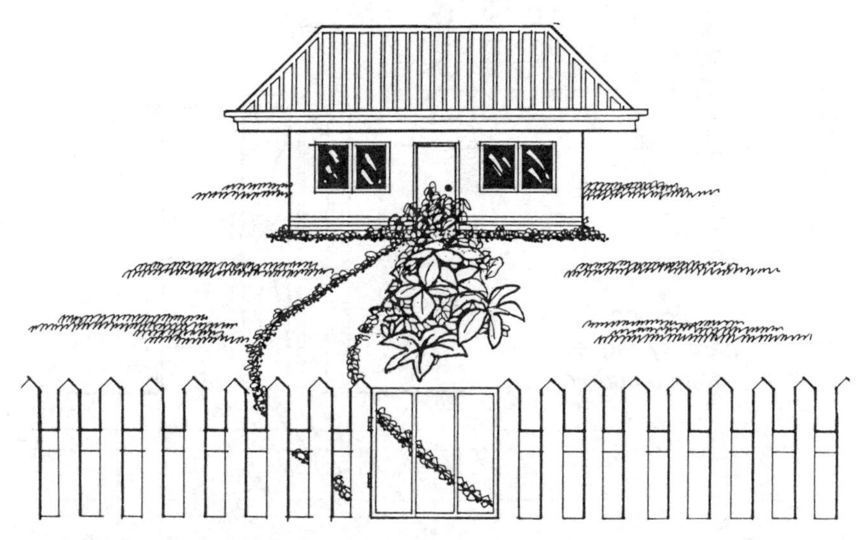

A front door facing the gate – with a curved path & plants between

CHAPTER EIGHT

FENG SHUI FOR A HAPPY MARRIAGE

A happy marriage is maintained in the bedroom and fortified in the kitchen. Good lovemaking and good food can keep a man contented and a woman fulfilled. It is argued that communication and sharing are the essential factors in maintaining a marriage, but isn't making love the deepest form of communication? And the family meal the very essence of sharing?

The bedroom is a pivotal point in the ***energy grid*** of a house. It is here that most arguments are settled, plans for the future are discussed and relationships are bonded in the physical act of love.

THE FIRST MARITAL HOME

Of the millions of snowflakes that fall, no two are exactly alike. The same is true of people; each person is unique. When two people with different qualities, personalities and preferences decide to set-up house together, it is certain that adjustments will have to be made.

Compromises and sometimes sacrifices are required to maintain a peaceful and happy marriage. The first few years together are crucial, as they set the pattern for a lifetime of personal interaction.

Most people do not realize how deeply the environment affects the human psyche and nervous system. Marriages are often unnecessarily strained because the couple live in an environment unsuited to their personalities, their backgrounds and their physical and psychological needs

The first conjugal home should be a place that provides an atmosphere of harmony, peace and inspiration. It does not have to be large and luxurious. A small apartment can become a cozy retreat from the outside world, and the bedroom a place where the couple can restore their energy and express their love. In most homes, the bedroom is not given the importance it deserves. It is, or should be a place dedicated to sustaining the bonds of marriage; a place for intimate personal communication and peaceful, restorative sleep.

SECRETS OF THE BEDROOM

Here are a few *feng shui* DO's and DON'Ts that can prolong the honeymoon of newly-weds, or restore that old magic to a tired marriage.

Bed Placements:

DO place the head of your bed against a solid wall:

A bed should have 'backing.' This rule of backing applies to all major *feng shui* placements and is particularly important for a bed. A firm solid support behind your head gives a comforting feeling of security. When you are sleeping, your subconscious mind will relax and let down its guard, providing you with a better quality of rest.

DON'T place your bed under a window:

This placement does not provide the essential backing, nor a feeling of safety. You will feel even less secure if the window is open. This sense of insecurity is often subconscious, but it is the subconscious mind that determines whether we sleep well, or are restless during the night.

A bed under the window

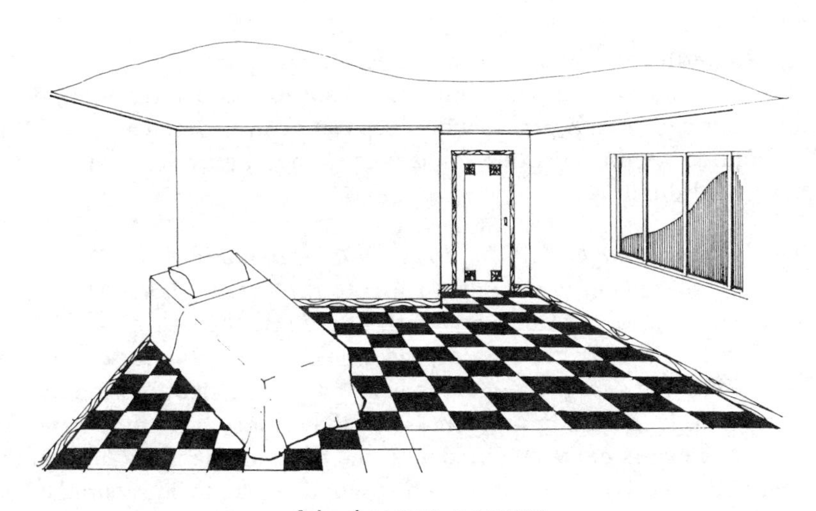

A bed across a corner

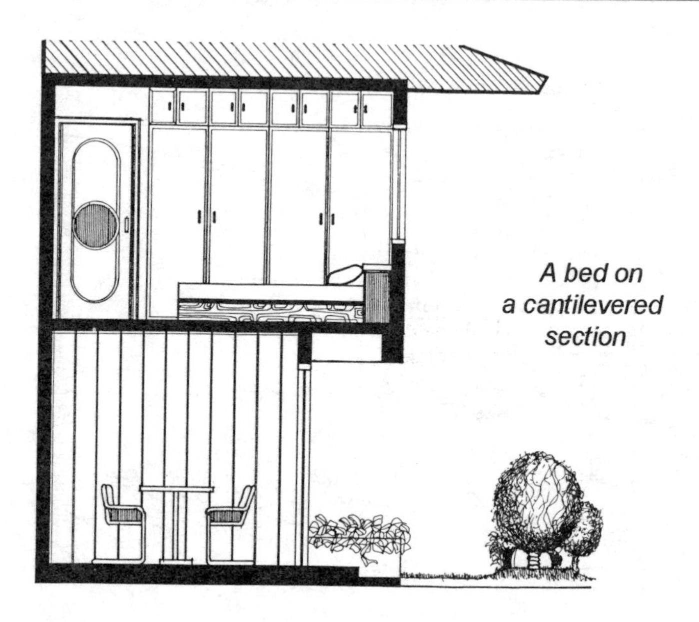

DON'T slant your bed across a corner:

The diagonal placement of a bed does not provide backing, it can also drain your energy because, *energy escapes through corners*.

DON'T sleep on a cantilevered area:

A cantilever is a protruded or over-hanging area that has no foundation or support. If a portion of your bedroom is cantilevered, don't place your bed on it. A person who sleeps on a cantilevered area will lose self-confidence, because the mind will always be aware that there is nothing solid below.

DON'T place your bed in the direct path of a door:

This placement is very disturbing to the *energy field* of the bed – every time the door is opened, a rush of *chi* hits the bed.

If the door opens to a toilet; the humid and fetid *toilet chi* will be absorbed by the *energy field* of the bed and the health of the couple will be affected. It is usually problems with the urinary tract that manifest.

If the bed is between two doors; the bombardment of *chi* from the doors will create chaotic energy – this will disturb the body/mind of the couple – short tempers and irritability will be the result.

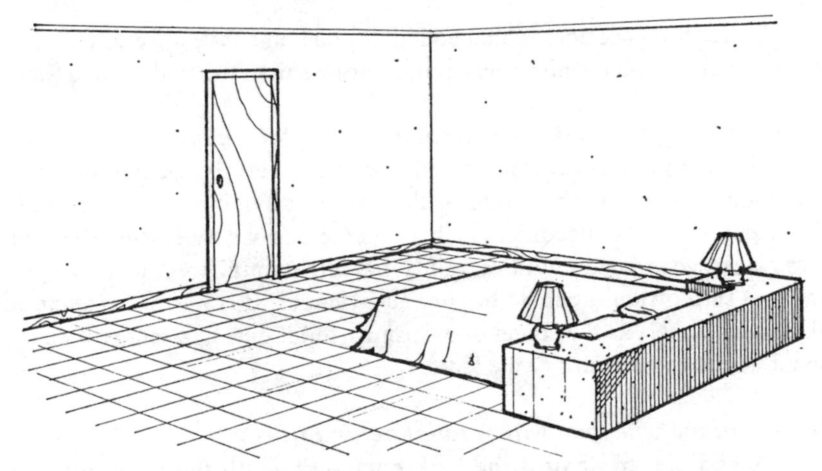

A bed in the direct path of the door

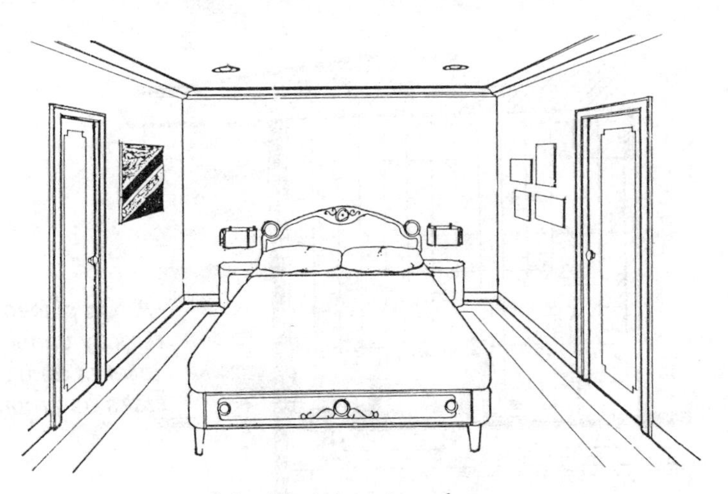

A bed between two doors

DON'T sleep too high above the ground:

If your bed is too high, you will be disconnected from the *ground chi*. Sleeping on the floor is actually the best way to get in touch with the Earth's energy. The higher the bed, the less *chi* you receive. If you are convalescing from an illness, you might recover faster if you sleep on a low bed or on the floor.

Water beds are not recommended. If you must have a water bed, use it in a vacation home which you occupy for less than thirty days at a time.

DON'T place your bed under a toilet of the floor above you:

Toilets are dirty elements and must be carefully located to avoid contaminating favourable areas of the house. Remember that water *chi* flows downward, consequently, dirty water and waste matter flushing away over your head could certainly be detrimental to your body *chi,* and just think what it can do to your self-image! It is hardly a romantic placement either, as the sound of a flushing toilet during a tender moment could be distracting, to say the least.

DON'T place your bed with a toilet behind it:

A bed placed against the bathroom wall, with the toilet directly behind it, is a no-no for reasons similar to the above.

A bed placed directly under a toilet of an up-stairs bathroom

A bed with a toilet behind it

DON'T sleep under a water tank:

Water chi flows downward and penetrates to the floor below. If a tank is over your bed, you will not only be oppessed by its weight but will also absorb the yin *water chi* – to the detriment of your health.

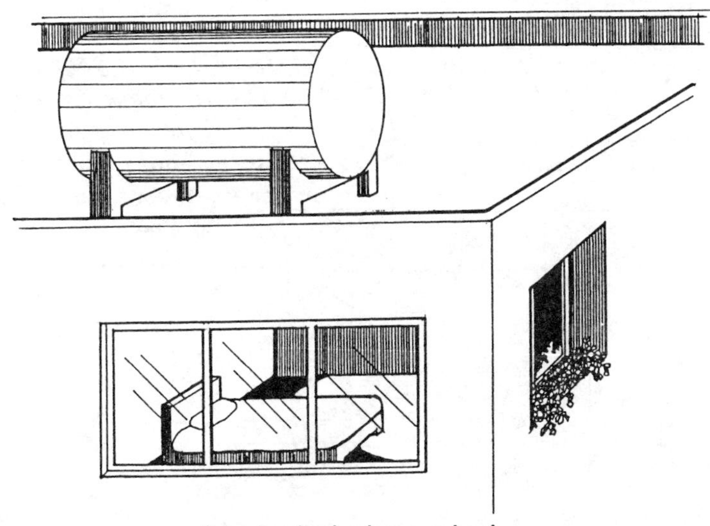

A water tank above a bed

Don't place a stove or heating appliance behind your bed:

The stove and other heating appliances emit the frequency of fire. If the appliance is used daily, a heat field will build up and penetrate the wall behind your bed. This subtle energy will affect you when you are at your most vulnerable, i.e., when you are sleeping. The result will be irritability and hot-headedness.

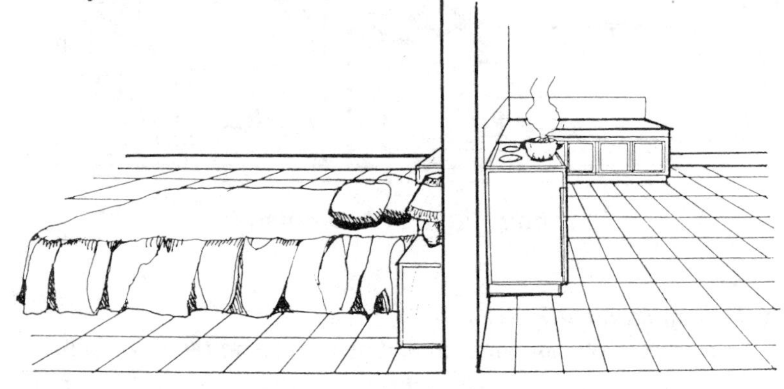

A stove behind a bed

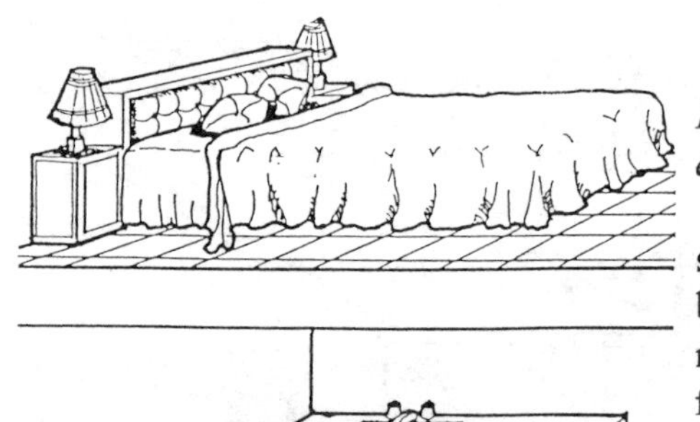

DON'T place your bed directly above a stove:

If you are living in a two-storey house, your bed might be over your stove. *Fire chi* rises and penetrates the upper floor. If you are bad-tempered or prone to fever, check what is downstairs under your bed.

DO avoid over-head beams:

Over-head beams exert pressure on whatever or whoever is beneath them. Some of the effects of a beam over a bed are:

a) Over the head or throat;
can give you a feeling of heaviness, headache, or sore throat.

b) Over the chest area;
will make you susceptible to coughs and colds and will aggravate an asthmatic condition.

c) Over the stomach area;
will make you prone to digestive and intestinal problems.

d) Running lengthwise down the centre of the bed;
will diminish your love life, as both you and your spouse will tend to stay on your own side of the bed to avoid pressure from the beam.

e) Over the reproductive organs;
If a man sleeps on his back, as most of them do, and if there is a beam over his reproductive organs, he will eventually have difficulty with his sexual performance. The subtle pressure of an overhead beam can also affect the sex drive of a woman. Childless marriages can often be attributed to this wrong placement of the marital bed.

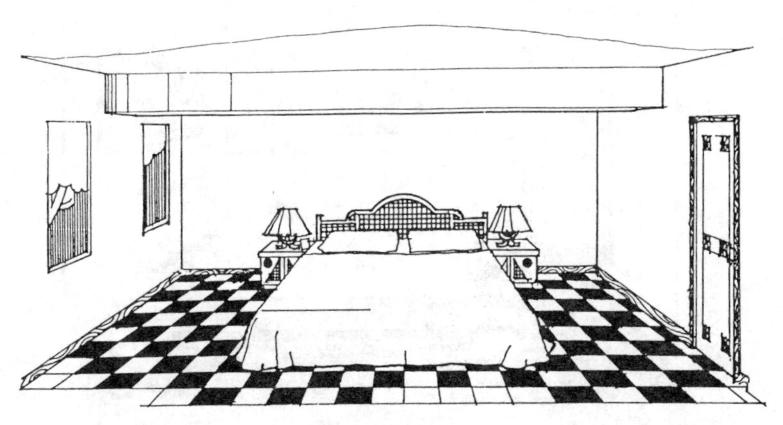

A beam over the chest area

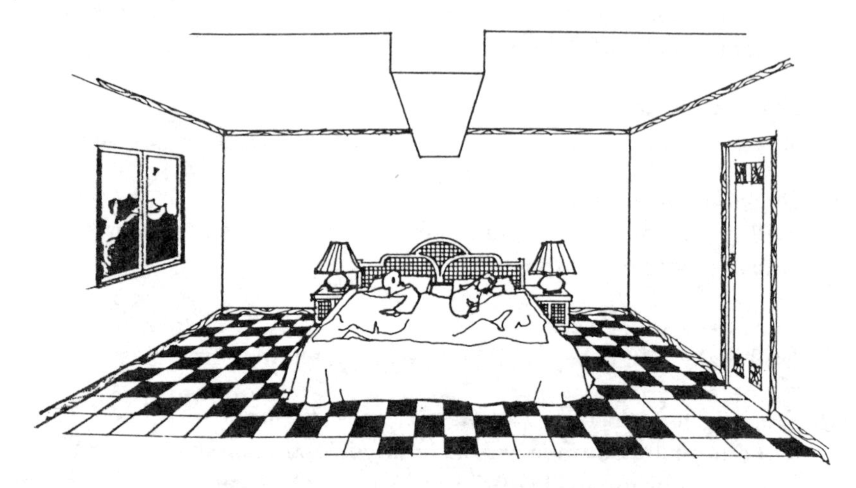

A beam lengthwise over the bed

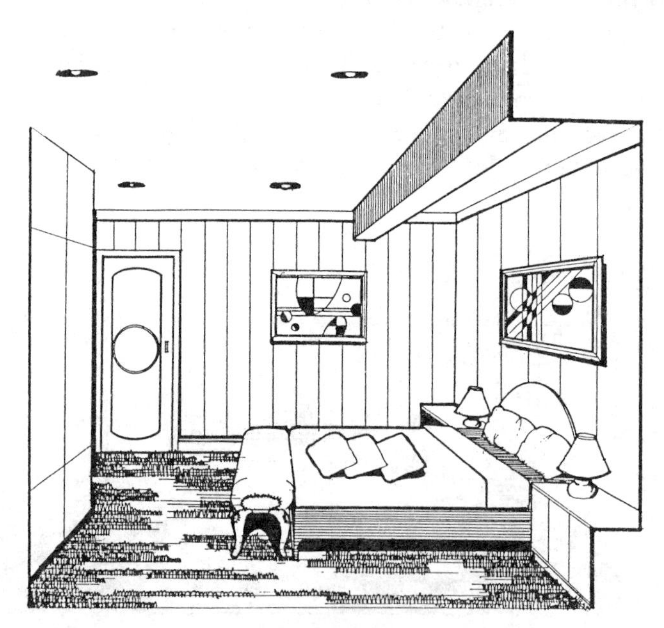

A beam over the reproductive organs

YOUR FENG SHUI CURES:

1] You can relocate your bed to avoid most of the preceding violations.

2] If there is no place for your bed other than under a window, then fit your window with venetian blinds and turn the slats upward to direct the *chi* over your head. Heavy curtains that hang considerably lower than the window can also help.

3] If you cannot avoid having a beam over your bed, you should drop the ceiling to the level of the beam. We sometimes recommend dropping the ceiling only over the bed area and placing lights behind the dropped section. This not only corrects the *feng shui* violation, it also gives attractive, indirect lighting to the room.

4] If you cannot avoid ***door chi*** hitting your bed, you should place a screen or divider between the door and the bed. If your room is too small for a divider, hang a curtain outside your door.

Dropped ceiling over the bed

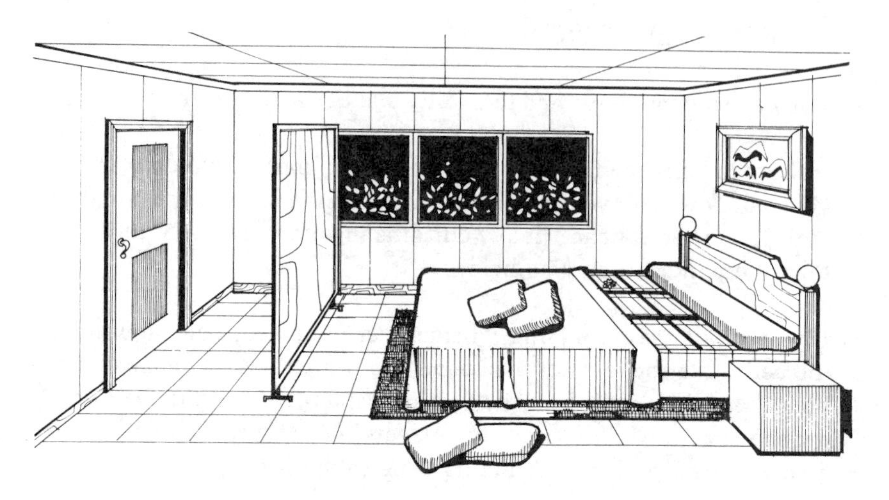

A screen between the bed & the door

OTHER THINGS UNSUITED TO THE BEDROOM:

a) *Round shapes, e.g., round beds, windows, tables or ornaments* – round shapes represent movement – a bedroom should be 'steady'.
b) *Metal beds or metal furniture* – these give off '*cold chi.*'
c) *Triangular shapes or pointed objects* – these emit *arrows of chi.*
d) *Irregular shaped rooms that have many angles* – these rooms have too many protrusions and hollows. Fill the hollows with furniture or plants. If protrusions are pointed, round them off or place a plant in front of them.

Bedroom Colours:

In *personalized feng shui* the colours in the bedroom should be those that correspond to the *elements* needed by the occupants, and the headboard of the marital bed should be placed in a direction that is favourable to them. In lieu of a personal analysis, you should select the location of your bed to avoid the preceding violations, and decorate your room in soft shades of harmonious colours – *see the chart on page 25 for the harmonious colours.*

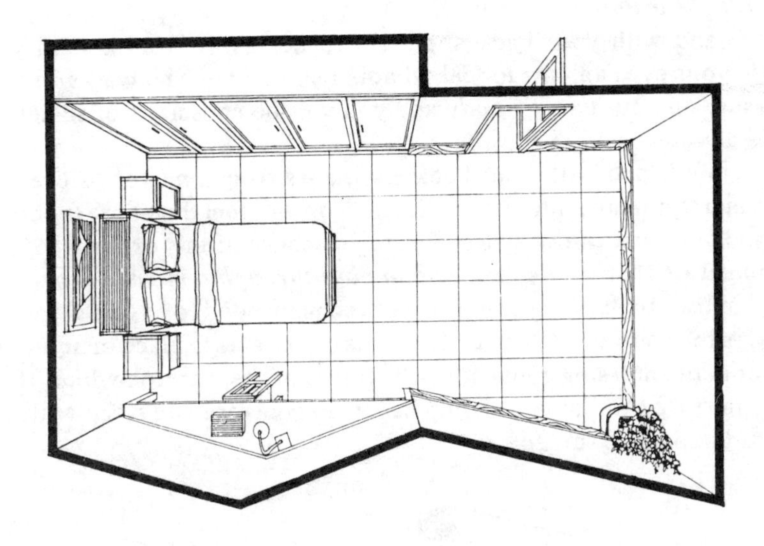

An irregularly shaped room – with the sharp corners corrected by a plant and built-in furniture

MIRROR, MIRROR ON THE WALL

A bed should never be reflected in a mirror. If the mirror is behind the bed, it voids the principle of 'solid backing.'

The worst mirror versus bed position is to have a mirror on the ceiling directly above the bed. This may be fun, but it is damaging to the psyche, as constantly seeing yourself lying prone on a bed suggests sickness or death to your subconscious mind.

In metaphysical practice, mirrors can be used as doors to other dimensions. When you sleep, your *astral form* moves out of the physical body, it can pass through the mirror and wander into *astral realms* – this causes morning fatigue and disturbed, restless sleep, sometimes with vivid, colourful dreams. Many of the people who come to us for *feng shui* advice, complain that they wake up feeling tired. When we inspect their house, we usually find that they have a mirror reflecting their bed

Try the following experiment:

Stand with your back about six inches away from a solid wall. Close your eyes and try to feel what is behind you. The wall will exert pressure on your *energy body* and you will be conscious of something solid at your back.

Now, stand with your back six inches from a mirror. Close your eyes and again tune into your feelings. You will feel that there is nothing behind you, just empty space. The significance of this experiment is to demonstrate that *subtle energy can pass through a mirror.*

In traditional *feng shui* it is not recommended to have any mirrors at all in the bedroom. We usually advise our clients to place their mirrors either in the dressing room or on the inside of the wardrobe door. If you have mirrored walls, you should cover them before you sleep with curtains, blinds or a screen.

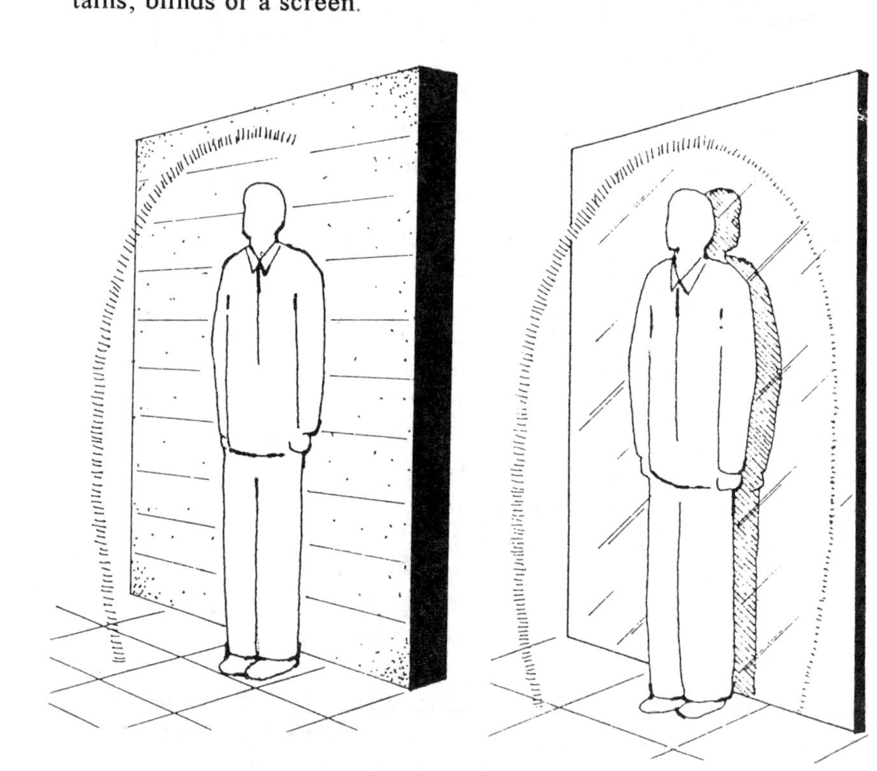

Experiment with mirror and wall

The bed reflected in two mirrors

A mirror on the ceiling over the bed

SUBTLE CURRENTS

A mistake made by many couples, is to have too many electrical appliances inside the bedroom. It is not uncommon to find in the bedrooms of modern homes, some or all of the following:

a) Television
b) Video player
c) Home computer
d) Electric clock
e) Radio
f) Tape or C.D. player
g) Mini-refrigerator
h) Coffee maker
i) Cellular phone
j) Intercom

The list is formidable, and with the new technology it could be just a foretaste of the future. Some beds have electrical wires and extension cords over, under and around them. The frequency of these subtle currents negatively affects the persons sleeping in the bed. It is often the case in a bedroom jammed with electrical gadgetry, that t.v. viewing and computer games take precedence over lovemaking.

Radiation from t.v. sets is decidedly unhealthy. The t.v. should not directly face the bed and should be disconnected from the wall socket (not just turned off) when not in use.

BEDROOM LIGHTING

The type of lighting you use can affect your body *chi* and your health. When you rest or read directly under an electric light, it has an effect on your mood. Light gives off a frequency of energy that is quite strong – it is also hot. If your bed is under an overhead light, you will wake up with a headache or feeling irritated.

We do not recommend flourescent lighting in a bedroom. Single colour lighting, such as that emitted by flourescent tubes, can throw the body's energy out of balance. Our bodies are composed of energy in the full spectrum of colour. Psychics see the *auric field* of the human body in multi-colours. This phenomenon can also be observed by using eyeglasses with special lenses, and to some extent, by kirlian photography.

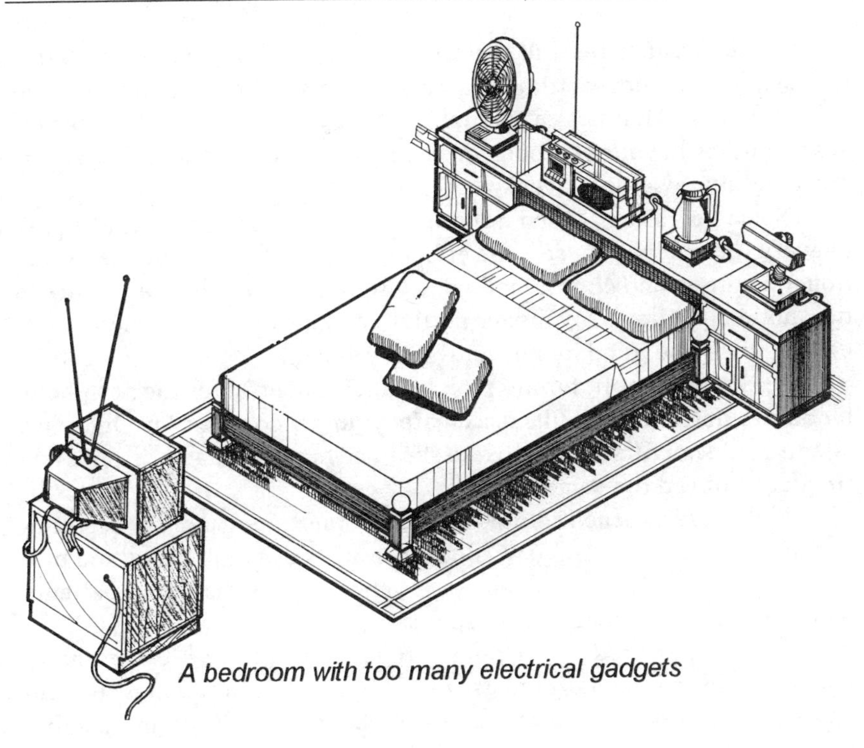

A bedroom with too many electrical gadgets

A bedroom with subtle lighting

In some countries, full spectrum lighting, which invisibly radiates the complete colour spectrum, is used in schools, offices, institutions and private homes. If it is not yet available where you live, you can use incandescent bulbs in your bedroom, or you may try the 'soft pink' bulbs that are generally available everywhere.

Some years ago, I used light bulbs in a very delicate shade of pink in every room of my house – the effect was fascinating. Without exception, my guests and clients mellowed within ten minutes of exposure to the subtle pink glow. My dinner parties and late suppers became events of happiness and good humor until the wee hours.

Basking in a soft, faintly pink light is wonderful for the peripheral blood circulation and results in a clearer younger complexion. One of my clients could not find pink bulbs, so she lined her lampshades in pink fabric and achieved the same effect.

Pink, rose or peach colours create an atmosphere that is absolutely conducive to loving feelings. Colour therapists use pink lights and pink walls to produce positive moods in psychologically disturbed patients. You can try it on a recalcitrant spouse.

Low wattage red lights can improve your sex life – traditionally, houses of pleasure make good use of red lights. Red stimulates the *base* and *sex* energy centers (*chakras*) of the body. Pink has a more subtle effect, it stimulates the *heart chakra* which enhances sensitivity and loving feelings.

A healthy and fulfilling love life is the true objective of bedroom *feng shui,* and it is certainly one of the most important ingredients in a happy marriage. No matter what arguments or problems occur during the day, when you are together in the warm and romantic atmosphere of a well-planned bedroom, all hurt feelings and resentments melt away.

CHAPTER NINE

FAMILY BEDROOMS

Childrens' Rooms

Study Tables

Rooms for the Elderly

CHILDRENS' ROOMS

When planning the bedrooms of young children, pay particular attention to those placements that engender insecurity. Children who are sick, nervous, hyperactive, who 'wet the bed' or have nightmares should have the *feng shui* of their bedrooms thoroughly checked.

Apart from the bedroom DON'Ts, which are enumerated in the preceding chapter, childrens' rooms should not have any of the following items visible from the bed:

a) Swords, weapons, or posters depicting violence.
b) Toys that are frightening or huge, i.e., bigger than the child.
c) Mobiles or moving objects.

Children enjoy these things, but when it's time go to sleep they should be out of view so that a peaceful, non-scary atmosphere prevails.

A nervous child should not sleep in total darkness. A small night light that does not hit the eyes can be installed, and objects that cast shadows can be placed inside the closet.

There should definitely not be any mirrors in the room of a highly sensitive child (except on the inside of a closet door).

Don't locate the bedrooms of children or elderly persons over a garage. Both these age groups are susceptible to respiratory problems. The polluted *chi* of garage fumes will exacerbate this susceptibility.

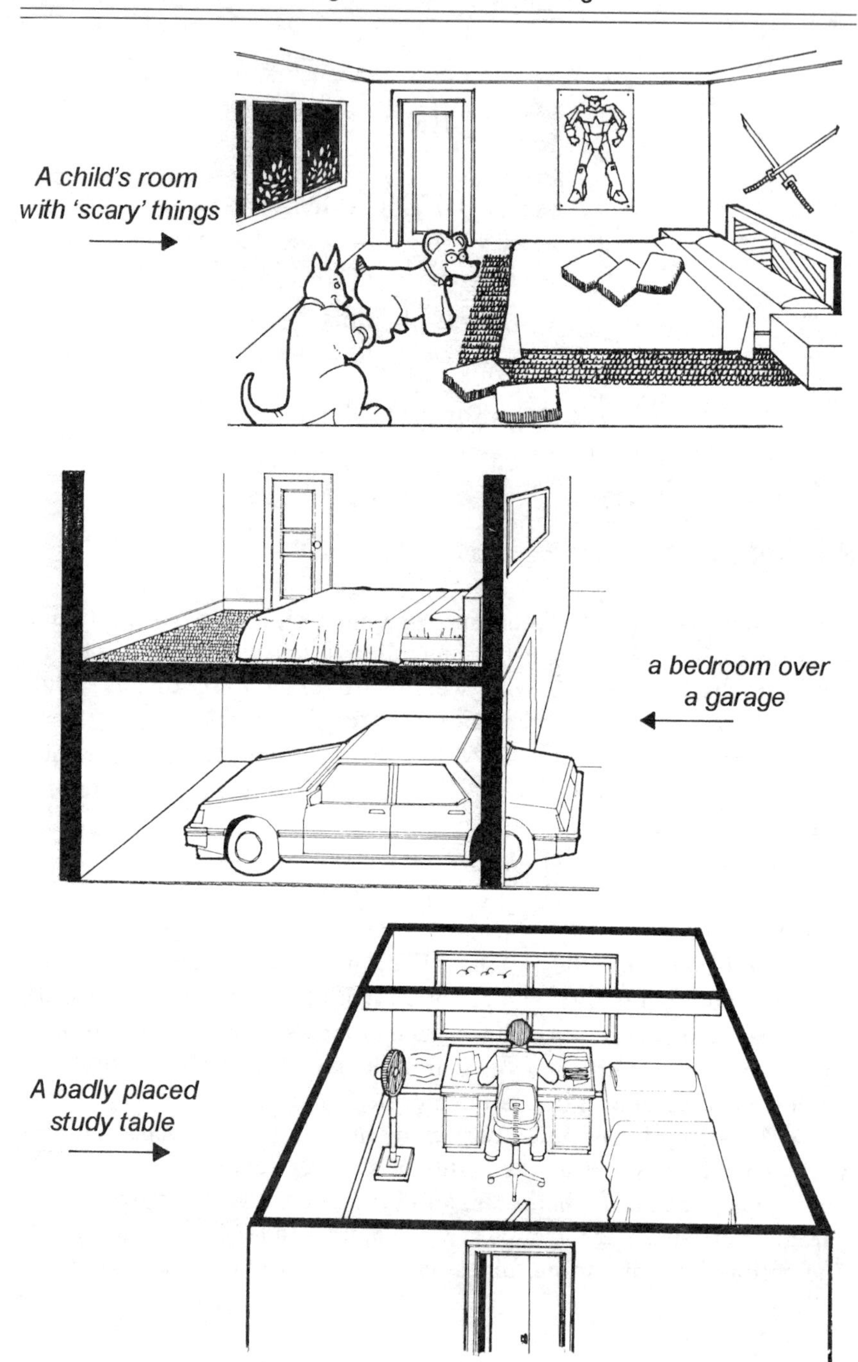
A child's room
with 'scary' things
a bedroom over
a garage
A badly placed
study table

THE STUDY DESK

The placement of a child's study table can spell the difference between passing and failing grades. To give your child the right environment for study, follow these guidelines when placing the table or desk:

a) *The table should not face a window* – this distracts concentration.
b) *A light should not be directly overhead* – this can be the cause of headache. A desk lamp that shines on the work (not in the eyes) focuses the student's attention.
c) *A study chair should not be under a beam* – the oppressive *chi* of a beam causes fuzzy thinking.
d) *A door should not be behind a study table* – this disturbs the student's concentration.
e) *A study chair should not be hit by a draft from an air-conditioner or electric fan* – this is not only distracting, it is also unhealthy.

Note: *These rules can also be applied to the placement of office desks.*

BEDROOMS FOR THE ELDERLY

Here too, you can apply the rules previously outlined in *Chapter 9*, but bear in mind that the elderly are particularly vulnerable to drafts and subtle *chi* from doors, windows and sharp corners.

Avoid the following:

a) *A beam over the bed* – this will precipitate aches and pains.
b) *The bed near a bathroom door* – a dressing room, hallway or screen should block the bathroom's *yin chi* from hitting the bed.
c) *Highly polished floors* – carpeted floors are better, but they must be vacuumed often. Wooden floors with non-skid mats are also good.
d) *Dark and gloomy colours and darkly varnished wood* – decorate the room in soft and light tones, have ample ventilation and natural light during the day, and bright lighting without glare at night.
e) *An elder's room on an upper floor* – if your house has two floors, allocate a room on the ground floor for your older folk – this avoids the stress of climbing the stairs.

The idea is to have a bright, cheerful and safe room wherein your elders can feel comfortable and secure. With good *feng shui* in the bedroom, an ailing parent can recover faster, and a healthy oldster can have a longer and more active life.

CHAPTER TEN

YOUR KITCHEN

Placing Your Stove
Feng Shui Cures

The house you live in can make or break your marriage, your health and your bank balance. The family wealth and health is linked to many placements in the home, one of the most important of these is the kitchen stove.

The stove represents the family's fortune. It is a symbol of the love and nurturing qualities of the home's breadwinner, (usually the father) who works and strives to provide food and sustenance for his family. For this reason, the stove should be placed in a position that will enhance his capacity to earn. Wrong placement of the stove alone, or in combination with other factors, not only adversely affects the fortune of family members, it is also damaging to health and family unity.

PLACING YOUR STOVE

Your *geomancer* will place the stove according to the life analysis of the breadwinner and ensure that it does not oppose the fortune of the wife. This book does not include these methods of personalizing your *feng shui*, but there are quite a few general rules you can use to safeguard your stove from harmful *chi* and improve the atmosphere of your kitchen. Observe the following DON'Ts when placing your stove:

DON'T place a stove opposite a sink, washing machine or refrigerator:

This placement, creates a conflict of frequencies. The stove emits *fire chi* and the faucet, refrigerator and washing machine emit the opposing *water chi*– since water puts out fire, the *chi* of the stove (and your fortune) will be diminished.

When the *water and fire chi* conflict, the atmosphere of the kitchen becomes discordant and irritating – the cook (usually the wife) becomes argumentative and nervous – the food she prepares absorbs the negative vibrations – and those who eat the food assimilate the negativity.

It is with good reason that the Chinese give such importance to the placement of the stove. Even in the West there is the expression 'You are what you eat,' which indicates an awareness that food affects your body chemistry, therefore your health, your disposition, and consequently your ability to earn.

If the energy in the kitchen is harmonious and the cook is in a calm and happy mood when preparing the meal, the whole household will benefit from the positive energy derived from the food.

The stove facing a sink

The stove facing a door to the outside

DON'T place your stove directly facing a door to the outside:

This placement will cause loss of fortune and health, as the *stove chi* will be disturbed and dissipated everytime the door is opened. Any negative factor, such as; a water tank or an electric post that is outside the door, or a corner of a building or roof ridge line that is pointed at the door, will send its *sha* directly to the stove. Traditionally, a stove should not be visible from the front door, or from outside the kitchen door.

DON'T place your stove facing a toilet door:

Everytime the toilet door is opened, the humid and fetid *water chi* will hit the stove. This again creates a clash between the *fire* and *water elements* and dissipates the *chi* of the stove. It is also a hidden cause of stomach ailments.

DON'T place your stove with a toilet behind it:

This placement signifies that your fortune and health will be flushed away. A stove in close proximity to a toilet, sewage or drainage pipe is also unhealthy, and health goes hand in hand with prosperity.

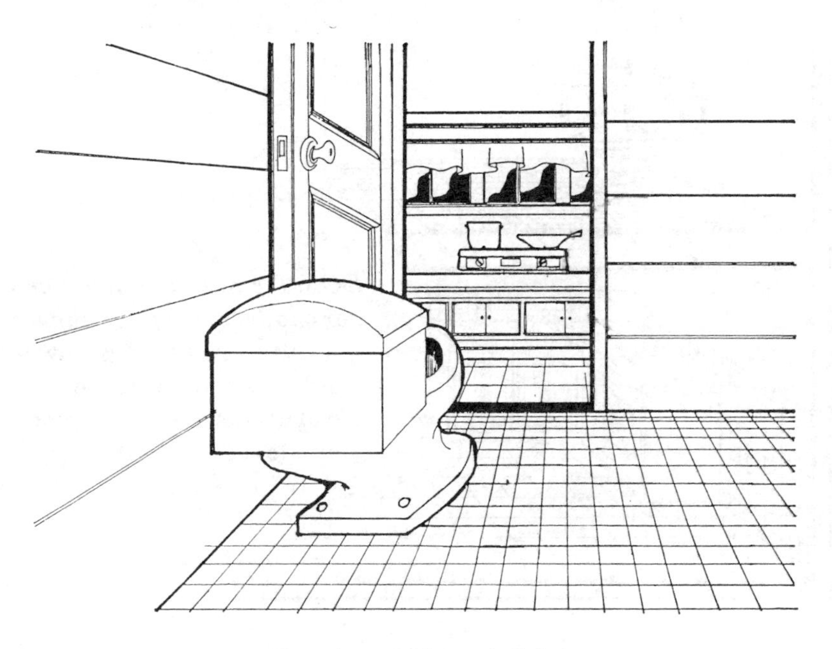

The stove facing a toilet door

A toilet behind the stove

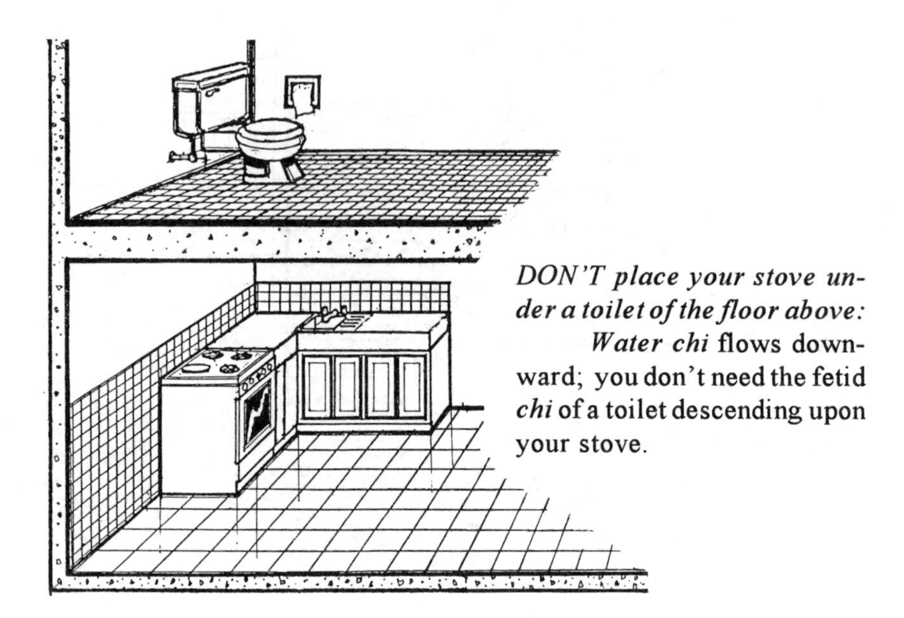

DON'T place your stove under a toilet of the floor above:

Water chi flows downward; you don't need the fetid *chi* of a toilet descending upon your stove.

The stove under a window

DON'T place your stove under a window:

There should be a solid wall behind your stove. This will provide backing – which translates into financial stability.

The modern cooking island, i.e., a stove in the centre of the kitchen, is considered to be unfortunate by traditional *geomancers*. In our practice, we can approve a cooking island for specialty foods, as long as the main staples are cooked on a well-placed stove.

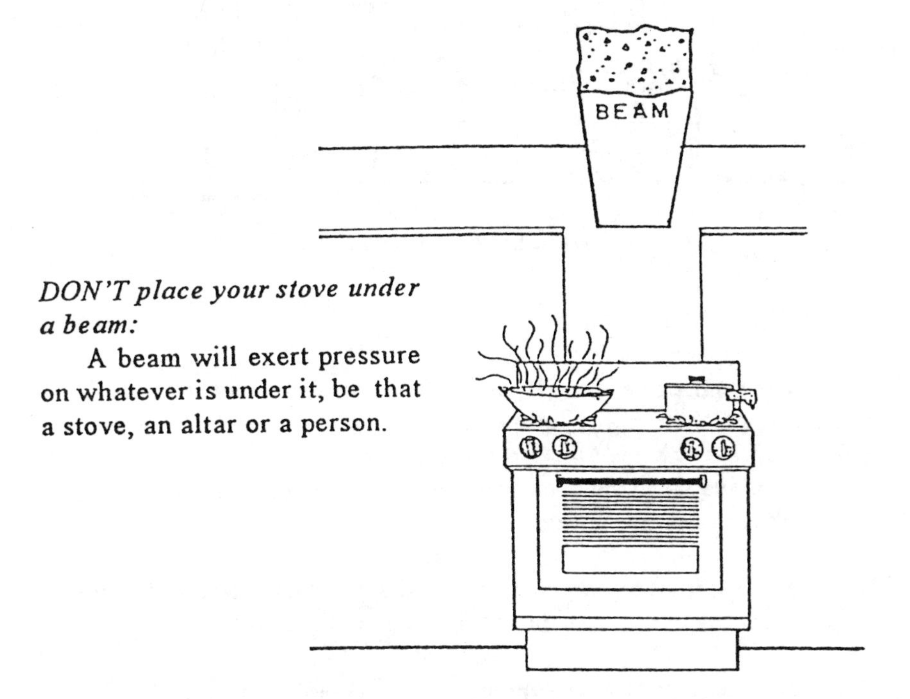

DON'T place your stove under a beam:

A beam will exert pressure on whatever is under it, be that a stove, an altar or a person.

A few more tips on stove placements:

a) A stove should not be 'hit' by the sharp *chi* of corners, walls or pillars.
b) Exposed water pipes should not run under your stove.
c) Your stove should not be placed between two water elements, such as a sink, a refrigerator or washing machine.
d) An exhaust fan can be close to, but not directly behind or above your stove – stove hoods are acceptable.
e) A water tank, laundry sink, garden faucet, or any other water placement should not be located behind your stove.

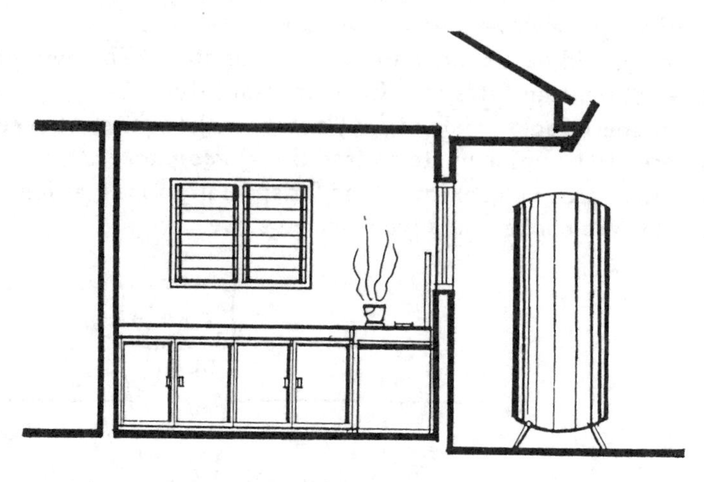

A water tank behind the stove

YOUR FENG SHUI CURES:

When your stove is negatively placed, the best 'cure' is to move it. If you cannot, then do the following:

1] If your stove faces the back door, place a convex mirror or a *ba-gua* over the outside of your door. (You can use the cut-out on page 269)

2] If your stove is hit by *sha chi* from the sharp corners of walls or pillars; round off the corners, or place plants or vines in front of them.

3] Cover water pipes under your stove with a plank of hard wood. *Water chi* from the pipes feeds the *wood chi* of the plank, and the *wood chi* feeds the *fire chi* of the stove. This is a clear example of how *geomancers* use the subtle energies of the *elements* as *feng shui cures*

4] A piece of wood can also be placed between a stove and an adjacent water placement; such as, a sink or a refrigerator.

5] A wooden table can be placed between a sink and a stove that face each other. A small live plant should be placed on the table. If there is no room in your kitchen for a table, use a swivel faucet on your sink and secure it so that it does not directly face the stove.

6] If you have a bathroom adjacent to the kitchen, and the door opens directly into, or facing the cooking area; fit the door with an automatic closer, and place a live plant inside the bathroom or outside the bathroom door.

7] If your stove is under a window and you cannot move it, block off the lower section of the window with strong non-flammable material – this will provide 'backing' for the stove.

Traditionally, a stove should be installed or transferred only on the special days that are recommended by your *geomancer*, however, if you do install or move it on a wrong day, the bad effects will usually not last longer than 30–45 days.

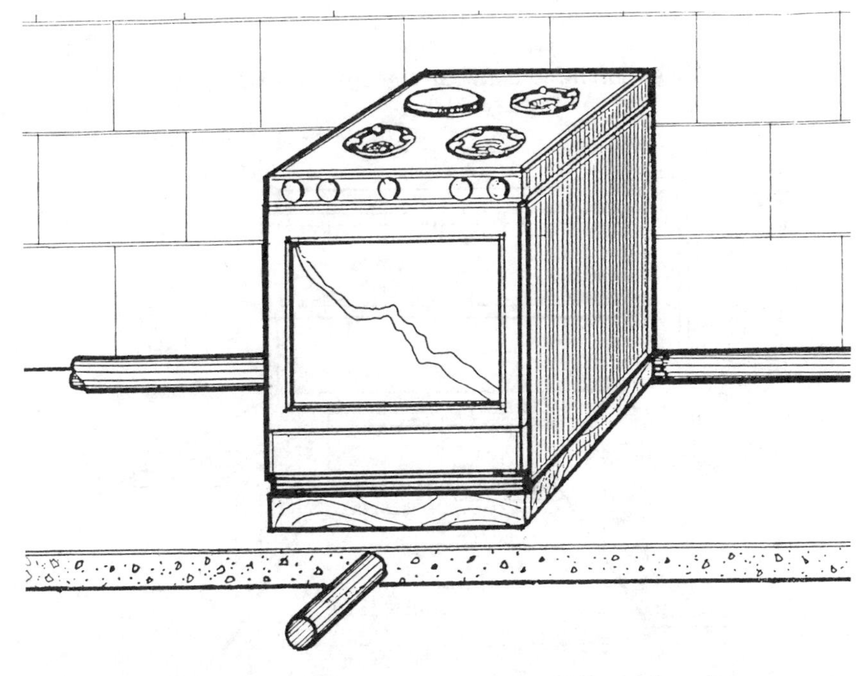

A plank of wood between the stove and the water pipes

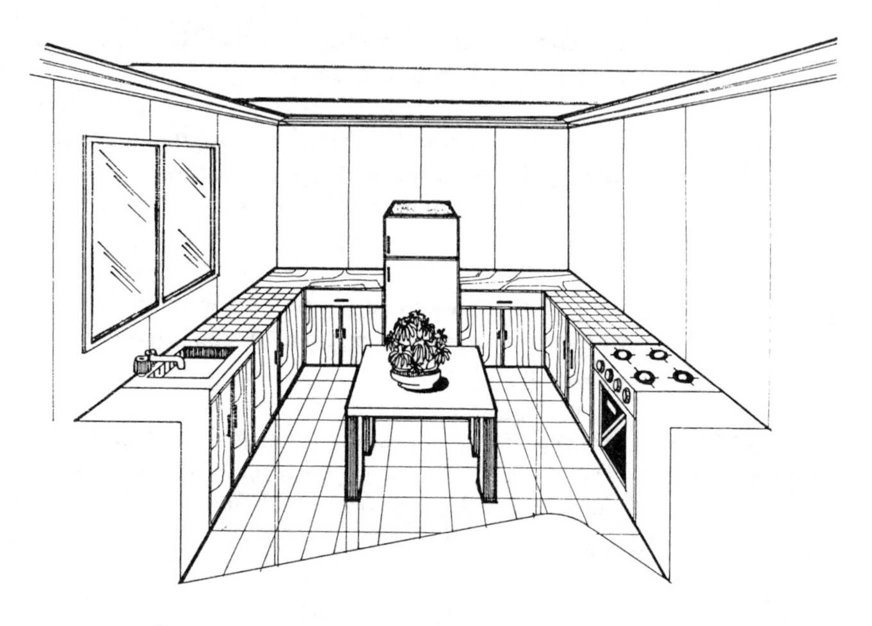

A wooden table between the stove and the sink

A swivel faucet to re-direct the water flow

CHAPTER ELEVEN

FAMILY AREAS

Living Rooms
Dining Rooms
A Word About Antiques

LIVING ROOMS

The living room of a house is meant to be used for family gatherings and for entertaining guests. It should be welcoming and attractive and not too stiff and formal. A very formal living room is not often used by family members because they can't relax in its atmosphere. Any room that is seldom used becomes *yin,* because the lack of movement creates stagnant *chi*. Unless you have many business or social commitments that necessitate a very formal entertainment area, it is preferable to make your living room 'livable'– this will encourage family members to spend time together.

Living and dining areas should be located at, or near the centre of the house. The centre, being the heart of the home, is an ideal place for family gatherings. The following are a few tips that will guide you in creating a living room that will indeed be the heart of your family activities and will attract and welcome your friends and guests:

a) The room should be regular in shape, i.e. square or rectangular. Any odd corners should be disguised with plants or furniture.

b) There should not be exposed beams on the ceiling. If beams are an essential factor in the architectural style of your house – avoid seating anyone directly under them.

c) Ceilings should not have excessive mouldings or designs.

d) Floors should have a smooth finish or be carpeted, and not be on a level lower than the rest of the house, i.e., sunken. If you have a sunken living room, bring up the *chi* of the sunken area with potted plants and overhead lighting.

A sunken living room – with potted plants and overhead lighting

e) The room needs adequate natural light and air, but not excessive cross ventilation.

f) Your furniture placements should not obstruct access to and from the door. Too much furniture not only clutters a room, it also impedes the flow of *chi*.

g) Sharp corners of walls or pillars can be rounded off or softened with plants or vines.

h) Colours should be harmonious – *refer to the colour chart on page 25*

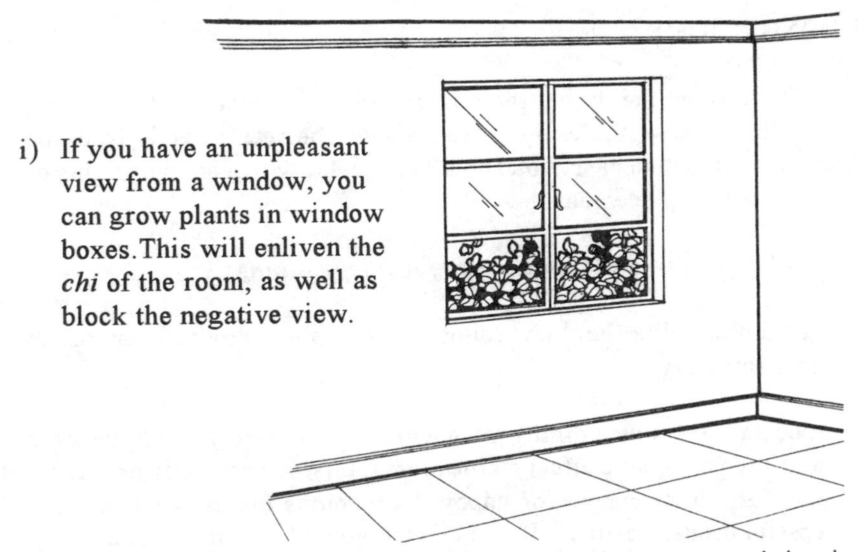

i) If you have an unpleasant view from a window, you can grow plants in window boxes. This will enliven the *chi* of the room, as well as block the negative view.

j) If there is a beautiful view outside your window, you can bring it into the room by using a well-placed mirror – make sure the mirror does not reflect a door to the outside.

A mirror reflecting a beautiful view

DINING ROOMS

Quite often the dining table is placed in one section of the living room. This is acceptable, provided it cannot be seen directly from the front door, in which case, you should conceal it with a screen, plants or artful furniture placements.

The following are some guidelines for happy dining:

a) The dining table should be round or oval – this allows the energy to flow smoothly.

b) A beam traversing a dining table will cut the *energy field* of the table and have a divisive effect on the diners; this will certainly not create the right environment for happy, harmonious family meals or successful dinner parties – If you cannot move the table, you can hang a light from the beam, over the table, to diffuse the heavy *chi.*

c) A mirror can be placed behind a buffet table on which food is served. This multiplies the food and suggests abundance and prosperity, but if the mirror is large, be sure it's not on the rear wall of the house.

d) A dining room should be well-lit, but without glare. Indirect lighting that is focused on the food, and not on the diners, is pleasant and comfortable.

e) Mirror on the ceiling over the dining table should be avoided as this disturbs the equilibrium of the diners by reflecting their bodies upside-down.

f) Make sure your dining table is not placed under an upstairs toilet.

g) Portraits or pictures of ancestors emit *yin chi.* They should not be hung in a dining room, especially not facing the table. *Yang* energy should be cultivated in any room where food is eaten.

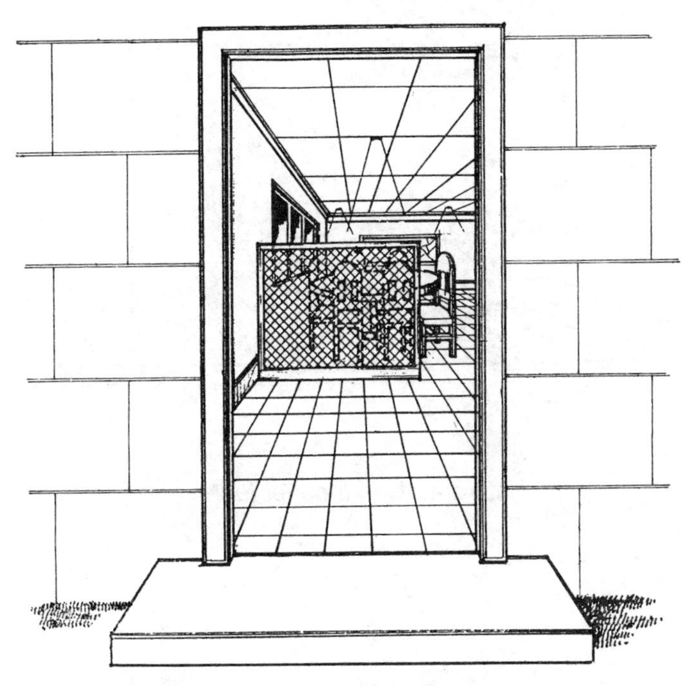

The dining table hidden from the front door

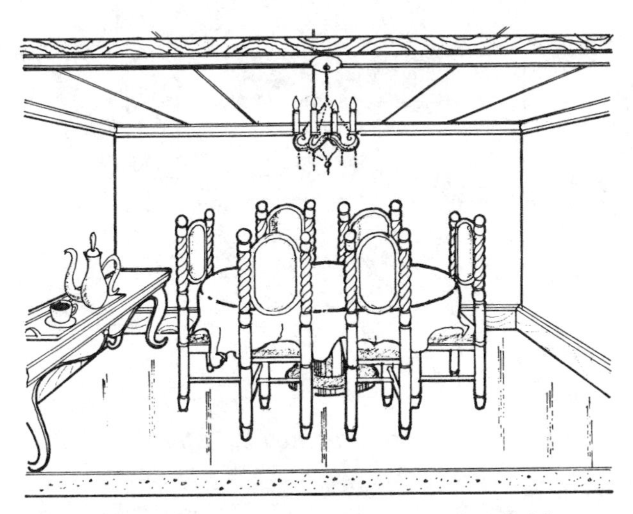

A beam over the dining table – with a light

Mirror behind a buffet table

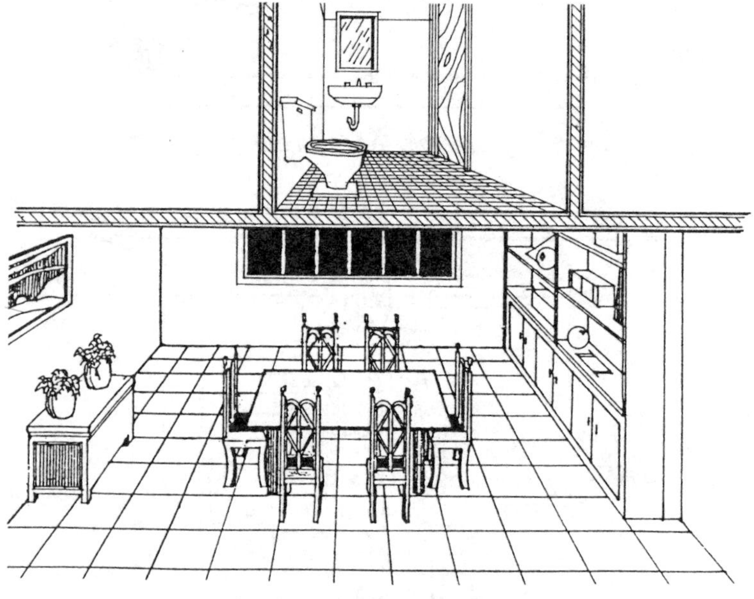

A toilet over the dining table

A WORD ABOUT ANTIQUES

Many people collect rare and/or old pieces of furniture and objet d'art. Undoubtedly these can add grace and beauty to a home, if they are well-chosen and suitably placed, but collectors should check the history of an antique piece.

Wood holds vibrations – some types of wood more than others. Wooden objects that stayed for many years in places where negative or unpleasant energy prevailed, will have that negative frequency instilled within them.

Old chairs – often contain the energy of those who constantly sat in them.

Statues and old religious objects – are very *yin*. They must be carefully placed within a house, so as not to imbalance the *energy grid*.

Portraits of dead persons (and some other yin types of paintings) – are not suitable in a dining room or in a bedroom – see, *'The Art of Feng Shui'– Chapter 17.*

Before you bring old things into your home, let them stand under the morning sun for at least one hour. If they have come from a 'doubtful' place, you can fumigate them. Sprinkle salt and cinnamon over burning charcoal and, for about five minutes, let the smoke to waft around them.

CHAPTER TWELVE

FLOOR MANAGEMENT

Perhaps you are experiencing changes of fortune. You make a little progress, then something unforeseen happens and you have another set-back. If this is the case read on – you may discover a possible cause.

It is an undeniable fact that everything in your environment affects you physically and psychologically. You are being continuously influenced by your surroundings, for example; everyday you walk several miles within your own home, back and forth from the kitchen to the living room, to the bedroom, to the bathroom, etc. If your floors are not even, smooth and comfortable to walk on, you will tire easily and your subconscious mind will register negative inputs. What your subconscious mind registers will ultimately reflect in your conscious thoughts and actions. If your fortune is 'up and down,' look for corresponding factors in the floors of your home, as in the following cases:

SPLIT-LEVEL HOUSES

In these houses the *chi-flow* is obstructed and uneven. Physically, floors on different levels require more effort to move around. Mentally, the inputs are, 'be careful not to trip' or 'here I go up again, down again.'

CANTILEVERED AND SUSPENDED FLOORS

Cantilevered floors:

These are floors that are not built on a solid foundation. Cantilevered floors are common in tropical countries, because the overhanging section of the second floor provides protection from the sun and rain for the ground floor. This type of architecture, although practical, is unfortunate for the person occupying the cantilevered room. If the bed is placed on the cantilevered section, it causes restless sleep due to a sense of insecurity and foreboding. A study table on the cantilevered section diminishes concentration. A small cantilevered area is acceptable but, a bed, study table, altar, safety vault or stove should not be placed on it.

Suspended floors:

These floors are supported from above and have no pillars below. An interesting example of a suspended floor is the banking hall of a large Hong Kong bank. When you stand in this hall, you do not feel that you are on anything solid, in fact, some sensitive people claim that they feel as if the floor is swaying. This is certainly not *good feng shui* for a bank, which should project a sense of stability and strength.

A split-level house

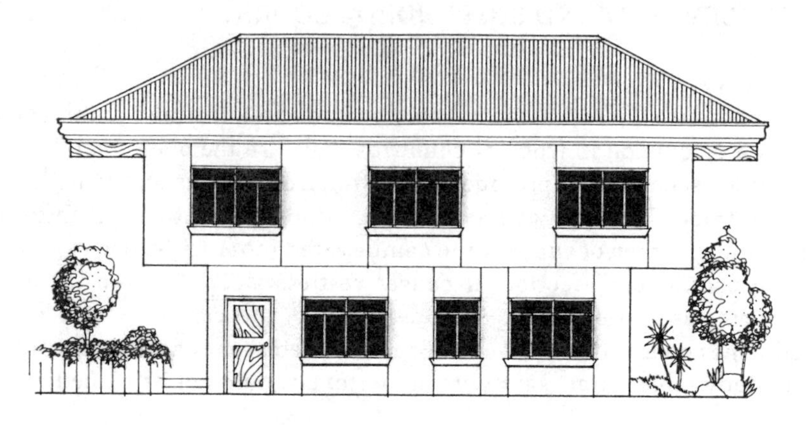

A house with the 2nd floor cantilevered

FLOOR PATTERNS AND FINISHES

Chaotic designs:

Crazy-cut floor designs impart a sense of disorder and confusion. If you have a patterned rug or fancy tiles on the floor, be sure the design is harmonious and balanced.

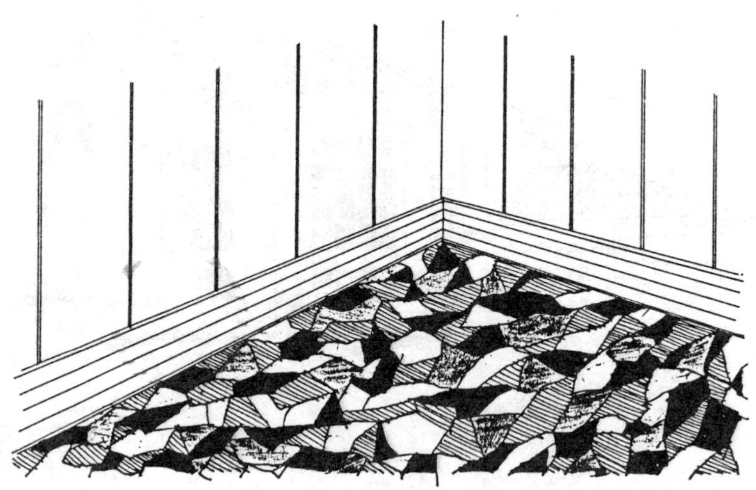

A crazy-cut floor design

Rough floors:

Constantly walking over floors that are made of pebbles, stones, or materials that are uneven gives a mental imprint that life is like a 'rocky road,' nothing goes smoothly. It won't take long before the 'bumps' start to manifest in your life.

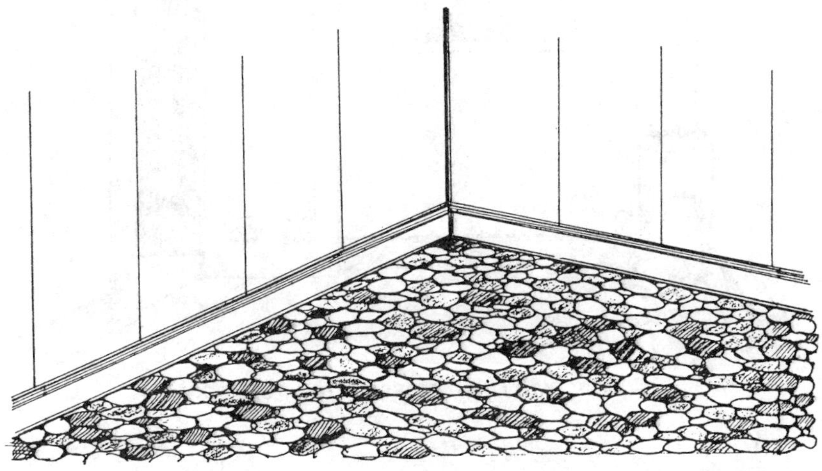

A pebble floor

Floors with a pattern of straight lines:

Quite often, the details of floor designs go unnoticed. As long as the floor appears to be attractive and clean, most people are satisfied. They do not even suspect that what they are constantly walking over can affect their mood, and pervade their mental outlook.

Becoming aware of the subtle energy around you is an important part of your *feng shui* training. If you can hone your powers of observation, and understand the subtle inferences of what you observe, you will begin to have more control over your life. With this in mind, look again at your floors and see if you can find a pattern of lines.

Lines in a floor pattern can be formed by wooden planks, tiles, and designs in cement flooring or rugs. Straight lines should not 'cross' the front door as this signifies obstacles to overcome. If your floor design has lines, they should run from the door into the house – this will draw in the *chi*.

A floor with lines 'crossing' the front door

A floor with lines 'entering' the front door

BEDROOM FLOORS

Bedroom floors should be smooth, even and comfortable. Marble flooring is too 'cold' for a bedroom. Wooden planks or parque are good, so are carpets in single colours or with unobtrusive patterns. Persian rugs in delicate shades are recommended for their beauty, balance and harmony.

BATHROOM FLOORS

Bathroom floors should be lower than bedroom floors. This will help to maintain the *water chi* within the bathroom.

CHAPTER THIRTEEN

CEILINGS – BE AWARE OF WHAT'S UP THERE

Good feng shui means having harmonious and balanced *chi* in your home or workplace. It is reassuring to know that if you do not now enjoy this harmonious energy, you can create it. You must first find out what is wrong, and then remedy it.

In order to achieve a smooth energy flow in your home, there should not be walls with acute angles, pillars with sharp corners, or ceilings with exposed beams or sharp mouldings that point downward.
An ideal ceiling is smooth and even, neither too high nor too low, but, of a height proportioned to the room.

COMMON CEILING MISTAKES

Sloping ceilings:

Sloping ceilings will direct the flow of *chi* to the area where the slope reaches its lowest level – this creates an imbalance of energy in the room. If a door is at the end of the room where the ceiling is lowest, the accumulated *chi* will rush out everytime the door opens – which causes the energy of the room to be depleted. Most attics have a sloping ceiling, plus the added *feng shui* violation of exposed beams – which is a good reason for not sleeping in an attic.

We recently did the *feng shui* of a lovely country home. The ceiling of the living room sloped from a height of 11 feet 6 inches (3.5 meters) on one side of the room to 6 feet 6 inches (1.98 meters) on the opposite side. We recommended that the ceiling be levelled at a height of 9 feet (2.74 meters) and the area lower than that be fitted with cabinets and bookcases and turned into a study nook.

A simpler remedy is to either hang a windchime or install a light at the lowest end of the ceiling to redistribute the *chi*.

Sleeping under a sloping ceiling & exposed beams

A ceiling sloping toward the front door – with a windchime

Ceilings with exposed beams:

It may add interest to some types of architectural designs to have exposed beams on the ceiling, but, it is not *good feng shui*. Beams exert pressure on the head of anyone seated under them. If you sit for any length of time under a beam you will be prone to headache, heavy head, aching shoulders and/or lack of concentration. The following are some negative placements of beams:

A beam over the bed:

Sleeping under a beam is decidedly worse than sitting under one. The aged, the ailing and children are first to succumb to the effects of a beam over the bed – see, '*Feng Shui for a Happy Marriage*' – *Chapter 8.*

Beams that cross the threshold:

Whether inside or outside the front door, beams will 'cut the *chi.*' This means that the energy entering the house will be blocked to some degree. The corresponding effect is a blockage in your fortune.

A beam crossing the threshold

A beam over a sofa:

Arrange your furniture so that nobody is seated under a beam.

Ceilings that are too low:

Low ceilings oppress the *chi*. Persons sitting or sleeping under them will feel this oppressive energy and will not be comfortable in the room. If your ceiling is low, give it a smooth and even surface and paint it white or a light pastel colour to give an illusion of space and height. If you use overhead lighting, it should be flush to the ceiling.

Mirrors on the ceiling:

This is not recommended. If a mirror is over a dining table, it can give a sensitive diner nausea or indigestion. Standing or sitting under a mirror can cause disequilibrium by reflecting the *energy body* upside down. For mirror on the bedroom ceiling – see, '*Feng Shui for a Happy Marriage*' – *Chapter 8.*

ABOVE THE CEILING

We should know what is on the floor above us. Heavy pieces of furniture , such as bookcases and marble tables can create pressure that will penetrate the floor below. If you live in a two-storey house or a multi-storey building, you will be affected by the overhead placement of the following:

group a: Heavy furniture or machinery; gym equipment with weights; and machines that vibrate, such as; air-conditioners, sewing machines, and power tools.

group b: Water tanks or coolers; water closets; faucets; washing machines; and other water placements.

YOUR FENG SHUI CURES:

All of the above send pressure and negative energy to the floor below. If any of these items are over your storeroom, bathroom, or areas that are not often occupied, then the damage is negligible, but if they are above frequently used areas, you should heed the following advice:

1] Offset the effect of '*group a*' by hanging a windchime from, or installing a light on, the ceiling directly beneath the heavy items. Either one will disperse the heavy *chi*.

A windchime under a heavy object

2] Hang or place plants under '*group b*' to absorb and balance the *yin water chi*.

3] If you are sleeping under any item '*a*' or '*b*' – move your bed.

Plants under water placements

ATRIUMS

If, inside your house, you have an open (unroofed) atrium, an internal garden or an open courtyard, it is like having a hole in the *energy grid* of your home. A hole allows energy to escape from, and rain to fall into the house, which can never be good. With a hole in the energy grid, not only will the *chi* escape, but so will all those things that the *chi* cultivates, like; good health, enthusiasm, money and good fortune.

An open atrium is particularly detrimental if it is located in the centre, which is the heart of your home. It is our observation that when the centre of the house has a hole, some members of the family will physically develop heart problems or become unloving.

Water placements such as toilets, pools, or fountains are also detrimental in the centre and can cause sickness and poverty

1] If you have an atrium in the centre of your house, you should place a roof over it. The roof can be of transparent material, to allow light to pass through. It can also be elevated above the main roof, to allow air to enter from the sides (but not all sides). This way you can still have light and air, but you minimize the loss of *chi* from the heart, or nucleus of your home.

2] The center is governed by the *earth element*, and the *earth* and *water elements* are inimical. Therefore, any water placements in the centre of your house should be de-activated, and pools and ponds that are centrally located should be filled in. The centre can then be beneficially used for dining or entertaining.

3] Having many plants in the centre of your house is also bad as, *wood* is destructive to *earth* – a few plants are acceptable – remove the rest.

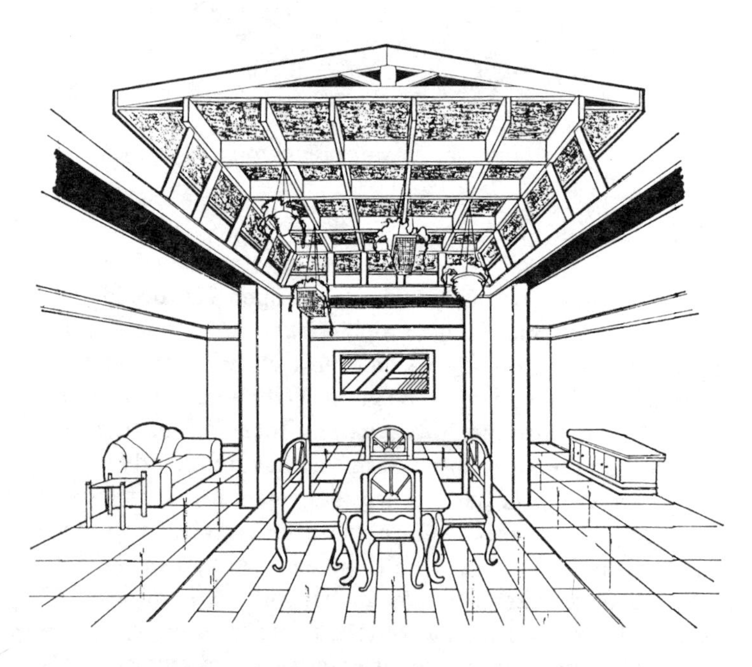

An atrium – with an elevated roof

CHAPTER FOURTEEN

STAIRS – CONVEYORS OF CHI

Counting Your Stairs
Types of Stairs
The Placement of a Staircase within the House
Feng Shui Cures

COUNTING YOUR STAIRS

It is common practice in some Asian countries to count the stairs leading to your front door, or to the upper level of your house. In fact, 'counting the stairs' can become quite addictive. If you start the habit of stair-counting you may find that you're doing it everywhere you go. Although it can be fun to count the steps and relate them to your fortune, or to the fortune of others, it does not have much significance in the overall assessment of the *feng shui* of your house. However, as I am constantly asked to comment on the lucky and unlucky number of steps, I will give you a simple formula.

Count your steps with four words, which translated from Chinese mean, 'going up,' 'peak,' 'decline,' and 'diminish.' You could substitute good, good, bad, bad. One step is good, two steps are good, three steps are bad, four steps are bad, five steps are good, etc.

Don't worry if you are lacking one step for luck, just place a mat at the bottom of your staircase – this will substitute for the missing step. If you're missing two steps, place another mat on the landing or on the top of the stairs. *Be sure that the mats are non-skid or you may get the wrong result!*

Note: *You should count the stairs continiously from one floor to the next, i.e., without stopping and starting again on the landing.*

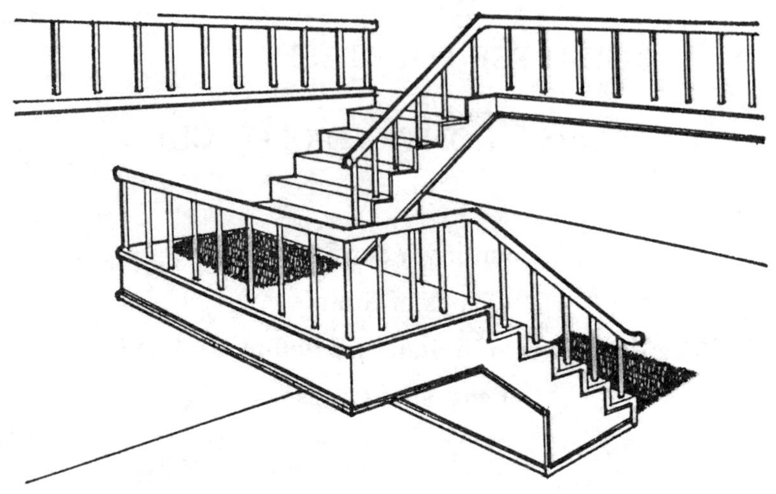

A mat on the landing and at the bottom of the stairs

TYPES OF STAIRS

Spiral staircases:

A spiral staircase is not recommended in *feng shui,* because it is like a 'screw hole' penetrating the grid of your house.

Cantilevered or open stairs:

Cantilevered stairs or stairs that have open spaces between them are also not good, as the *chi* escapes and is not carried to the higher floor.

Cement, metal and wooden stairs:

Cement, metal or wood are the most common materials used in constructing stairs. Before deciding which material to use, you should consider its relationship to the *elements*, for example:

a) Do not place wooden stairs in the West or Northwest, which are *metal guas*, or in the South, which is the *fire gua.*
b) Do not install stairs made of metal in the East or Southeast, which are *wood guas.*
c) If you must have stairs in the North, which is not really recommended, they should not be made of cement (*earth*) – see, *page 124*

PLACING THE STAIRS WITHIN YOUR HOUSE

Stairs convey people and *chi* from one level to another, but the movement or traffic flow within the stairwell, causes the *chi* to be destabilized and dispersed, hence, a stairwell is like a 'hole' in the *energy grid* of your house.

A staircase in the centre of the house:

This placement is detrimental to family unity. The centre of the house being its heart, should be 'steady' and have a good accumulation of *chi*. If the stairs are located in the centre, it disturbs the equilibrium of the house and is tantamount to a 'hole in the heart' – certainly not a good prognosis for a home.

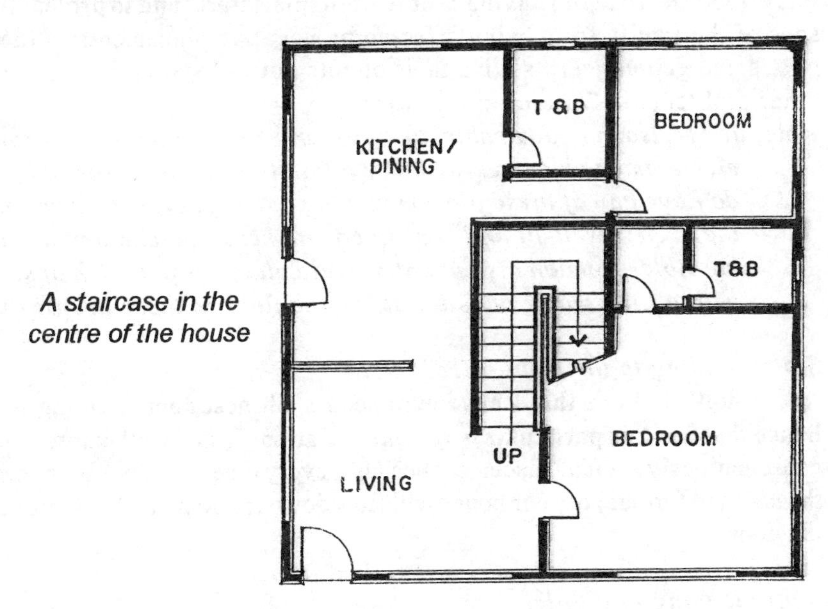

A staircase in the centre of the house

A staircase in the Northwest:

The Northwest section of the house is designated to male authority or the father. The moving *chi* of a staircase in this section could undermine the authority of the father or master of the house – this will lead to a household without discipline and order.

A staircase in the North:

This is an unfavourable placement. *Yin* energy emanates from the North, which is said to be the dwelling-place of immortals and spirits; consequently, a stairwell, toilet, drain, garbage chute, or any hole or passage should not be located here.

Note: *In China, it is thought to be unfortunate to place your front door facing the direct North, as you may invite spirits to enter your house – not to mention the icy winds from Mongolia.*

A staircase in the Northeast:

The Northeast (which is the *gua* of young sons) is also known in *feng shui* as '*the Devil's gate*' because it is here that the energy deviates from the norm. The *chi* becomes harmful if a malefic star moves to this direction. To avoid having problems of this nature, and to protect the sons of the family from being affected by negative placements in their *gua*, some *geomancers* advise their clients not to locate stairs, or any other problematic feature, in the Northeast.

Note: *It is also not advisable to have any unsanitary or odorous elements; such as, a kitchen or a toilet in the Northeast. If you do have any of these placements in your house, make sure that the area is well-lit and ventilated and kept as clean and dry as possible. You can also unobtrusively place a small dish of salt, with a little water added to it, on the floor in these areas.*

Stairs leading to the front or rear door:

I don't believe that I have ever seen a Chinese family living in a house that has this particular *feng shui* violation. It is a well-known and conscientiously avoided placement because, every time your door is opened, the *chi* (and fortune) of your house will flow down the stairs and out through the door.

Stairs leading to a toilet:

This placement leads to the loss of energy and fortune. Because *chi* has a propensity to flow downward, it will flow down the stairs and into the toilet, and your fortune will be flushed away

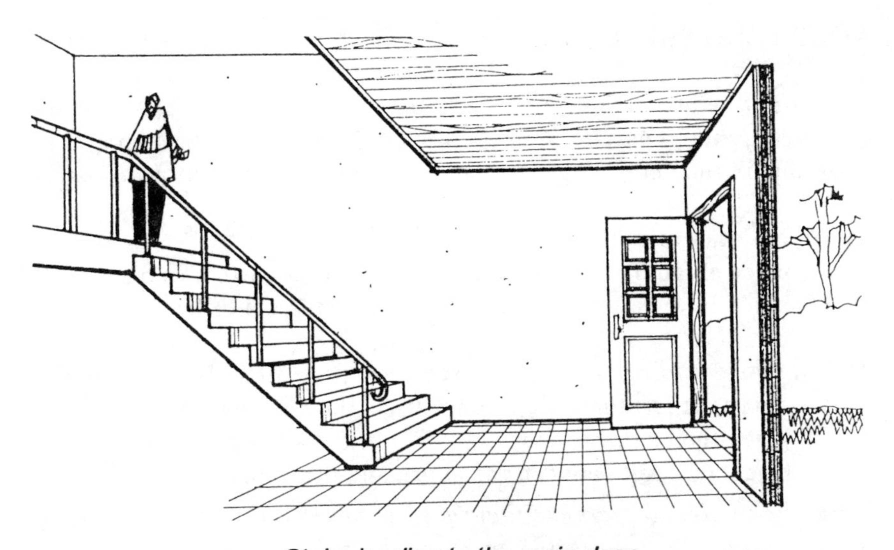

Stairs leading to the main door

Stairs leading to a toilet

YOUR FENG SHUI CURES:

1] Stairs that are in the centre of the house, or are otherwise wrongly placed, should have a 24-hour light on the ceiling of the stairwell to stabilize the *chi – This cure can also be used for spiral staircases.*

2] If your stairs lead to a toilet door:
   a) place an automatic closer on the door, or a curtain in front of it;
   b) place live, potted or hanging plants inside the toilet.

3] For stairs leading to a front or rear door; do any of the following:
   a) curve the last three steps to re-direct the *chi* away from the door;
   b) place the last three steps at 90° to the door, after a landing;
   c) place a screen between the stairs and the door.

Note: ***bannisters or screens that face the door, should have a base of wood or other solid material, to block the chi from flowing through.***

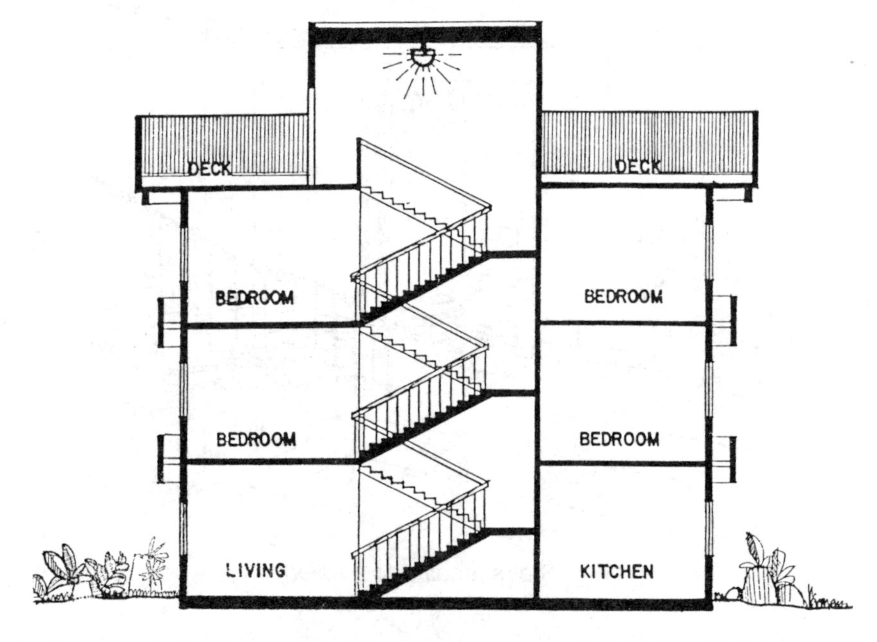

A staircase in the centre of the house – with a light in the stairwell

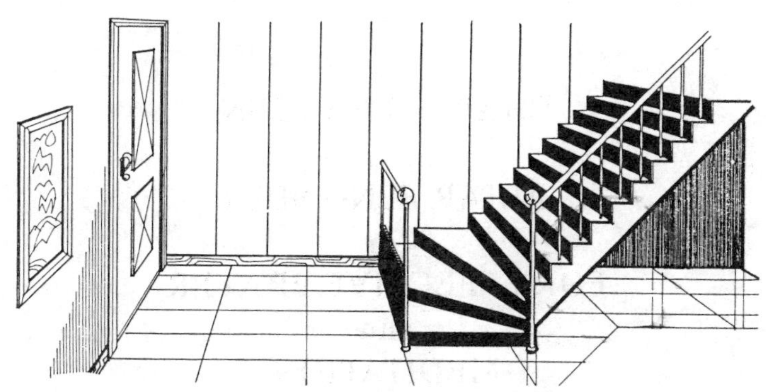

The last three steps (with a solid rail base) – curved away from the door

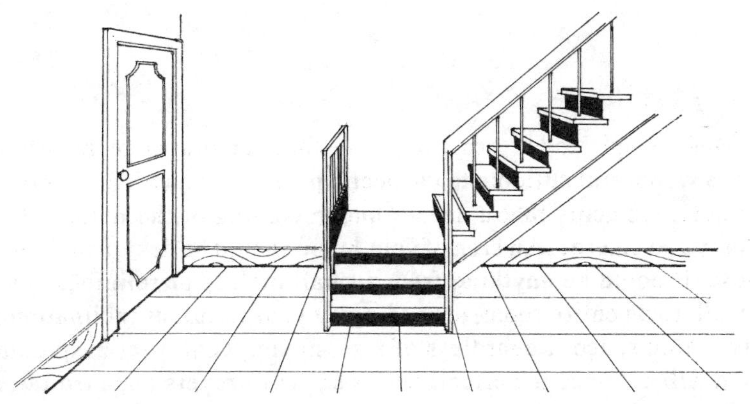

The last three steps (with a solid rail base) – at 90° to the door

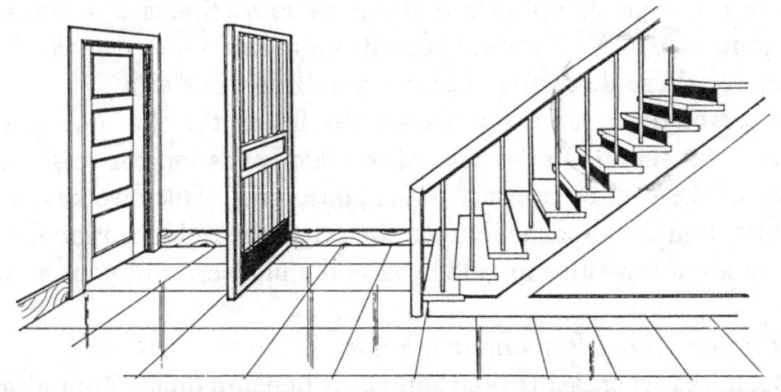

A screen with a solid base – between the stairs and the door

CHAPTER FIFTEEN

ALTAR FENG SHUI for FOR EFFECTIVE PRAYER and MEDITATION

Most people today practice some form of prayer or meditation. This is a wonderful antidote to the hectic pace of modern life. It is during these quiet moments that a deeper understanding of the nature of man and deity can emerge. An area of your home should be designated for this purpose. It could be anything from a small picture or religious symbol on a wall, to an entire room, depending on your religious inclination and the available space. Regardless of size, having your altar auspiciously located will enhance the effectiveness of your prayers and meditations.

Where, when and how to install an altar is an important part of *feng shui*. The direction the altar faces is the first consideration. Every year there are different compass directions or *guas* that are designated as either good or bad. You should consult your *geomancer* or the Chinese almanac for these directions before installing your altar.

In personalized *feng shui*, we usually install the altar facing a direction that is favourable to the head of the family (as long as it is not a bad direction of the year or contrary to the house grid). Once we have decided which direction the altar should face, we select the right location for it. The following are a few rules to guide you in the placement of your altar:

Do not place your altar under a beam:

Beams exert pressure on whatever is beneath them. Your altar must be protected from all suppressive or negative energy.

Your altar should be against a solid wall:

Having a solid wall, i.e., without windows, behind your altar will give it backing or support. One of the most basic rules of *feng shui* is that *all important placements should be solidly supported.*

Do not place your altar directly facing a door:

This rule applies in particular to a toilet door, a bedroom door or a door to the rear of the house. The altar can face the front of the house, but in most circumstances should not directly face the front door.

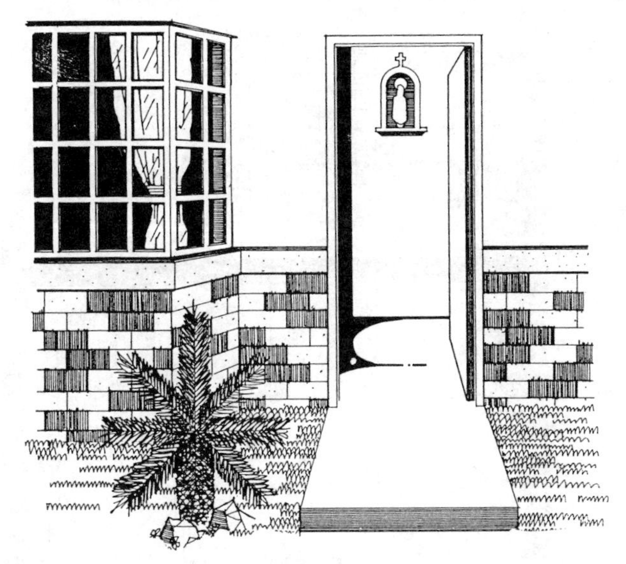

An altar facing the front door

If you live in a two-storey house or a high-rise building, be sure that you do not place your altar under any of the following:

a) *Directly under a bed of the floor above:*
   It is not respectful to deity, if people are sleeping or making love above the altar.

b) *Under a corridor:*
   To have people walking over the altar is also disrespectful, and will lower the quality of the *altar chi.*

c) *Under heavy objects or vibrating machinery of the floor above:*
Having these objects above will oppress or distort your *altar chi.*

d) *Under water tanks or other water placements:*
The *water chi* will seep to the floor below and permeate the altar.

e) *Under a toilet:*
A flushing toilet over your altar will not enhance its spiritual energy.

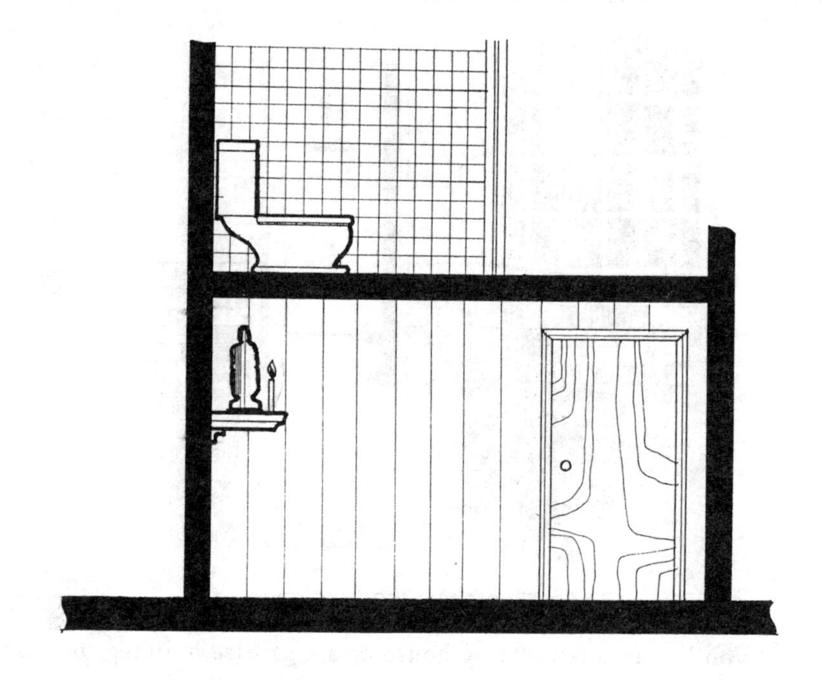

f) *Under the stairs:*
An altar under the stairs will be constantly walked over.

g) *On the landing:*
An altar on the landing is another wrong placement. Stairs convey people and *chi* up and down, so there is no way to stabilize the *chi* around the altar.

An altar under the stairs

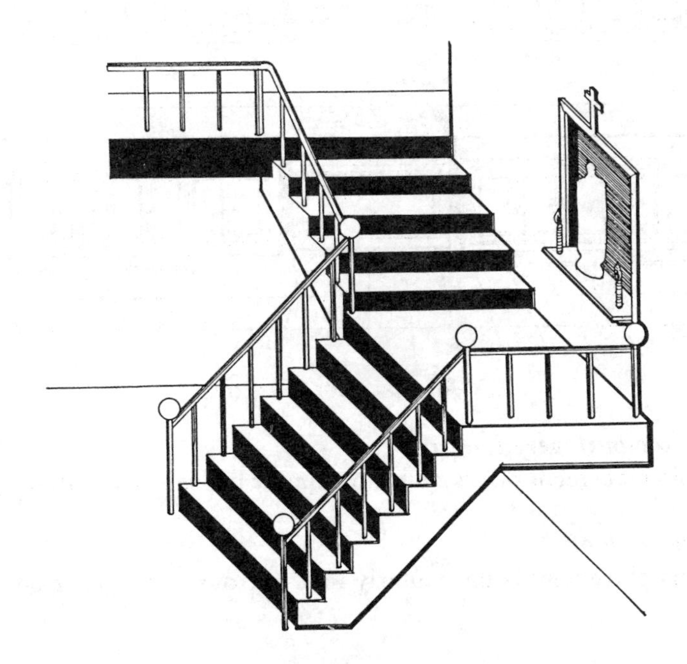

An altar on the landing

h) *Over the stove or a heating appliance:*
Fire chi rises – it is not good to have your altar over a 'hot' area.

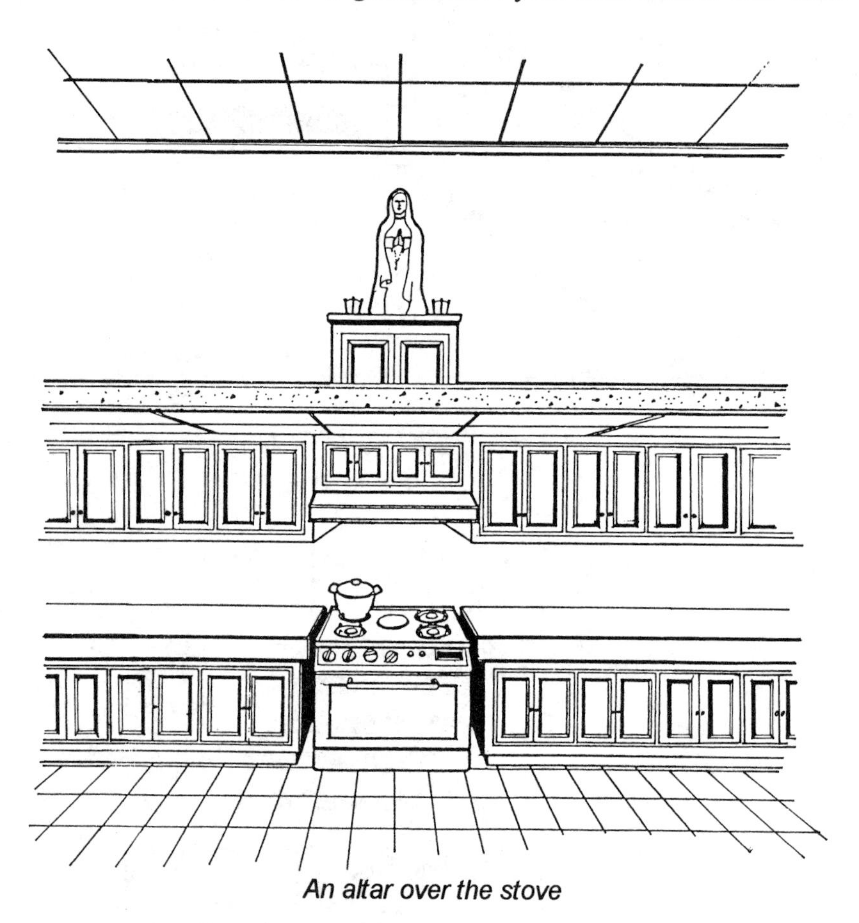

An altar over the stove

i) *On a cantilevered area:*
This placement offers no solid support beneath your altar.

j) *Over a door:*
This placement is particularly inauspicious over your front door.

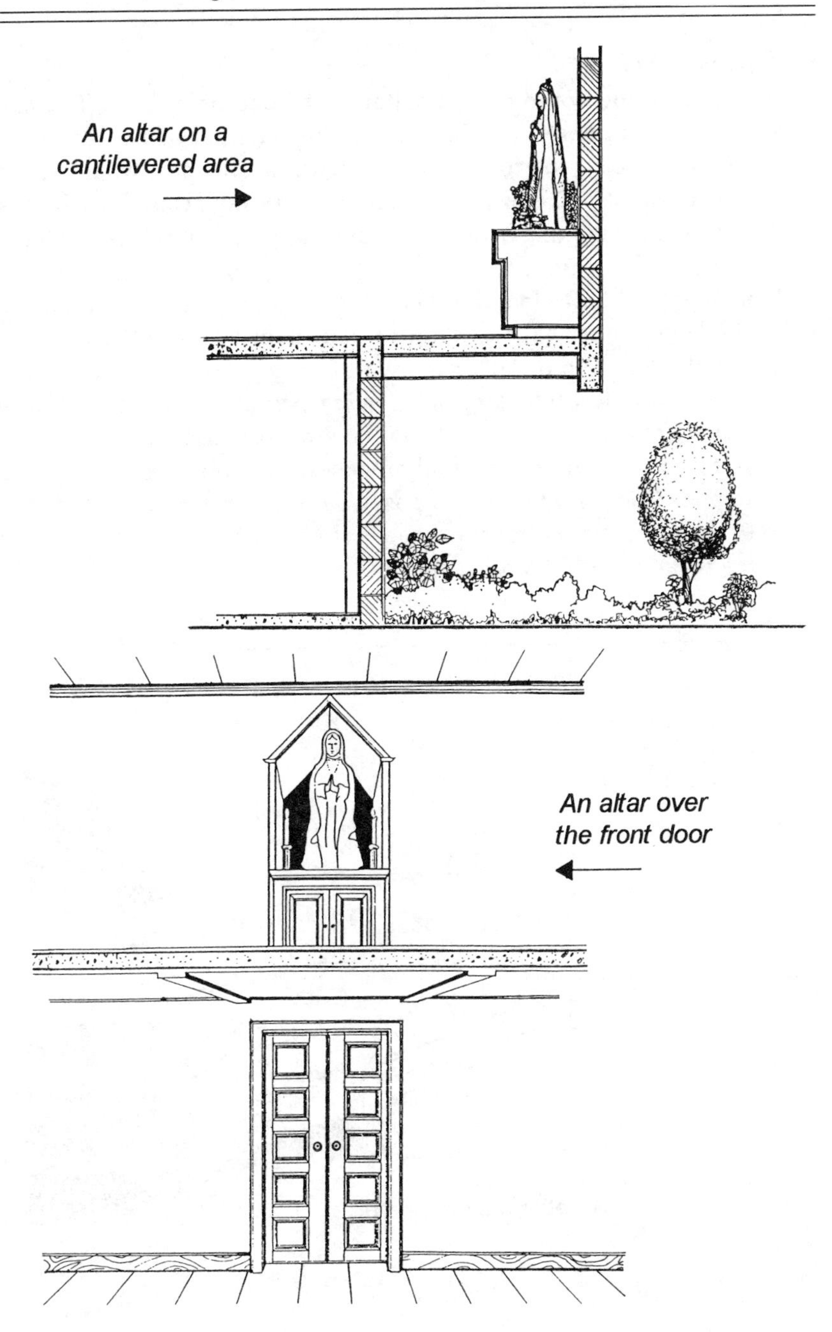
An altar on a
cantilevered area
An altar over
the front door

k) *Facing a bed:*

It is preferable not to have an altar in the bedroom at all. The altar is dedicated to deity, and belongs to the spiritual or *yin* dimension living persons belong to the *yang* dimension. Besides, would you do in church what you do in the bedroom? Walking around partially or fully naked, or making love in front of an altar will surely not enhance its spiritual energy.

Some people like to feel that God is watching over them when they sleep. If you must have an altar in your bedroom, don't place it on the wall behind your bed or the wall facing your bed, and do cover it with a curtain when you plan to engage in activities that will lower its vibrational frequency and show disrespect to deity.

If you live in a house of more than one-storey, placing your altar on the upper floor eliminates the possibility of it either being 'walked over' or sustaining other overhead violations. Just be sure you do not place it on the other side of the wall behind your bed.

An altar facing the bed

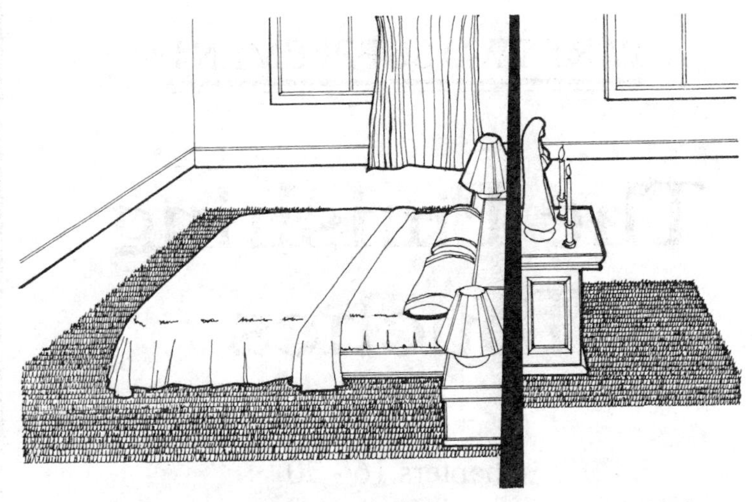

An altar on the other side of the wall behind your bed

In traditional *feng shui*, the size of the altar and its height from the floor should be of auspicious measurement. The day and time you first install your altar is very important as well.

If you want to be absolutely correct in all things concerning the installation of an altar, you will have to consult a professional *geomancer*. Once your altar is installed you need not change its location to correspond to the annual good and bad directions, as these directions only apply to the initial installation.

PART TWO SUPPLEMENT

The Finishing Touches

Chapters 16 - 20

CHAPTER SIXTEEN

MIRRORS – POTENT TOOLS OF FENG SHUI

Mirrors are magical. They can reflect, deflect, invert, reverse and absorb subtle energy or *chi*. The use of mirrors in *feng shui* is only limited by the training and skill of the *geomancer*.

Because mirrors are one of the most potent tools of *feng shui*, they must be placed with great care. The wrong placement of mirrors cause conflicting and distorted patterns of energy that disturbs the harmony of a house or building.

Geomancers use three kinds of mirrors; concave, convex & plain.

a) Concave mirrors are used to invert the image or *chi* of a reflected object, thereby neutralizing its effect.
b) Convex mirrors reduce and disperse the image or *chi* of a reflected object, thereby minimizing its effect.

c) Concave and convex mirrors are not always available. For the inside of a house plain mirror can usually suffice as a cure.

The following are some basic rules for placing a mirror:

A mirror should not face the front door:

Yin chi may be absorbed through the mirror and *yang chi* could be reflected back. Either way the implications for the household will not be beneficial.

A mirror should not reflect a bed:

This placement often results in disturbed rest, vivid dreams, and morning fatigue – see, *'Feng Shui for a Happy Marriage' – Chapter 8.*

A mirror should not reflect a door:

Movement activates the qualities of a location. If a mirror is in a negative area of the house-grid, and it reflects a door, the movement and the changing light exposure created by the opening and closing of the door, will be reflected in the mirror. This reflected movement will activate the negative qualities of the mirror's location.

A mirror can bring in light and chi:

Beautiful outside views can be reflected into the house by placing a mirror at an appropriate angle to the view. This can also bring more light and *chi* into a room.

Mirrors can change the shape of a room:

They do this by adding depth or width, depending on where they are placed. Many interior designers mirror a whole wall to give the illusion of more space, which etherically makes the wall 'disappear.' It also changes the *chi-flow* in the house – whether it is for better or for worse depends on the house design.

A mirror can be used to 'move out' negative placements in the house:

If there is a negative element in your house, e.g. a toilet facing the main door or on a *horoscopic zone*, a mirror can be used to reflect the toilet and reverse its position – *for horoscopic zones see, Chapter 21.*

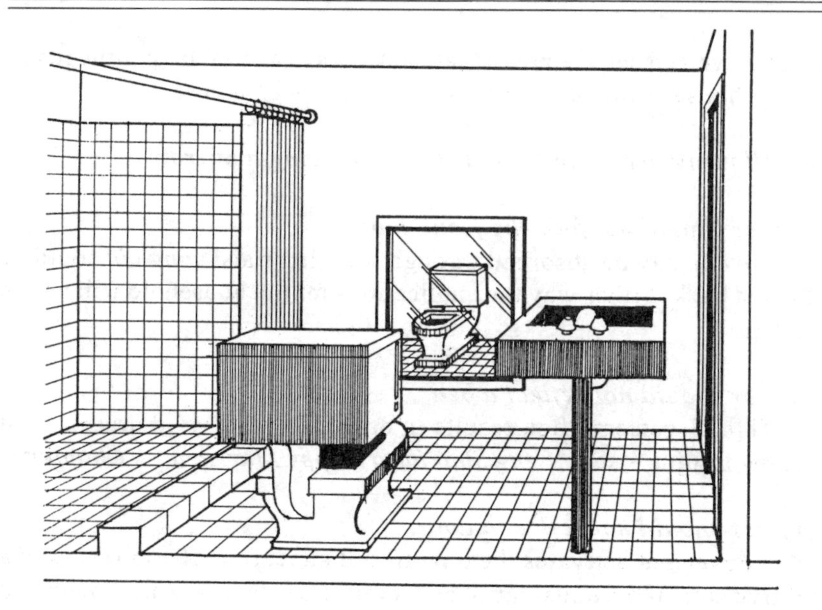

A mirror 'moving out' a toilet

Cracked or broken mirrors:

Broken mirrors are unfortunate and should not be used. They can be re-cut to delete the cracked parts.

Mirror tiles:

These are not recommended as they give a distorted view of whatever or whomever they reflect.

More About Mirrors:

A mirror can be used as a means of entering other dimensions or planes of existence – *try the test described on page 84 of this book.*

If a mirror is placed in a negative or *yin* zone of a house, particularly if it reflects a door, it can be used by elementals and spirits to penetrate our human dimension. This is sometimes the cause of hauntings, strange occurrences and spirit possession.

Mirrors reflect light and images, therefore they create movement. If a mirror is placed on the *tiger-wall* (the wall to your right when you are inside your house facing the street) it can 'arouse the *tiger*' and make the household members prone to accidents or surgery.

If a mirror is placed on the rear wall, it negates the steady backing required for *good feng shui*.

Mirrors can be placed on the *dragon-wall* (to your left when you are inside your house facing the street), or on the front wall.

A basic rule in *feng shui* is, the rear and the *tiger-side* should be steady, and the front and *dragon-side* should have activity.

Geomancers generally do not recommend the placement of mirrors without a thorough analysis of the house. Although mirrors can be wonderful tools for enhancing or directing the *chi*, they can also be hazardous to health and harmony if they are wrongly placed.

At this point, you may be thinking that it is better to forget about mirrors and place paintings on your walls instead. Paintings can also be 'lucky' or 'unlucky.' But don't give up, you will be relieved to hear that paintings are a lot less complicated than mirrors.

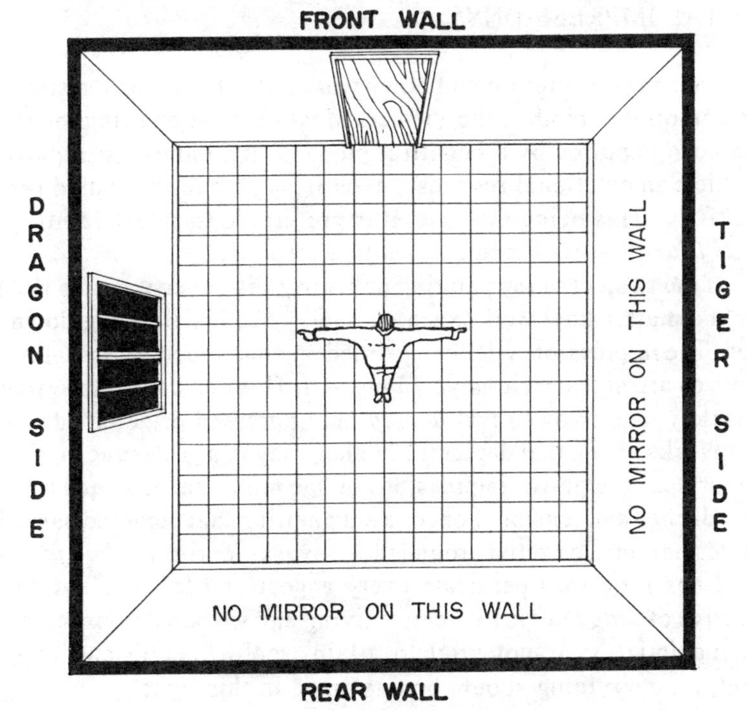

Where not to place your mirror

Note: ***The mirror 'cures' given in this book are simple and safe to use.***

CHAPTER SEVENTEEN

THE 'ART' OF FENG SHUI

Mental Impressions
Guidelines For Artists And Buyers
Where To Hang Your Paintings

MENTAL IMPRESSIONS

Paintings, sculpture and other works of art can leave a strong impression on the mind of the viewer. Most of us at one time or another have been captured by a beautiful piece of art. Paintings in particular can elicit an emotional response, even from persons not noted for their sensitivity. This being the case, it is preferable to select paintings and *objets d'art* that will create a positive response.

If the subject of the painting or art work is poverty, grime and ugliness, no matter how well executed it may be, it will bring down your mood. The impression will be imprinted on your subconscious mind even when you are not consciously looking at it. This constant imprinting will ultimately cause you to feel depressed, oppressed or defeated.

Works of art, that depict the human body in a grotesque or distorted manner, leave negative impressions on the mind that are often the cause of headaches and tension. I once saw a painting that depicted parts of the female anatomy scattered around the canvass – definitely *bad feng shui*!

Does *feng shui* permeate every aspect of life? Yes indeed! The objective of *feng shui* is to create a living and working environment that will maximize your potential to attain wealth, health and happines, therefore, everything should be examined in this light.

When you are in doubt as to whether a painting or an object is positive or not, ask yourself the following questions:
a) Does this painting/object uplift me?
b) Do I look at it often?
c) Do I avoid looking at it or only look briefly?
d) Do I feel uneasy when I look at it?

If your answer is yes to (a) and (b), buy it. If it is yes to (c) and (d), pass it by.

Recently, we suggested a few alterations to improve the *feng shui* of a leading art gallery. After the adjustments were made, we attended the blessing of the newly-arranged gallery. As there were many artists and buyers present, I was asked to give an impromptu talk on art, from the perspective of *feng shui* – the following are some of the pertinent points of that talk.

GUIDELINES FOR ARTISTS AND BUYERS:

I offer these guidelines, not to influence the creative expression of artists or the personal preferences of buyers, but simply to demonstrate that art should be considered as a contributing factor to *good feng shui.*

Avoid paintings that have harsh, conflicting colours:

Colour is a radiation of energy. Each colour ray corresponds to a subtle emotion. Conflicting colours produce conflicting emotions that can disturb the nervous system of the viewer. Do not place a painting of this kind in your bedroom or office.

Avoid scenes of disaster:

Earthquake, flood, massacre and other violent subjects will arouse in the viewer a subtle reaction of aggression or anxiety.

Avoid scenes of poverty and despair, or dull and lifeless colours:

The mental imprint of these paintings will lead to fatigue, depression, and a lack of enthusiasm.

Abstract and impressionist paintings:

These can be beautiful if they are well-balanced and capture the viewer's imagination. The paintings of many modern masters fall into this category. If they are clear in colour and beautifully composed, they can draw the viewer into the 'space' of the painting. This can have a very relaxing and refreshing effect on a tired businessman or a tense home-maker.

Paintings of sun-splashed houses and gardens:

These exude peace and a feeling of security.

Landscapes with roads, pathways, rivers or creeks:

Roads, pathways, rivers, etc., should enter the room from the painting. To get the right effect, the artist can paint a person walking, or a vehicle moving into the room or toward the viewer. This concept especially applies to boats. You may be familiar with the expression 'my ship has come in,' which means that fortune has arrived, so be sure that a boat in a painting does not appear to be sailing away from the viewer, or toward a door or a window.

WHERE TO HANG YOUR PAINTINGS

Mountain scenes:

A painting of mountains can be placed on the wall behind a study chair. This will give the feeling of solid backing and stability.

Water scenes:

Water corresponds to movement and/or money. Water flowing into a room from a picture can be fortunate as long as it is correctly placed. It is good if it flows onto the desk where you do your household accounts or office work, but it should not flow behind your study chair or into your bedroom. Be sure that water does not appear to be flowing out a window or a door.

Still life, landscapes and garden scenes:

These paintings can enhance the ambience and the *feng shui* of a dining room.

Pictures or portraits of saints or of people who are dead:

These should not be displayed in a bedroom, as they emit *yin chi*. The saints and deities should be confined to the altar area.

If your deities are Bhuddist or Hindu they should not overlook a dining table laden with meat. Pictures of dead family members can be placed on the ancestral altar (if you have one),in a reception room or in an upstairs family hall.

If you buy paintings as an investment, and are in doubt about the effect they will have on the atmosphere of your home, you can place them in areas that are used only for entertaining.

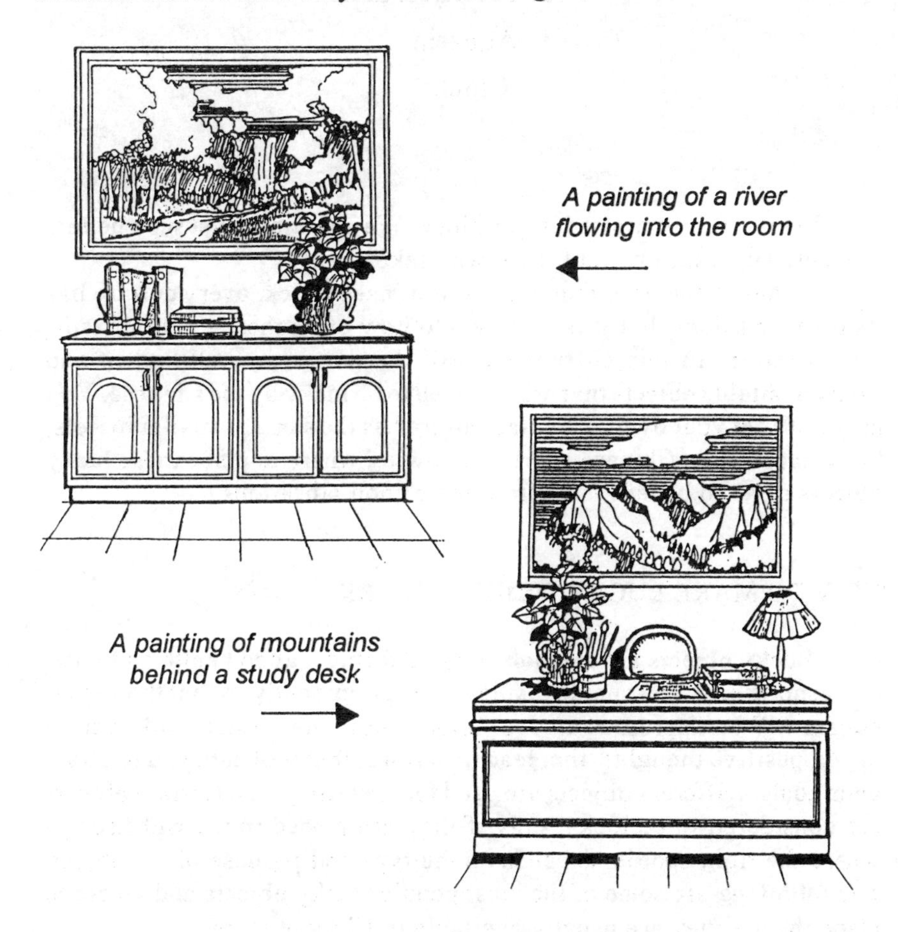

A painting of a river flowing into the room

A painting of mountains behind a study desk

CHAPTER EIGHTEEN

LUCKY OBJECTS – WHAT AND WHERE

How To Make Lucky Objects Work
Your Fortune Table
Aquaria
Clocks

Everyone is interested in good luck. We may claim that such beliefs are mere superstition – but then, why take chances?

When it comes to that elusive stuff called luck, every culture has its own traditions, but it is remarkable how often these cultural traditions overlap. In this chapter we will discuss some well-known and easily available objects that are believed to be lucky by the Chinese. You may find that your own particular culture has the same or similar beliefs, but what sets the Chinese apart, is knowing where to place these lucky objects so as to benefit most from their good vibrations.

HOW TO MAKE LUCKY OBJECTS WORK

Lucky objects are symbols of good fortune, good health and positive aspirations. You should display them prominently so that their symbolism will be impressed on your mind. These impressions will inspire in you positive thoughts, that lead to actions, that will help you to attain your goals. Different objects are used for specific goals. Certain objects are considered to be lucky, only if they are placed in the right spot – where the right spot is, depends on the type and purpose of the object. The following are some of the most popular lucky objects and where to place them – they are usually available in Chinese stores.

The Dragon:

The dragon is a symbol of authority, it can be strategically placed in an office to symbolize the authority and power of the chief executive. Place your dragon on the dragon-wall (your left when you face the door) but be sure it does not appear to be heading toward the door or a window.

The Phoenix:

The phoenix is a symbol of renewal. It is well-placed in the front section of the house – just be sure the bird is not 'flying toward the door.'

The Tiger:

Tigers represent bravery and strength. They can be placed in a den or an office. A tiger should not have its mouth open or look as if it is 'ready to pounce.'

The Horse:

The horse symbolizes power and movement. It is often used by people who would like to travel. There is a special *feng shui* technique in placing a horse, that is said to aid an applicant for visa or emigration.

A horse painting or sculpture can be placed on, or near an executive's desk to reinforce his image as a powerful and dynamic man, but it should not be headed toward the door or a window.

The Elephant:

Elephants should always have their trunks turned upward, as if trumpeting – this is meant to herald good news. They can be placed in an the entrance hall, but not directly facing the door.

The Turtle:

Turtles symbolize longevity and constancy. They can be placed in the rooms of the elderly, but as they are slow moving creatures, they are not recommended for an office or workplace. Sometimes several small turtles are placed in a circle, preferably on a circular table. This symbolizes perpetuity.

Money Cats:

These cute cats are very popular lucky objects. Although originally Japanese, they are presently the craze in Hong Kong. Money cats can be seen hanging from the rear vision mirrors of most Hong Kong taxis. The more expensive models are in restaurants, shops and private homes. They are meant to be white, with gold and black spots on their fur that look like coins, but there are now some plain gold versions available. They can be placed facing the door or on a fortune table. If you have a live cat with this colouring, take good care of it, it may attract money into your house.

Fortune Frogs:

Fortune frogs are great conversation pieces. Some are very large and quite garish in colour. The frog (actually a three-legged toad) holds a coin in its mouth and has strings of coins around its feet. It should be placed facing the door to catch the money of passers-by. In a store, it can be on or near the cash register, facing the direction of the door.

Natural Quartz Crystals:

Natural quartz crystals are very much in use by modern *geomancers* because of the piezo-electric energy they generate. A crystal ball, a cluster or a terminator, if well-placed, can diffuse its good energy throughout a room and can neutralize some types of *yin chi.* Sometimes multifaceted, man-made, crystal balls are used in *feng shui,* but these are only capable of refracting light; unlike natural quartz, they do not generate energy. In order for them to be beneficial, they must be placed or hung where there is natural sunlight, or a good incandescent light source.

Golden Taels:

In China, gold is not sold in ounces, but in *taels.* A *tael* is slightly heavier than an ounce and has a particular shape. Imitation *taels* made of shiny golden metal or plastic are considered to be symbols of prosperity – they are usually placed on a fortune table.

A Laughing Buddha:

This jolly fellow is a symbol of prosperity, joy, and the proliferation of the family. He is usually prominently placed in the living room, dining room or family hall.

Money Cat

Fortune Frog

Crystal Cluster

Crystal Ball

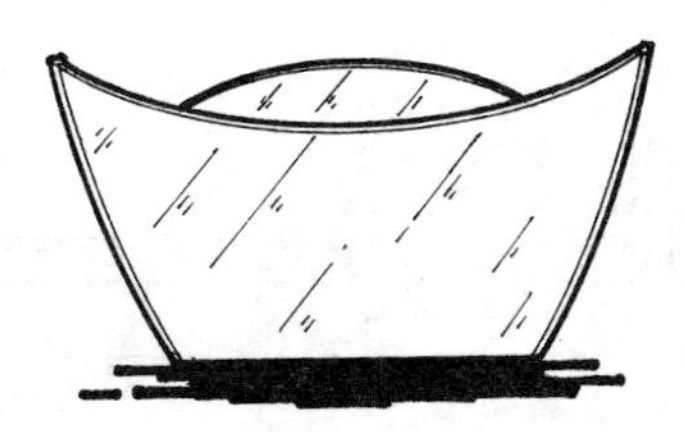

Golden Tael

Laughing Buddha

YOUR FORTUNE TABLE

One of the most interesting ways of attracting luck is to have a fortune table. An ideal location is a corner that is well-protected by solid walls on either side, has no beam or light directly overhead, and is furthest from the door.

Some of the items that can be placed on your fortune table are; quartz crystal balls or clusters; a fortune frog; a money cat; golden taels; a small dish of chocolate gold coins, or other round gold candies (which can be eaten and replaced occasionally).

A live plant can be placed on or beside your fortune table. It should not have spikey leaves or thorns. If it wilts, replace it with a fresh one.

An open-mouthed earthenware jar with a few coins inside can be placed next to your table – this is said to attract money.

A prosperity painting should be on the wall behind your fortune table. Prosperity paintings can be; lucky calligraphy or poems; scenes of farmers harvesting golden grain; fishermen netting abundant fish; fresh food and fruit; or beautiful houses and gardens.

A fortune table accumulates wealth by stabilizing the *chi*, therefore, do not place on it or near it, any item that either moves or depicts movement, e.g., galloping horses; flying birds; cars and conveyances; mobile sculptures; fish tanks; etc.

A fortune table with prosperity items

AQUARIA:

An aquarium is considered lucky and can bring prosperity into the house, if it is properly positioned. Fish can also absorb negative *chi*, particularly the blackmole (blackmoor) variety, which are very sensitive. If you have blackmoles in your tank, and they die easily, check the water temperature, the aerator and the type of fish food. If all these are correct, but the fish are still dying, their death can then be considered as an indication that the house has negative energy.

In Hong Kong, when locals move into new premises, they install near the door, a fish tank containing six or eight blackmoles and one gold fish. The blackmoles absorb negative vibrations that are inherent in the place, or left behind by the previous tenants – dead fish are immediately replaced, and the process continues until all the bad luck is absorbed.

Locate your aquarium in areas of your house or room that require activity. That would generally be defined as the left (dragon) wall, and the front wall. Do not place your aquarium on the right (tiger) wall, or on the rear wall, as these areas should be steady.

The shape of your aquarium:

Round, cylindrical, hexagonal or rectangular shapes are suitable for an aquarium.

It is better not use square or triangular tanks, as these shapes represent *earth* and *fire* which are inimical to the *water element*.

Your aquarium should be aerated to enhance its capacity to activate the *chi*.

Colour and number of fish:

A predominance of black, gold or silver fish are good. Limit the number of red fish, as red conflicts with the *water element*.

The number of fish in the aquarium are also considered. When the purpose is to enhance prosperity, you can have, 1, 6, 8, or 9 fish. Avoid having 2, 5, 7, or 10.

Your *geomancer* should consider the *energy grid* of the house and calculate the influence of the annual moving stars before recommending the positioning of your aquarium.

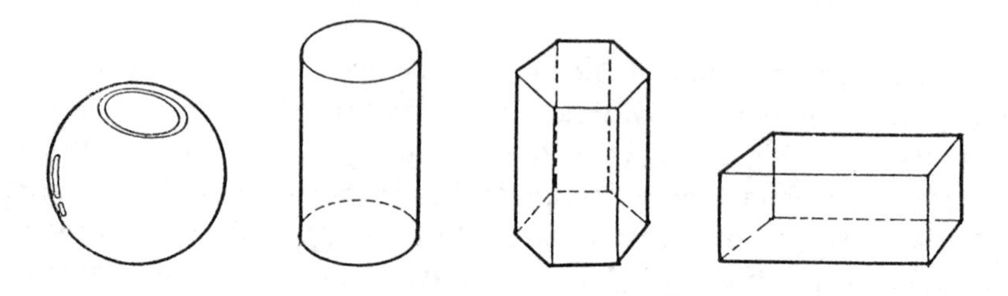

Good shapes for your aquarium

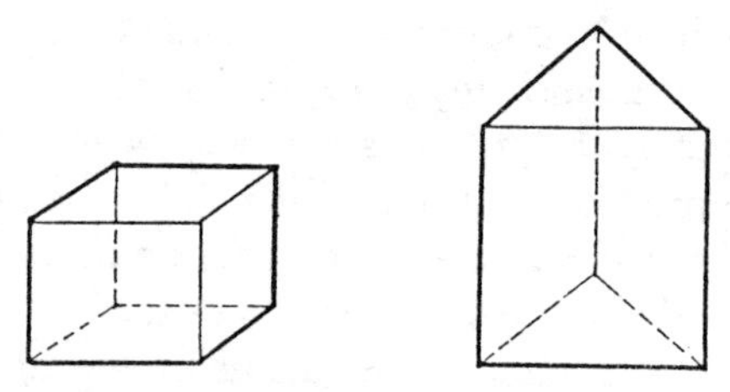

Bad shapes for your aquarium

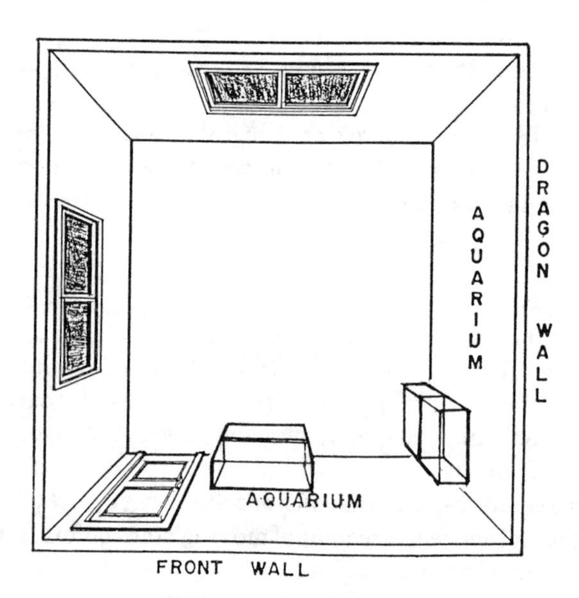

Aquaria correctly placed

CLOCKS

Feng shui consultants often place a clock in an area of the house that has good *chi*, so that the movement of the clock's hands or pendulum will stimulate the *chi* and let it circulate throughout the house. If you are unable to get expert advice, it is acceptable to place a clock on the left (*dragon*) wall or on the front wall of the room – it should not be placed facing the main door.

Clocks remind us that 'time is running out,' this is the reason why Chinese people don't use them as a gift item. Clocks come in all shapes and sizes – the best shapes are round, oval, hexagonal, and octagonal.

A clock facing the front door

CHAPTER NINETEEN

WHEN MONEY FLOWS LIKE WATER

Water Placements and Their Effects
Leaking Roofs and Clogged Drains
The Esoteric Side – Wells and Ponds

Water is synonymous with movement, travel, traffic flow and cash. In fact, in Hong Kong, *shui* (water) is a slang expression for money.

When your *geomancer* assesses your house, great importance is given to the placement of toilets, faucets, water tanks, pools, fountains, aquaria, etc. The professional methods of calculating the good and bad areas for water depend on the orientation of the building and lot, the personal data of the occupants, and other considerations.

Correct placements of the *water element* inside and outside your house can enhance your fortune. Incorrect placements can be detrimental to your health as well as to your cash flow.

Below is a compilation of the water placements we have mentioned in previous chapters of this book, plus some additional advice for those planning to buy, build or renovate a home.

WATER PLACEMENTS AND THEIR EFFECTS:

a) A toilet bowl that faces the front entrance – *depletes wealth*.

b) A water placement in the centre of the house, such as; a pool, a fountain, a fish tank, an open atrium that allows rain to fall inside the house, and particularly a toilet – *depletes wealth and health*.

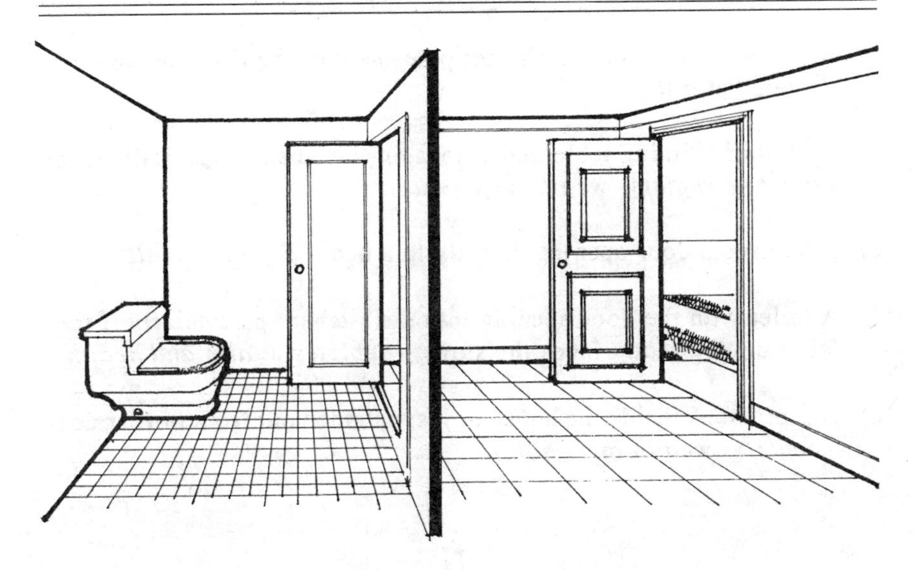

A toilet facing the front door

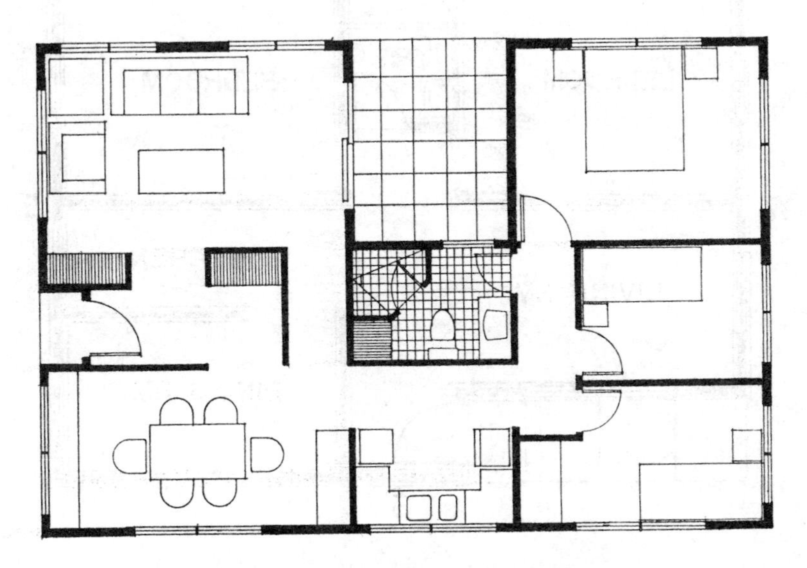

A toilet in the centre of the house

c) An altar or stove under a water placement of the floor above – *depletes wealth.*

d) A bed or a dining table under a water placement; especially under a toilet – *depletes wealth and health.*

e) A bathroom door opening directly to a bed – *depletes health.*

f) A toilet with the door opening into the kitchen; particularly if the toilet bowl directly faces the stove – *depletes wealth and health.*

g) A septic tank inside the house or just outside your front or rear door – *depletes wealth and health.*

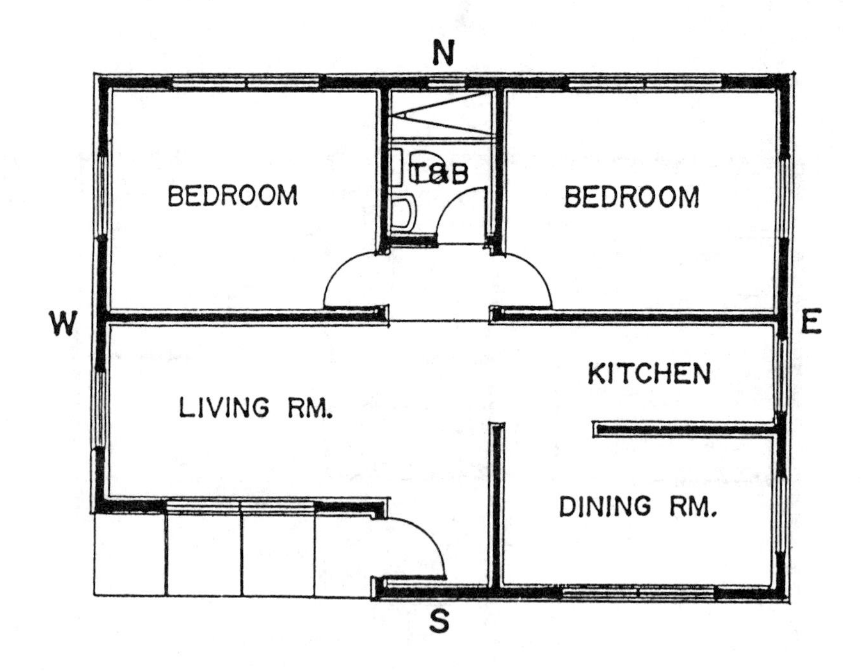

h) A bathroom in the North of the house

h) A bathroom in the North section of your house – *depletes wealth and health.*

i) Dirty or stagnant water in the North section of your lot – *depletes wealth and health.*

j) A drain outside your front or rear gate or door – *depletes wealth*

k) A sewage or drainage pipe flowing out under your front or rear gate or door – *depletes wealth.*

l) A view of water flowing away from your house; especially from your front door – *depletes wealth.*

j) A drain outside the front door.

k) A sewage or drainage line flowing out under your front door

l) A view of a river flowing away from your house

FENG SHUI CURES:

1] For items (e) (f) (h) – fit your toilet door with an automatic closer and place live plants and a small dish of salt inside the toilet.
2] For item (i) – grow tall plants around the water tank.
3] For items (g) (j) (k) (l) – place potted plants either side of your door.
4] For item (g) – you can also place a yellow or brown mat outside the door, or place potted plants directly on the septic tank.

Note: *Other cures for the above feng shui violations are given elsewhere in this book.*

LEAKING ROOFS AND CLOGGED DRAINS

Everything in your house has a correspondence in your life, and will eventually affect your health, for instance:

Leaking roofs, dripping faucets, running toilets, seepage, etc., all mean loss or wastage of water. The correspondence in your life is loss or wastage of money. The eventual effect on your health will be a runny nose, watery discharges, loose bowel movements and/or incontinence.

Clogged or blocked drains, toilets, sinks, downspouts, etc., correspond to blockages in cash flow, stopped or delayed collection of payments, and sometimes to delay or curtailment of travel plans, business expansion and/or career opportunities. The health correspondences are; sinusitis, constipation, clogged arteries and other physical blockages.

For the sake of your prosperity and your health, be sure that the water elements in your house and workplace are located properly and are functioning smoothly.

THE ESOTERIC SIDE – WELLS AND PONDS

Are you planning to build a house or cultivate a garden? Before doing anything else you should inspect your lot to see if there is an old well or pond on it.

When a well or pond has been abandoned or filled with rubbish, it can harbour *yin water chi* as well as noxious fumes. If a house is built over it, the *yin chi* will seep throughout the house and cause sickness and misfortune to the occupants.

Unused or unwanted wells or ponds should be filled in a proper way and on an appropriate day. There are special methods to dissipate the *yin chi* harmlessly.

One simple method is to first remove whatever you can of the dirt slime or garbage, then insert a hollow bamboo or a piece of pipe quite deeply into the centre of the well or pond. Fill it with fresh earth or clean materials, then cover the area with top soil and grow plants on it. Be sure that the pipe is unclogged and protruded about one foot above ground level. It will take six months to one year for the *yin chi* to be dissipated, depending on the depth and condition of the well or pond.

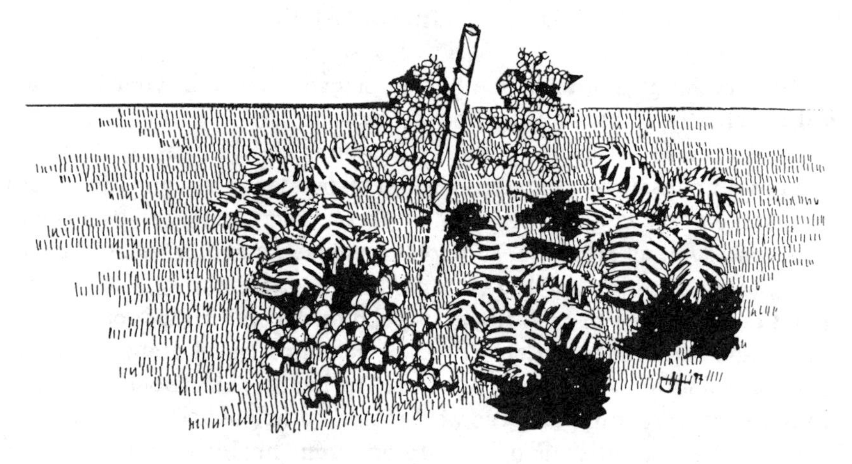

A filled well – with protruded pipe and plants

CHAPTER TWENTY

YOUR GARDEN

How to Prune or Cut Down a Tree
Traditional Interpretations of Trees
Flowers
Indoor Plants

When assessing the *feng shui* of a property, it is necessary to consider every factor that can influence the balance and harmony of the lot and building.

External factors such as; electric posts, water tanks, sharp corners of neighbouring buildings, nearby creeks and waterways, all have an effect on the *feng shui* of your home. An even closer external factor to consider are the trees in your garden.

Trees and plants are living entities, and like everything else in this universe, they have consciousness, albeit on a different level to our own. This has been proven in extensive laboratory tests using sensitive instruments attached to plants.

In one famous experiment, several potted plants were placed in an empty room. They were then hooked up to machines that could register minute changes in energy levels. A lab attendant went into the room and hacked one of the plants to pieces – the other plants registered acute shock on the biometer. The next day people entered the room one at a time – the plants did not react. When the 'murderer' came in, the plants registered a movement on the biometer that, in human terms, would be interpreted as absolute terror. All living things on this planet interact on a consciousness level. Even things we consider inanimate register subtle energy on a sensitive biometer

As everthing has energy and awareness, consider then a tree. It is a well-known fact that when you prune a tree by cutting large branches, the sap 'bleeds' and the tree takes some time to recover. Gentle pruning of old or excessive leaves and twigs can benefit a tree, but drastic and careless pruning will always damage the tree and offend the tree spirit.

HOW TO PRUNE OR CUT DOWN A TREE

Pruning a tree:

According to *feng shui* practice, you should first find a suitable day for cutting or pruning a tree by consulting an almanac. For three days before the designated day, (preferably at twilight) you should communicate your intention to the tree by placing your hand on the trunk and visualizing that you are cutting the parts in question. If you feel uneasy, or experience a tingling sensation in your fingers when visualizing the cutting of a certain section, it indicates resistance from the tree – it is better to cut less in that area. If you follow the above procedure when the branches are cut, there will be no bleeding, because the tree will have withdrawn the sap.

Cutting a tree:

If you have to cut down a tree, you should follow the same procedure as above, but visualize that you are cutting the tree, and ask the tree spirit to vacate peacefully. In some asian countries it is customary to leave an offering of food and drink under the tree. If the tree spirit is willing to co-operate it will extract the *chi* from the food within thirty minutes or so; you can then remove the offering and dispose of it. You may want to try the food; if it is flat and tasteless it means that the *chi* has been extracted and the spirit has accepted your offering. It is also customary to plant a young tree somewhere else; this practice shows concern for the plant kingdom by giving back to nature what you have taken from it. Remember to dig out the roots of the cut tree so that the spirit has no place to linger and the tree will not grow again.

Note: *The above procedures are mainly used when a tree is old and well-established, particularly if the tree is of a type noted for in-dwelling spirits.*

TRADITIONAL INTERPRETATIONS OF TREES

Trees are sensitive to their environment and to the energy of the people around them. This sensitivity affects their growth pattern. Study the trees in your garden to find clues to the family fortune.

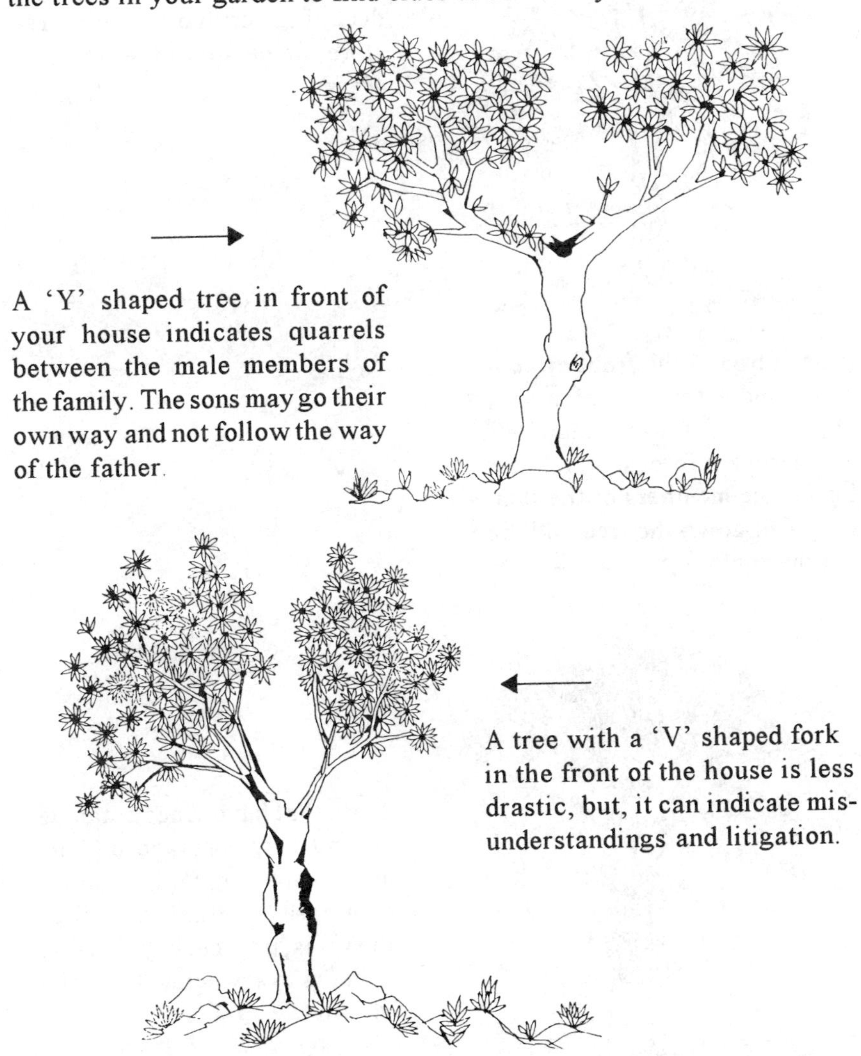

A 'Y' shaped tree in front of your house indicates quarrels between the male members of the family. The sons may go their own way and not follow the way of the father.

A tree with a 'V' shaped fork in the front of the house is less drastic, but, it can indicate mis-understandings and litigation.

Sick or sparsley leafed trees in front of the house can forecast declining fortune – Try to restore the health of the trees.

A dead tree in the front of your house indicates loss of money or prestige. If the tree has a hole in the trunk it forecasts sickness for female members of the family – Cut down the tree and dig out the roots.

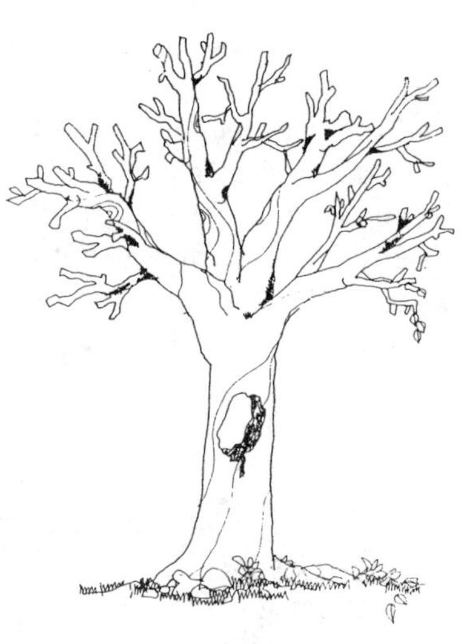

Trees that have vines entangled around them presage personal and business entanglements or courtcases – Prune or pull out the vines, particularly if the tree is being overwhelmed by them.

Trees that grow leaning away from the house mean that the children of the family will not be lucky there and may leave home. It can also indicate that the energy of the house is negative.

A tree that bears white flowers should not have branches overhanging the roof. If the white flowers drop onto the roof, it foretells of a death in the family. This belief is based on the fact that white is the Chinese colour of mourning, it was also the custom for widows to wear white flowers in their hair – If you have a white flower bearing tree near your house, cut the branches overhanging your roof in the manner prescribed in this chapter.

Bamboo plants that dip their branches toward a pond or waterway are said to warn the family of the danger of children drowning.

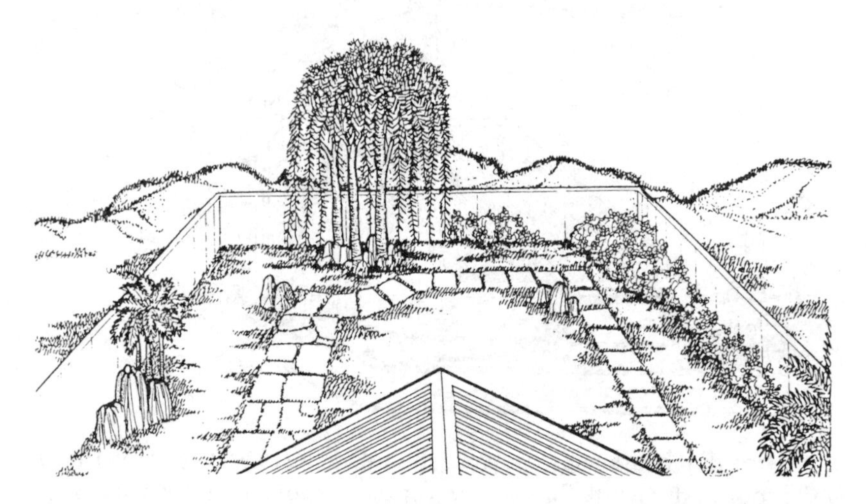

Willow trees should not be planted near the house. They should be at the far end of the garden as, in both Western and Chinese *geomancy*, they are thought to be inhabited by strong spirit entities.

In Europe, willow branches are used to make wands for the purpose of magical practice. European *geomancers* also use a forked willow twig to divine for water. A willow twig is very effective indeed for water divining as the willow tree always dips its branches to water.

In Taoist temples, willow branches are used to write channelled spirit messages. These messages are written by the temple mediums in powdered cork or sand.

A row or 'stand' of trees is used in *feng shui* to give backing to the rear of a house or building. It also provides a protective screen from the negative influences of disorder, poverty and sickness that emanate from rubbish dumps, shanties or hospitals.

Trees planted in the North or the Northwest are considered beneficial, particularly if these directions are at the rear of the house.

FLOWERS:

Flowering trees, shrubs and plants have special significance according to their colour. Each direction brings to the house its own qua-lity of *chi*. The flowers in your garden should complement the *directional chi* and the family correspondences.

Apply the following guidelines only if your flower beds are large and close to the house:

Do not plant white flowers in the East and Southeast:

a) White flowers in the East sector of your garden can be detrimental to the health of the eldest son.

b) White flowers in the Southeast can be detrimental to the health of the eldest daughter.

Do not plant red flowers in the Northwest, East or Southeast:

a) Red flowers in the Northwest can undermine family discipline.

b) Red flowers in the East or Southeast can trigger susceptibility to drinking, gambling and other indulgences.

Do not plant red or yellow flowers in the North:

a) Yellow flowers in the North can lead to genito-urinary tract or kidney problems in susceptible persons.

b) Red flowers in the North may lead to family quarrels.

A garden is a place in which to commune with nature, a refuge from the harshness and pollution of the city. If you plan your garden with an awarness of plant and directional compatibilities, and tend it with care and affection, you will create a harmonious outdoor environment that will enhance the *feng shui* of your house.

INDOOR PLANTS

The best plants to place inside your house are those with rounded or oval leaves. They should be healthy and not sparse.

Do not use plants with thorns or spikey leaves inside, or even outside your home. It is better to have plants with spikes or thorns as far from the house as possible – this includes the very popular bougainvillaea (unless you find a thornless variety).

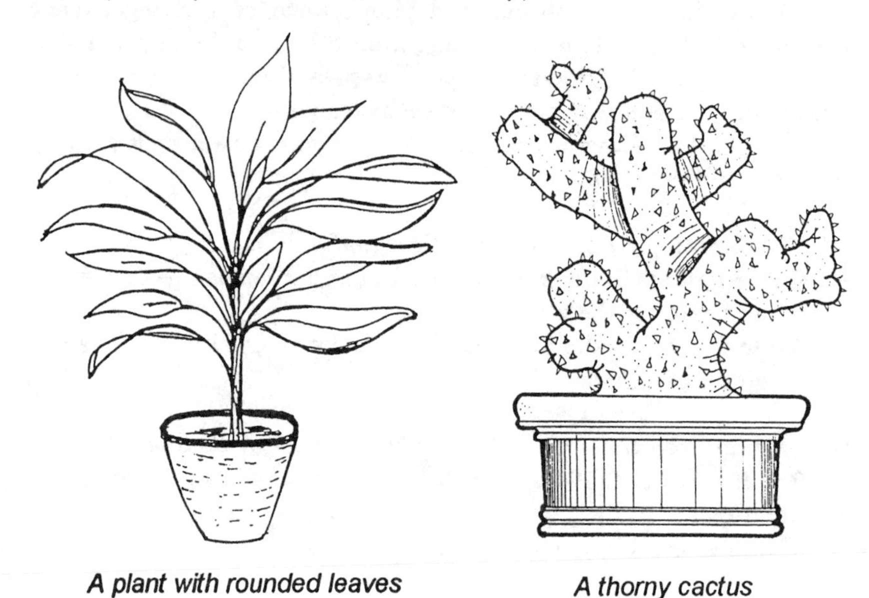

A plant with rounded leaves *A thorny cactus*

Part Three

Case Histories – Causes & Cures
(Feng Shui Analysis)

to preserve client confidentiality,
names, and some personal information, have been withheld
and house plans have been re-drawn.

CHAPTER TWENTY ONE

HOROSCOPIC ZONES

A Tiger On The Toilet
Health and the Horoscopic Zones
Finding Your Horoscopic Sign
Finding Your Horoscopic Zone
Locating The Zones Within Your House

"Oh look, the Tiger is on the toilet," Victor said. "That explains it," I agreed. "And what about this! The Rooster is on the stove and the Dragon is on the septic tank, no wonder they are getting sick." No, we were not discussing the *feng shui* of the zoo, we were analyzing the home of one of our clients whose problem was ill health in the family.

The previous day, we had visited her house. She sat dejectedly on the sofa. "I am having stomach pains and cramps, our little girl is constantly getting skin rash and fever, and our son is always nauseus and irritable. It all began after I made major renovations to the house last year," she recalled. "Could you please check the *feng shui*? I really don't think I can take much more of this."

We asked for her birthday information, the birthdays of her husband and three children, and the house plans. We took a compass reading of the site and inspected the property for any external *feng shui* violations. While our staff measured the doors, beds and some other items of furniture, we checked the water and fire placements, i.e., toilets, sinks, bathrooms, and cooking or heating elements. Then we returned to our office to study the house plans.

Taking the orientation and completing a thorough inspection of the property is an important and essential part of a *feng shui* assessment, but often, it is when we work on the house plans that hidden violations are discovered. These violations sometimes involve the Chinese horoscopic zones of family members.

In the case of our client, who was born in 1962, the year of the Tiger, we discovered that a toilet was within her horoscopic zone. This placement made her prone to minor illnesses; such as, the cramps and stomach aches from which she was suffering.

Her young son, who was born in the year of the Dragon, (1988) had the septic tank in his horoscopic zone. This placement was undoubtedly a contributing cause to his nausea and irritability.

The little girl was born in 1981, the year of the Rooster. We found that the stove, the rice cooker and the toaster were all located in her zone, no wonder she had chronic fever and skin rash.

HEALTH AND THE HOROSCOPIC ZONES

The twelve-year cycle of Chinese astrology roughly corresponds to the twelve-year orbit of the planet Jupiter. This powerful planet influences your personality, your health, and your preferences. It also gives you an affinity with the direction that Jupiter occupied when you were born. This direction is your ***horoscopic zone.*** A toilet, septic tank, stove, or any unsanitary or heating element located in your zone, can negatively affect your health and your fortune.

Each of the eight directions (*guas*) contain either one or two horoscopic zones, each *gua* is governed by one of the ***five elements*** and each ***element*** rules certain body parts and functions. These correspondences enable us to predict what sicknesses the house occupants will be prone to, and which members of the household will be the most susceptible.

For instance; a house with a toilet in the North could foster kidney and urinary infections or problems with the bones. The family members that will be most likely to succumb to these afflictions are those born in the year of the Rat as, the Rat's horoscopic zone is in the North. The young men of the household might also be affected as the North *gua* is associated with the middle son – *refer to the chart on page 24.*

DIRECTION	ELEMENT	VISCERA	TISSUES	SENSE
S & SE	WOOD	LIVER & GALL BLADDER	MUSCLE	SIGHT
SOUTH	FIRE	HEART & SMALL INTESTINE	BLOOD VESSELS	SPEECH
SW, NE & CENTER	EARTH	SPLEEN & STOMACH	FAT & FLESH	TASTE
W & NW	METAL	LUNGS & LARGE INTESTINE	SKIN & HAIR	SMELL
NORTH	WATER	KIDNEY & GENITO-URINARY	BONES	HEARING

Health correspondences of the guas

FINDING YOUR HOROSCOPIC SIGN

The twelve years of the Chinese horoscopic cycle are named after twelve animals, these are: Rat; Ox; Tiger; Rabbit (Cat); Dragon; Snake; Horse; Goat (Sheep); Monkey; Rooster; Dog; and Pig – each horoscopic animal governs one year of the cycle.

Chinese years are based on the lunar calendar. They begin sometime between mid-January to mid-February. This means that if you were born before Chinese New Year, you should adopt the sign of the previous year.

For example: If you were born on February 16,1950, (a Tiger year) you are an Ox not a Tiger, because in 1950 the year of the Tiger began on February 17.

To find your horoscopic sign, see the chart on page 174. Look for your year, then look at the column on the left for the day your year began, then see the column on the extreme left for your horoscopic animal.

TABLE FOR FINDING YOUR HOROSCOPIC SIGN

RAT	JAN 31	1900	FEB 18	1912	FEB 5	1924	JAN 24	1936	FEB 10	1948	JAN 28	1960	FEB 15	1972	FEB 2	1984	FEB 19	1996
OX	FEB 19	1901	FEB 6	1913	JAN 24	1925	FEB 11	1937	JAN 29	1949	FEB 15	1961	FEB 3	1973	FEB 20	1985	FEB 7	1997
TIGER	FEB 8	1902	JAN 26	1914	FEB 13	1926	JAN 31	1938	FEB 17	1950	FEB 5	1962	JAN 23	1974	FEB 9	1986	JAN 28	1998
RABBIT	JAN 29	1903	FEB 14	1915	FEB 2	1927	FEB 19	1939	FEB 6	1951	JAN 25	1963	FEB 11	1975	JAN 29	1987	FEB 16	1999
DRAGON	FEB 16	1904	FEB 4	1916	JAN 23	1928	FEB 8	1940	JAN 27	1952	FEB 13	1964	JAN 31	1976	FEB 17	1988	FEB 5	2000
SNAKE	FEB 4	1905	JAN 23	1917	FEB 10	1929	JAN 27	1941	FEB 14	1953	FEB 2	1965	FEB 18	1977	FEB 6	1989	JAN 24	2001
HORSE	JAN 25	1906	FEB 11	1918	JAN 30	1930	FEB 15	1942	FEB 3	1954	JAN 21	1966	FEB 7	1978	JAN 27	1990	FEB 12	2002
GOAT (SHEEP)	FEB 13	1907	FEB 1	1919	FEB 17	1931	FEB 5	1943	JAN 24	1955	FEB 9	1967	JAN 28	1979	FEB 15	1991	FEB 1	2003
MONKEY	FEB 2	1908	FEB 20	1920	FEB 6	1932	JAN 25	1944	FEB 12	1956	JAN 30	1968	FEB 16	1980	FEB 4	1992	JAN 22	2004
ROOSTER	JAN 22	1909	FEB 8	1921	JAN 26	1933	FEB 13	1945	JAN 31	1957	FEB 17	1969	FEB 5	1981	JAN 23	1993	FEB 9	2005
DOG	FEB 10	1910	JAN 28	1922	FEB 14	1934	FEB 2	1946	FEB 18	1958	FEB 6	1970	JAN 25	1982	FEB 10	1994	JAN 29	2006
PIG	JAN 30	1911	FEB 16	1922	FEB 4	1935	JAN 22	1947	FEB 8	1959	JAN 27	1971	FEB 13	1983	JAN 31	1995	FEB 18	2007

THE HOROSCOPIC ZONES

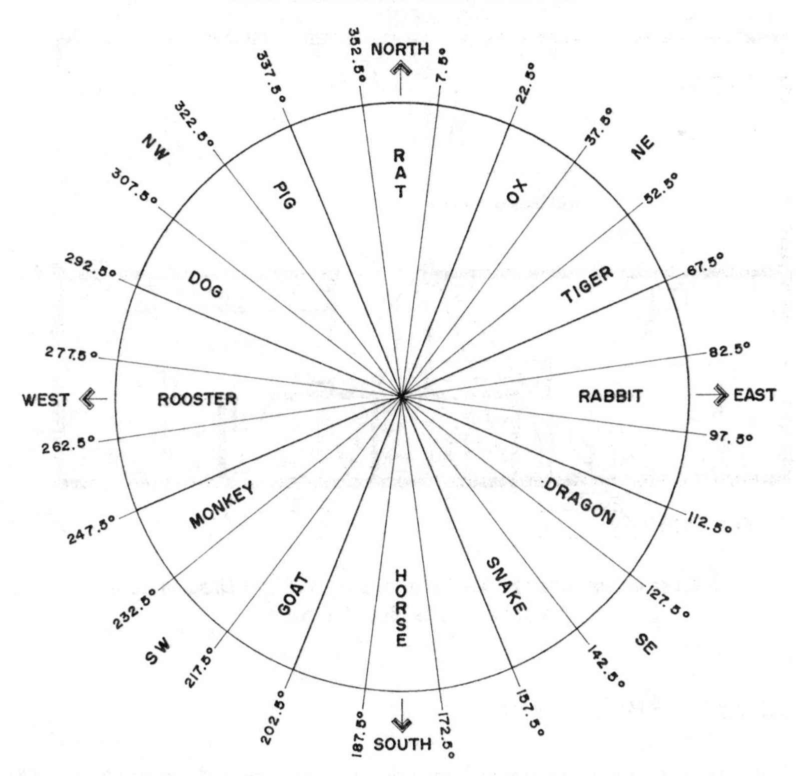

Each horoscopic zone occupies a 15° segment of the compass

LOCATING THE ZONES WITHIN YOUR HOUSE

To locate the horoscopic zones within your home, you should have a scaled floor plan of the house. Then get the centre point (refer to page 41 for instructions). Find the direct North by either using a compass, or more accurately, by using the bearings or the North arrow indicated on the architectural drawings of the house. Now, draw in the North/South line and the East/West line through the centre point. Use these four main directional axes as guidelines for finding the horoscopic zones on your house plan.

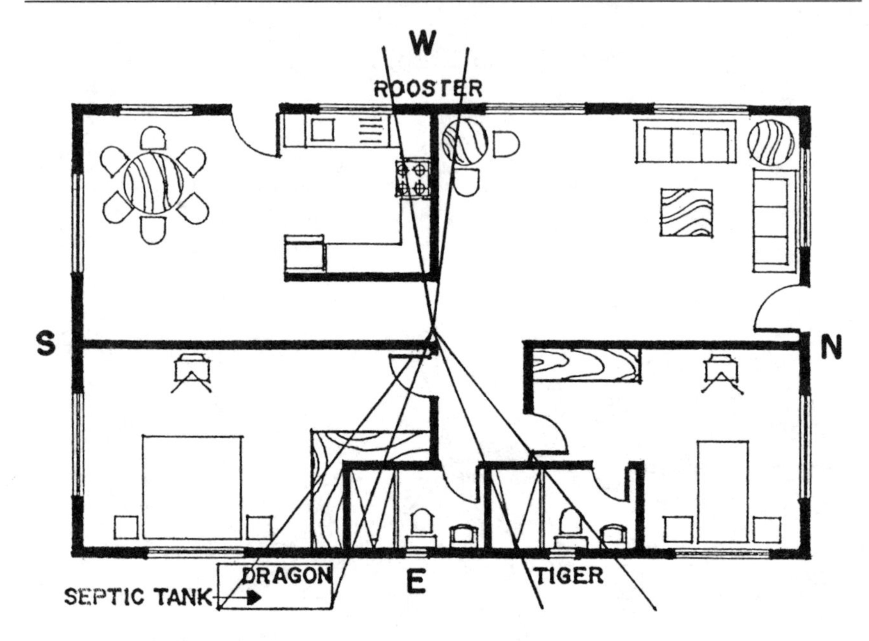

** a toilet in the Tiger zone * a septic tank in the Dragon zone*
** a stove in the Rooster zone*

YOUR FENG SHUI CURES:

1] *For a toilet that is in your horoscopic zone or otherwise wrongly placed, you can do any or all of the following;*

a) Hang a mirror on the wall fronting the toilet or on the side of it; this will 'move it out'– be sure that the mirror is large enough to reflect the whole toilet bowl as well as the person seated on it. A convex mirror can also be used; this will not only 'move it out' it will also 'diminish it.'

b) Place or hang live potted plants in the bathroom; they will absorb some of the *water chi*.

c) Keep the area as clean and as dry as possible, and cover the toilet bowl with the seat when it is not in use.

d) Place a small dish of rough kitchen salt, with a little water added to it, in a corner of the bathroom.

2] *For a septic tank that is in your zone or otherwise wrongly placed:*

a) Cover the tank with potted plants or a layer of soil and grass.

b) If the tank is in front of your main or rear door – place plants on either side of the door.

3] *For a stove or heating element in your zone:*

The obvious 'cure' is to relocate them. If you cannot do that, use the mirror cure #1.a) on the opposite page.

** A mirror relocates a toilet * plants & salt neutralize yin chi*

A septic tank – with plants

CHAPTER TWENTY TWO

THE DISINTEGRATION OF A FAMILY

A Case History

They were considered an ideal family. The husband was successful in his business, the wife was a good homemaker and a devoted mother, and their children were well-behaved and studious. They had their ups and downs as all people do, but in general their problems were minor ones and they usually worked them out together.

Their children had many friends, so the house was always full of happy and noisy young people. They had lived in this house since they were married, but now, with all the teenage activity, it suddenly seemed too small for them. They decided that they needed a larger home with more entertainment space. After months of looking at properties, they finally found a house that suited them and moved in. One year later they were in our office almost in despair – this is their story...

About three months after moving into the new house, arguments between the husband and wife began to occur; we will call them Mr.& Mrs.'B' They would quarrel about small things that never bothered them before. As the months passed, they became constantly irritated with each other and with their children as well. A tense atmosphere prevailed in the house. Mrs.'B' began to suffer from minor ailments and nervousness.

It was well into the sixth month after their transfer that Mrs.'B' noticed that their youngest son, who was 16 years old, was not behaving normally. He was not eating well and was losing weight. Most of the time he was out of the house, and when he was at home he stayed mainly in his room. At the same time, money and small items of jewelry began to disappear. One day, Mrs.'B'caught her son going through her handbag. When she confronted him, he complained that his allowance was not enough for his needs, but she suspected he was using drugs and stealing to finance his habit. She also noticed that the friends he now associated with were ill-mannered and indolent.

Their 18 year old daughter was giving them a problem as well. She neglected her schoolwork and came home late at night. It seemed that Mr.and Mrs.'B' no longer had any control over their children's behaviour, and the closeness once shared by the family was lost.

We discussed their situation at some length, and asked them for the birthday information of the family members and a copy of the house plan. We then set an appointment to inspect the house.

FENG SHUI ANALYSIS:

For a *feng shui* analysis, we divide the house into eight sections or *guas*. Each *gua* is associated with a member of the family. If a *gua* is hollow, the associated family member will lose his/her effectivity in the household. If a *gua* is protruded, the family member associated with it will become dominant – see, *'Shape & Direction' – Chapter 6.*

The Northwest and Southwest hollow:

In this house, the *guas* of the 'father' and 'mother,' i.e., Northwest and Southwest, were hollow – this diminished the parents' influence over their children.

The West gua protruded – with a water placement:

The *West gua*, which is associated with the youngest daughter, was protruded – this influenced her to be willful and disobedient. There was also a bathroom in the West. As the *water element* governs the genito-urinary tract, this placement can precipitate sickness or promiscuity of the young females of the household.

The stairs and the stove in the Northeast:

The Northeast section of the house, which is the *gua* of boys or the youngest son, was occupied by the stairs. A stairwell is equivalent to a hollow or a 'hole' in the *energy grid* of the house. Because stairs are also conveyors of people and *chi*, the constant movement destabilized the area, which correspondingly destabilized the youngest son. The kitchen stove was also located within in his horoscopic zone, which made him hot-headed and prone to erratic behaviour.

The marital bed between two doors:

In the master bedroom, the marital bed was hit by the *chi* of both the bedroom and the bathroom doors. This disturbed the *energy field* of the bed, and it was here that most of the couple's arguments began.

RECOMMENDATIONS:

1] The bathroom in the West should be kept clean and dry and live plants placed or hung inside it.

2] Relocate the kitchen stove.

3] Place a 24-hour light on the ceiling at the top of the stairwell – see, *'Stairs – Conveyors of Chi'– Chapter 14.*

4] Relocate the marital bed to avoid the two doors opposing it, or place a screen between the bed and one of the doors, and an automatic closer on the other door.

We were able to remedy the *feng shui* of this house. The son is currently undergoing treatment for his addiction, the daughter is attentive to her studies, and Mr.and Mrs.'B' have kissed and made up – A happy ending to what could have been the disintegration of a family.

The preceding analysis and recommendations are based only on the aspects of feng shui that are discussed in this book, as such, they are valid but incomplete.

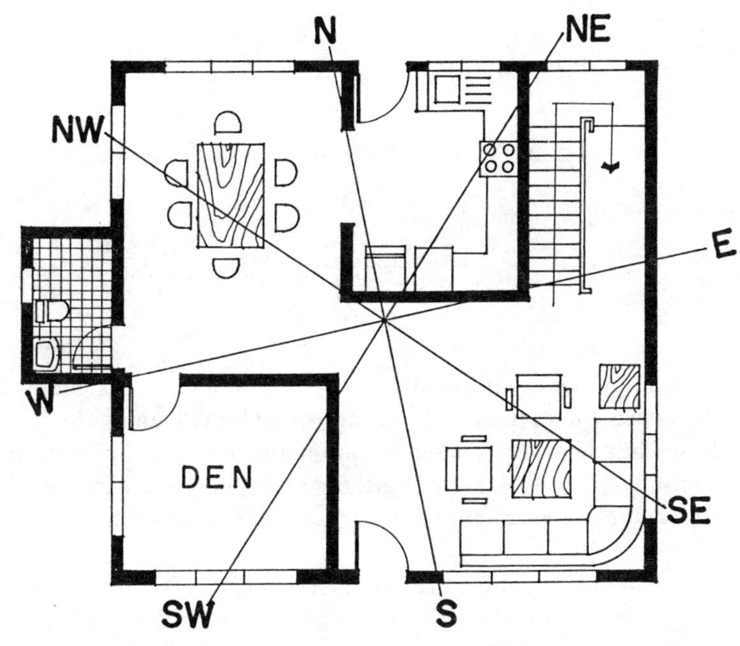

** West protruded – with a toilet * Stairs and stove in the Northeast*

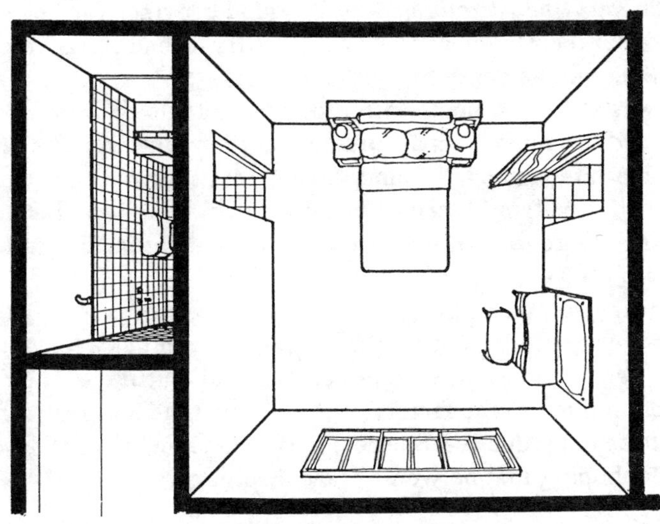

A bed between two doors

CHAPTER TWENTY THREE

THE MAKING OF A MATRIARCH

A Case History

Although most families are headed by a male, we sometimes encounter a case where the family is controlled by a female. The wife runs the family business and makes all the major decisions concerning the household, while the husband is either sickly, lazy, or leaves the family to live elsewhere. One of our recent cases was typical of the 'matriarchal syndrome.'

Mrs. 'L' was running the family business, which was their only means of support. She asked us to check the *feng shui* of her house to see if anything could be done to encourage her husband to be more helpful. She explained, that for the first ten years of their marriage, her husband had been very industrious and was a good provider for her and their children. For their tenth wedding anniversary he had bought them a new house. She and the children were very happy.

It was about six months after they moved into their new home that she noticed her husband's attitude toward his business was changing. He became careless and off-hand, sometimes he did not want to go to the office at all. The family income began to dwindle. It was then that Mrs. 'L' decided to go to their office and small garment factory to see if she could help out.

As the years passed, Mrs. 'L' became more proficient. Her husband progressively withdrew from the business, eventually leaving all the work in her hands. Dismayed at her husband's attitude, she recruited her eldest son to run the factory, but the little time he spent at his work proved to be unproductive. She decided to send him to live and work with his uncle, hoping that he would learn discipline.

Now her two daughters are assisting her. The eldest manages the factory and her second daughter takes care of the retail outlet. Her husband is sickly and only leaves the house to play mahjong with his group of friends. Her youngest son is still in college, so she and her daughters are undertaking the entire burden of supporting the family. "What can I do?" she asked, "I know that we can expand our business and improve our lives, if only my husband and sons could help us."

We have had several cases similar to this. In some instances, the woman enjoys the dominant role and is more capable than the male, so it works out quite well for everyone. But in generally, a woman prefers her mate to be the more active one so she can attend to the raising of the children.

We asked Mrs.'L' to show us the plans of her lot and house; we made a thorough inspection of the house and took note of the birthday data of all the family members. We then returned to our office to analyze the case.

FENG SHUI ANALYSIS:

A stairwell and a toilet in the Northwest:

In the house of Mrs.'L' the northwest section or 'master zone' was occupied by a staircase and a toilet. Both these placements were detrimental to the authority and the health of the husband.

A hollow in the East:

The second major problem of the house was the missing east section, which is the direction designated to the eldest son. A hollow in this area will often be the cause of the eldest son wanting to leave the house or, of his being ineffective within the family. If and when he leaves, the effect will sometimes pass on to the second son, who has then become the eldest male child in the house.

The female zones of the house, i.e., Southeast, South, Southwest and West, were strong. Indeed, a classic case of the house *feng shui* creating a matriarchal family.

In *feng shui*, there are so many aspects to be considered. An analysis of a home means weighing one aspect against another to get to the cause of a problem. Once the cause is known, a cure can be applied.

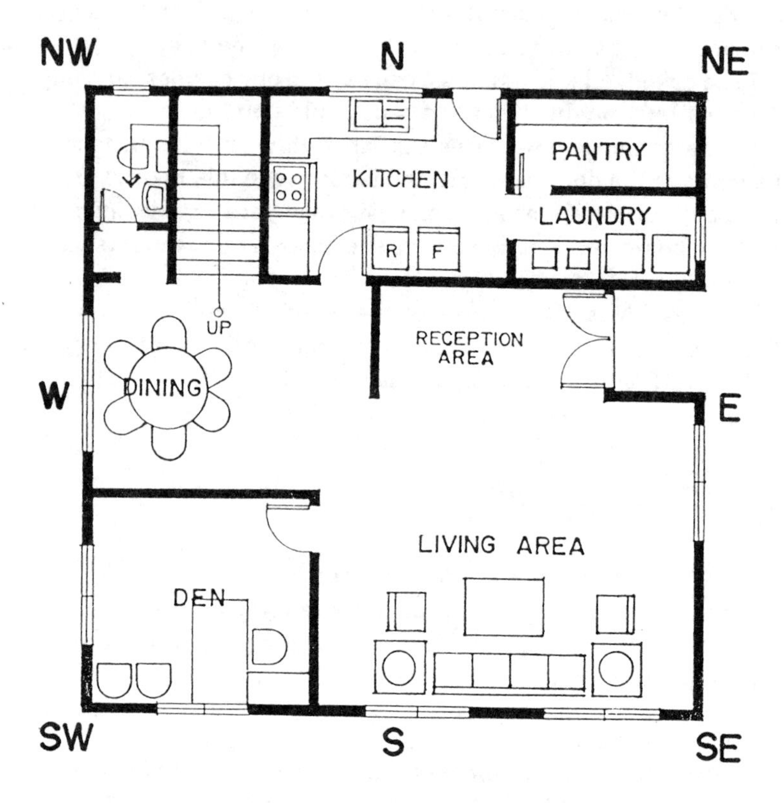

**The stairs and a toilet in the Northwest * A hollow in the East*
(This floor plan has been revised to placed the North at the top)

RECOMMENDATIONS:

1] *Maintain the chi in the stairwell:*
This can be done by installing a low wattage light bulb on the ceiling of the stairwell and keeping it lit 24 hours a day.

2] *Diminish the yin chi of the toilet, by:*

a) keeping live plants in the bathroom, and
b) making sure it is kept as clean and dry as possible; you can also
c) place a small dish of salt under the toilet bowl; this should be flushed away each week and replaced.

If the sickness of the husband becomes serious, the use of the bathroom should be minimized and the toilet bowl removed or sealed.

3] *Enclose the East section of the house:*

This can be done with grills, trellis, mosquito wire or screen.

The preceding analysis and recommendations are based only on the aspects of feng shui that are discussed in this book.

CHAPTER TWENTY FOUR

ARE YOU ACCIDENT PRONE?

A Case History

"I have become accident prone," she said. Mrs.'K' was sitting uncomfortably on the edge of the chair in my office, it was quite obvious that her nerves were frayed. "Within the past twelve months, I have had two accidents while driving my car. In both cases I was at fault, I just don't know how that could happen."

I asked if other members of the family were also having accidents. "Oh yes," she said, "a few months ago my son drove our car and had a collision with a jeep. Fortunately, he was only slightly hurt, but our new car was badly damaged. Not only that, my husband slipped in the shower and hit his head on the faucet."

Her list of accidents and mishaps went on to include, an 'almost' fire in the kitchen, when she neglected her frying pan to talk to a visitor, as well as minor cuts, burns and bruises, which were almost an everyday occurrence. "I am always paying for repairs to the house and the cars, not to mention medical bills. It's impossible to save money!" she added.

I asked Mrs.'K' how long she had been living in her present house. "We moved in one year and two months ago," she said, "and it was about one year ago that the accidents started."

The following week, we inspected her house. We checked the orientation, the external and internal factors, the water placements and various other elements important to our assessment. Then, armed with a copy of the house plan, we returned to our office to study the case.

FENG SHUI ANALYSIS:

Both the house and the lot of Mrs.'K' were protruded in the Northeast, which in *feng shui* parlance is rather colourfully known as, '*the Devil's gate.*' The Southwest is sometimes referred to as, '*the Devil's back door.*' The Northeast/Southwest axis creates a pathway of deviate energy. It is not advisable to place active, accident prone, or unsanitary elements in this zone, such as; doors, stairwells, electric panels, stoves, toilets, and garbage cans.

Front and rear doors hit by directional axes:

If a directional axis passes through or 'hits' a door, it can be the invisible cause of accidents and misfortunes. Because these directional lines have intense *chi,* they can trigger the energy of whatever they hit or pass through.

The front door of Mrs K's house was located directly on the Southwest axis and the rear door was on the Northeast axis. With both doors being hit by '*the Devil's axes,*' it is not surprising that so many negative incidents happened to the family.

A directional axis hits the stove:

When a directional axis passes through or 'hits' a stove, a heating appliance or an electrical box, it can create a fire hazard. This is often the hidden cause of electrical fires, or fires that seem to begin by spontanious combustion.

It is not easy to calculate the position of the axes. The bearings must be absolutely precise in order to get the exact North, and subsequently the other directions. The centre of the house is the point of reference for imposing the axes on the floor plan. The compass degrees of the axes are: N.0°: NE.45°: E.90°: SE.135°:-S.180°: SW.225°: W.270°: NW.315°

A toilet near the front door:

A toilet near a front door can lead to the loss of the family's fortune, as the *yang chi* that enters through the door, is either neutralized by the *yin toilet chi*; or it is 'flushed away' before it can circulate throughout the house.

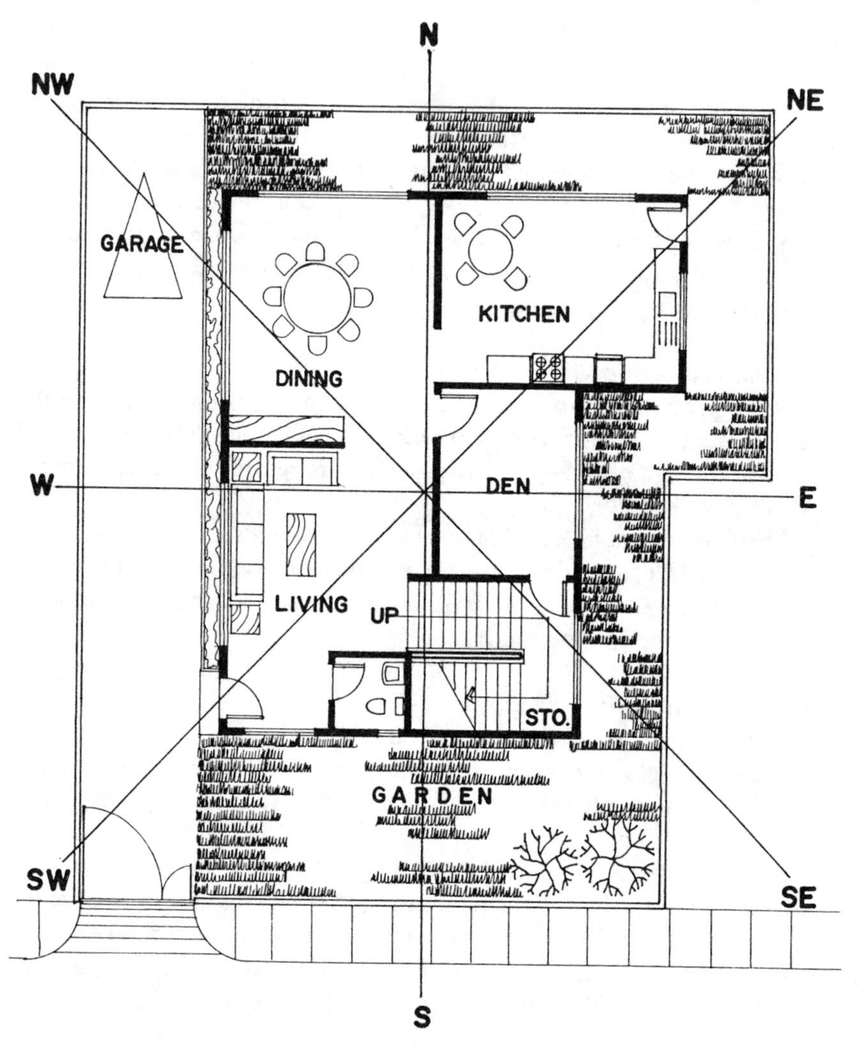

** The Northeast (Devil's gate) protruded*
** The stove hit by the Northeast axis*
** A toilet near the front door*
** Northeast/Southwest axis passing through the front & rear doors*

RECOMMENDATIONS:

1] *Recess the front and rear doors to avoid the axes.*

2] *Interchange the stove and the refrigerator.*

3] *To prevent the loss of money and the neutralization of yang chi:* treat the toilet near the main door in any, or all of the following ways;
   a) place a screen between the front door and the toilet door and/or,
   b) place live plants inside the toilet and/or,
   c) fit the toilet door with an automatic closer.

We were able to neutralize the negative factors of this house and give the family a chance to function without the weakening effects of an unsupportive environment.

The preceding analysis and recommendations are based only on the aspects of feng shui that are discussed in this book.

CHAPTER TWENTY FIVE

CAUSES OF 'BAD LUCK'

A Case History

Have you ever wondered why bad luck comes in cycles? Quite often these unlucky cycles can last for many years.

It is widely accepted that the environmental factors of the places in which you live and work, influence the events in your life. If these events are negative, the psychological effect of repeated misfortunes can lead to loss of confidence and negative thinking. Negative thinking creates a negative *energy field,* a negative *energy field* attracts more negative events, and negative events create more negative thoughts, and... this is how a cycle of misfortune is perpetuated.

If you trace this cycle of 'bad luck' to its beginning, you may discover that it began soon after you moved into a new home or renovated your old one. Sometimes problems arise after you change your office address or your job.

The following is the case of a reader of one of my columns who wrote to me about the long chain of unlucky happenings that had been dogging both him and his wife. We will call him Mr.'C.'

Mr.and Mrs.'C' enjoyed a happy marriage which produced six children. Although they were not prosperous, they were able to save part of their income. Some seven years ago they bought a lot and built a small house on it.

A short while after moving into the house, they began to experience the start of their 'bad luck.' Mr.'C' lost one job after another, even though he was highly qualified for the work. Whatever business venture the couple began, ended in failure, and they were constantly having misunderstandings with their neighbours.

Note: *Our analysis is based on the drawings enclosed in Mr. 'C's letter.*

FENG SHUI ANALYSIS:

A bow-shaped road hits the house:

The lot was on a curve of the road. The curve formed a 'bow' (as in bow and arrow) facing the lot. The *cutting chi* of this type of road configuration is often the cause of afflictions to the family, sometimes in the form of harmful gossip and ill will.

Flowing water at the rear:

At the rear of the lot was a flowing creek. This meant that the family had no solid backing or support.

Dead trees and thorny cactus in the garden:

There were two dead trees in the lot. Dead trees have a correspondence with ill health and misfortune.

Another violation was that the lot was bordered on all sides by prickly cactus plants, which may have done a good job of warding off intruders, but the thorns were also pointing inward toward the house. This created very irritating *chi*, which not only adversely affected the fortune of the occupants, but also caused them to quarrel among themselves and with others.

It is difficult to give a very detailed or accurate analysis by mail, as we need to visit the site to thoroughly inspect the surroundings, however, we were able to give the following advice to Mr. 'C.'

RECOMMENDATIONS:

1] *Plant trees and shrubs between the curve of the road and the house.*

2] *Build a wall or artificial mountains at the rear of the house:* mounds of earth planted with grass or shrubs, or a high wall between the house and the creek will effectively give backing to the house.

3] *Cut the dead trees and remember to dig out the roots:* this will remove any remaining *elemental energy* of the trees.

4] *Either pull out the cactus or plant rows of shrubs with round or oval leaves inside the perimeter of the cactus border:*
This will shield the house from the prickly *chi* of the thorns.

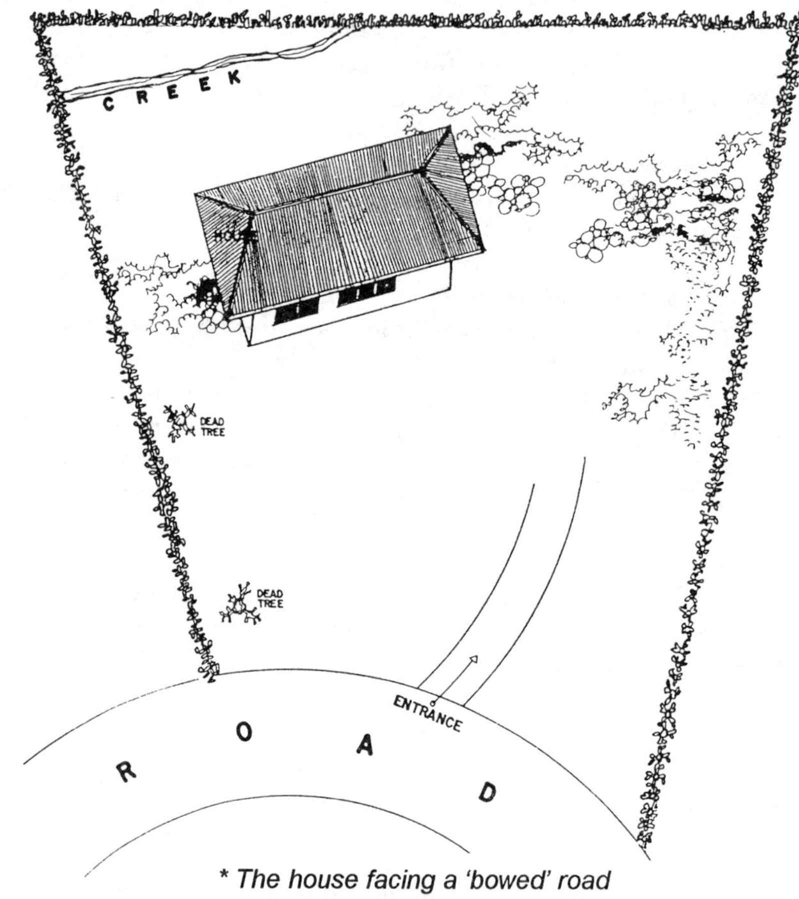

** The house facing a 'bowed' road*
** A creek at the rear of the lot*
** Two dead trees in the garden*
** The lot bordered by prickly cactus plants*

CHAPTER TWENTY SIX

RENOVATION – FOR BETTER OR FOR WORSE

A Case History

When you decide to renovate, you should be aware that any change you make, whether structural or superficial, can affect the balance of energy of your home or workplace, for better or for worse.

A typical case of 'for worse' is that of a family who had lived happily in a comfortable home for more than ten years. The house was starting to look shabby and, as their business was prospering, they decided to make some major renovations. Their plans included; building a den, modernizing the kitchen and master bedroom, and changing most of the furniture. They hired an interior designer and spent somewhat more than anticipated, but the results were beautiful and they were satisfied that it was worth the cost. Only the eldest daughter, who was quite sensitive, remarked that the house did not feel comfortable anymore.

Some weeks later, the husband began spending more time at the office and most of his weekends on the golf course. The eldest daughter developed almost daily headaches, the household expenses were over budget, everyone's nerves were on edge and family quarrels ensued. The wife decided to call us to check the *feng shui* of the house.

FENG SHUI ANALYSIS:

The family had extended the perimeter walls of the house by adding a den, thus changing the centre point of the house.

When the centre changes, all the *guas* and zones (which are calculated from the centre) also change, and the *feng shui* of the house has to be re-assessed.

The stove facing the rear door:

In the newly designed kitchen, the position of the stove now directly faced the rear door. This placement depleted the family's finances.

The front door within the daughter's horoscopic zone:

The horoscopic zone of the eldest daughter moved to the front door, which was why she did not feel 'comfortable' and had headaches.

Wrong placement of the marital bed:

The master bedroom had been redesigned and the colour scheme changed. Neither the new position of the bed, nor the colours of the room were suited to the husband's personal *chi*. The combination of negative factors caused him to sleep badly, and to feel uneasy and slightly nauseous – no wonder he spent so much time away from home.

We found quite a few other problems caused by the renovation. After some adjustments were made, the *feng shui* improved and harmony was restored.

When you are planning a renovation, one of the most important considerations is when to begin the work. Tearing down structures, banging on walls, and sawing and hammering distrupt the established *energy grid* of the house. A construction or renovation that is started on an inappropriate day can precipitate a series of accidents or costly errors and disputes with the contractor or decorator.

Chinese almanacs give auspicious and inauspicious dates for just about everything, but this is general information and does not take into consideration all the necessary factors. It is best to consult a *geomancer* before doing any major work that will disturb your home environment.

Note: *Do not renovate your house if one of the occupants is pregnant Wait until after the baby is born.*

CHAPTER TWENTY SEVEN

IS YOUR HOUSE HAUNTED?

CAUSES OF HAUNTINGS

Some houses and buildings, because of certain configurations in their design and layout, attract *nature spirits (elementals), ghosts* and *astral or spirit entities.*

The orientation of the building, topographical features, and water placements play a significant role in the analysis of a supposedly haunted site. In some cases the *yin* energy of a property can be so heavy that just driving past it causes a reaction in the bio-energy of a sensitive person. When we are selecting a site for a client, I sometimes reject a property without even entering the premises, because I can detect the presence of *elementals* and *spirit entities* from my seat within the car.

In other sites that are less *yin,* it is necessary to enter and spend some time inside before a reaction is felt. When the energy is so subtle that it cannot be felt; it can be detected by analysis. Orientation analysis is highly specialized – the orientation of a lot or a building can have a tremendous influence on the health and fortune of the occupants.

There are 360° (orientations) on the compass. Around 20% of these have a frequency or resonance that attracts negative energy. Although this 20% are all generally bad, some have their own dominant focus. There are orientations that are detrimental to health, others that are unfortunate for business, and still others that are destructive to relationships and family life.

Some orientations have a frequency similar to that of *elemental, astral, or spirit entities*. Houses with these orientations have 'invisible doors' that allow other life-forms to pass through into our dimension. This is one reason for the haunted house phenomenon.

Buildings undergoing construction on a site with a negative orientation often have more than the normal amount of accidents and problems, both during the construction period and after. Business establishments that have bad orientations are prone to prolonged labour disputes, strikes, and violence.

Skilled *geomancers* assess the subtle energies of the various compass points and determine how to close an 'inter-dimensional door,' but there are some clues that can be easily detected by everyone – these are placements within a home that provide access to the lower life-forms. I have listed some of them below.

Note: *It usually requires more than one of these violations, plus a negative orientation and/or a negative annual star grid to create an inter-dimensional door.*

A room without a window:

Windowless rooms are sometimes found in homes where a large room has been divided into two, with all the windows being in one room. The other room, having no natural light and only an air-conditioner or a fan for ventilation, will accumulate *yin chi* – light and fresh air give positive *yang chi*. The darker and more airless a place becomes, the more it is likely to attract *nature spirits,* and *ghosts*.

A mirror facing your bed:

This can be a dangerous placement, especially if your house has a negative orientation. If you cannot move the mirror, then cover it before you sleep. We do not recommend the placement of mirrors in a bedroom (except inside the closet door). Improper use of mirrors anywhere in the house can upset the energy balance and open a doorway to the lower planes. It again depends on other factors of the analysis.

A toilet door facing the bed:

The *yin* energy of a toilet can permeate the *energy field* of the bed and make the occupants vulnerable to sickness and spirit possession.

An unoccupied house:

If your house has been unoccupied for a long time it will become progressively more *yin,* and will attract *yin entities*. Human life-forms are *yang* – a house full of busy people is not an ideal site for *ghosts.*

Facing an unoccupied house or building:

If the door of your house faces an unoccupied house or building, it can absorb some of its *yin chi.*

Cracks, leaks, mildew and mould:

If your house has a leaking roof, rising damp or cracked walls, it will be *yin* and unhealthy, and will attract *yin entities*. It is also said that cracked walls in a master bedroom contribute to 'cracked marriages.'

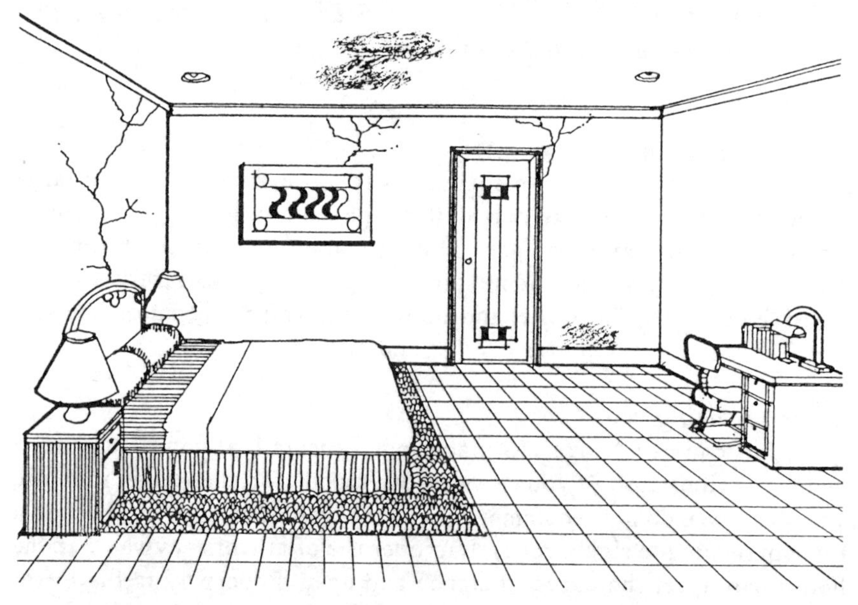

A bedroom with cracked walls and mildew.

A big tree outside the window:

A big tree outside a window can provide an ingress for *elementals*.

A bedroom in a basement:

A bedroom below earth level does not have enough exposure to sunlight (*yang chi*) and will consequently accumulate *yin chi*.

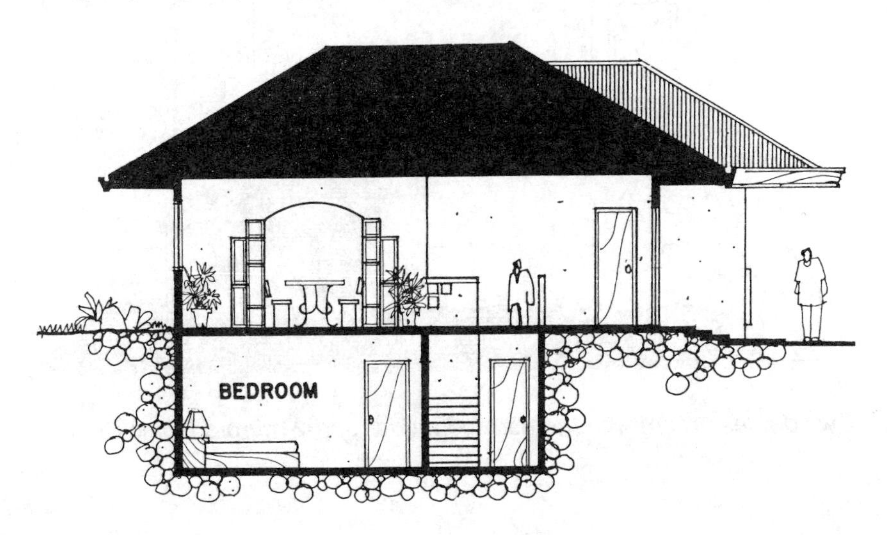

Sometimes a *geomancer* will detect an entity through the use of a compass. If, while he/she is taking a bearing, the compass starts to fluctuate or tremble, it usually indicates the presence of a non-human life-form.

On a recent trip, I experienced a haunted hotel room. This room had four *feng shui* violations that attract *ghosts*:

a) The room was very dimly lit.

b) Both the dresser mirror and a full-length mirror reflected the bed.

c) The toilet door faced the mid-section of the bed.

d) There was no window in the room.

Needless to say, I was disturbed during the night by *astral entities,* and I promptly moved out the next morning. My clients later informed me that the hotel was well-known for '*ghosts* on the 3rd floor.' So travellers beware, make sure you get a room with natural light and not more than one of the preceding *feng shui* violations.

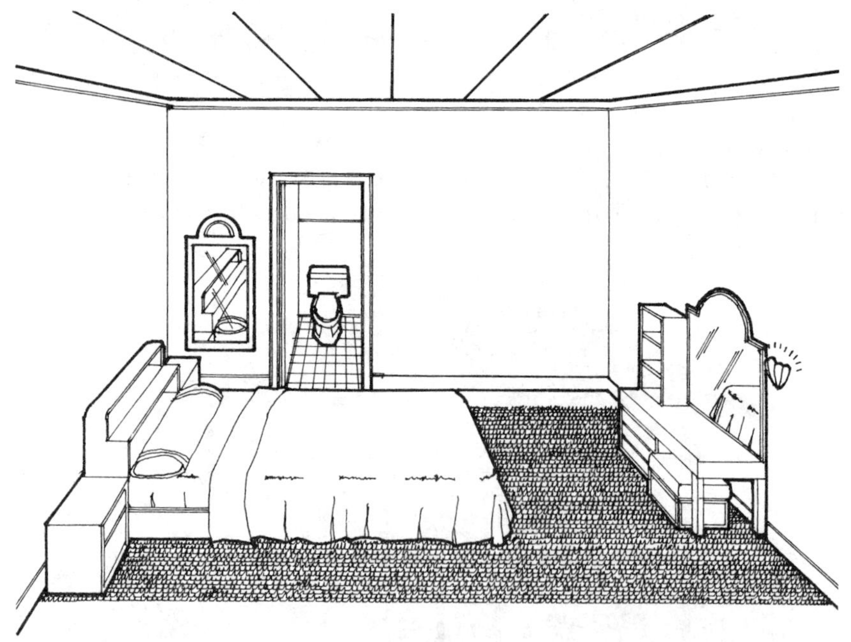

A windowless room with the bathroom door and 2 mirrors facing the bed

YOUR FENG SHUI CURES:

1] *If you have a room without windows in your house or in your work place, you should do the following;*
   a) leave a light on inside it 24 hours a day. A low wattage bulb is suitable; and
   b) ventilate the room by leaving the door open as much as possible;
   c) If the room is air-conditioned, clean the filter often; and
   d) be sure it has no mirrors that face the bed – preferably, do not sleep in the room.

2] *If you have a tall tree near the window of your room:*
   cut the branches that touch the house – see, '*How to prune a tree*' – *page 162.*

3] *If your toilet door opens to face your bed:*
   a) move your bed away from the toilet area, and/or
   b) fit an automatic closer on the toilet door, and
   c) keep the seat cover down over the toilet bowl, and
   d) place a small bowl of salt (with a little water added) under the toilet bowl.

4] *If doors or windows face a view of an empty or dilapidated building:*
   a) place a *ba-gua* or a convex mirror over the door;
   b) place venetian blinds on the windows and adjust the slats to block the view and divert the *chi*

5] *If you think your house may be haunted:*
   make sure that you do not have exposed mirrors in the bedroom, or a mirror reflecting a door anywhere in the house.

6] *If you are moving into a house that has been empty for some time:*
   you can clear the property of *yin* energy with lots of human activity – throw a noisy party.

7] *If you have leaks, rising damp or clogged drains:*
   you should get yourself a good plumber.

A final word about haunted houses:

A house or building has an *energy field* around it that is similar to the *auric field* of a person. This can be seen as either, 'bright' (positive) 'dim' (negative) or 'dark' (disastrous). A house with many *indwelling-spirits* and *elementals* appears to be covered in shadow, just like the *auric field* of a sick person.

Although *elementals* may not necessarily be bad or evil, they exist on a lower frequency of energy, hence, interaction or communication with them should not be encouraged. If we must have inter-dimensional contact, it is preferable for it to be with beings on a higher level of consciousness, such as saints, angels, and enlightened masters.

Your level of consciousness can be elevated by *good feng shui* and lowered by *bad feng shui*.Truly, it is not yet fully comprehended how vital a good living and working environment is to our health, our mental attitudes, and our interactions with others. *Feng shui* can spell the difference between a life that is happy and prosperous, and an unhappy life full of problems.

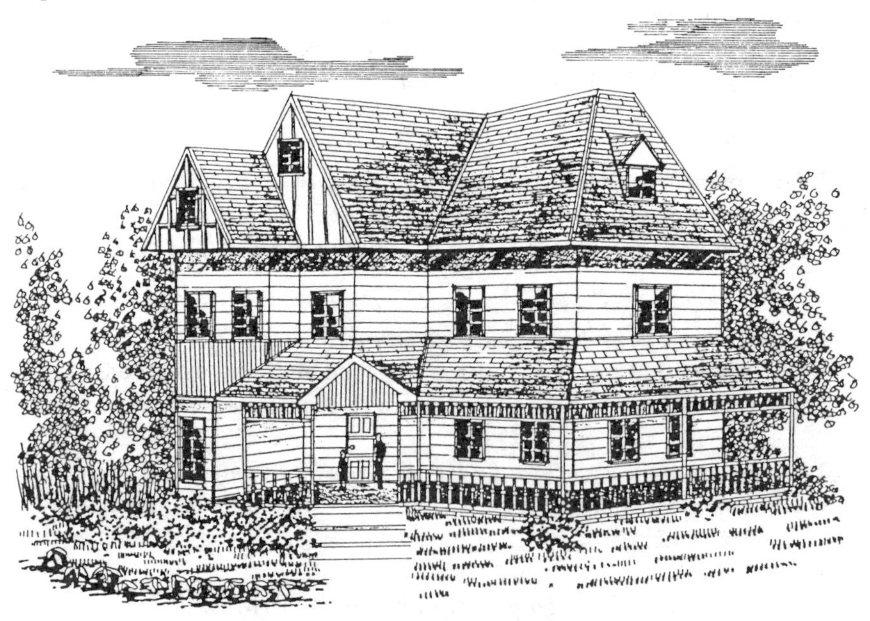

A haunted house

CASE HISTORY #1 – SPIRIT POSSESSION

If you suspect that you have anything like the following situation in your house or office, we recommend that you do not try to cope with it yourself, it is preferable to consult your geomancer or your spiritual counsellor.

A client asked for our help with a personal problem. It seemed that lately he was always tired and irritable. He suffered from frequent headaches and made wrong decisions. Consequently, his business was losing money and his health was deteriorating. "I seem to be undergoing a personality change," he said, "I can't control my temper and my family and staff are being affected. What can I do?" We suggested that we check his office for *feng shui* violations.

Our client's office was located in a high-rise building. We checked the orientation of the building and the unit, the location and measurements of the main door, the placements of the internal doors, toilets, desks and furniture, and the office pantry. We also checked the exposure of the unit and the view from the windows. Everything connected with *'office feng shui'* was thoroughly noted by us and drawn up by our staff architects. We then returned to our workroom to study the plan.

FENG SHUI ANALYSIS:

Chi is a living force. It moves in rhythmical cycles, therefore its movements can be charted. We use the *sixty-year*, *twenty-year*, *twelve-year*, *annual*, and *monthly cycles* for *feng shui* assessments and predictions. *Daily* and *hourly cycles* are mostly used for finding suitable dates for special *feng shui* events, such as ground-breaking, pillar erecting, opening a business, or moving into a house.

The progression of the *twenty-year cycles* explains why a house, which was lucky for its owners for many years, suddenly changed when the new *twenty year cycle cycle* began. The *annual cycle* affects our luck on a year to year basis.

A study of the *energy grid* of the building showed that a negative star of the *annual cycle* had moved right into the *gua* where our client's unit was located. There was also a convergence of negative aspects on the position of his personal office and desk. This kind of configuration acts like a magnet to *elemental, astral* or *ghostly entities*, particularly in certain lunar months when the *yin* energy prevails.

The *astral body* of the dead takes time to disintegrate or 'transform', especially if the death was sudden and violent. *Astral* and *ghostly entities* dwell in a different frequency to our physical world but, they can enter our dimension if an opening or 'door' is created by a location that has become too *yin*.

I checked the history of the building and found out that, during its construction, a workman was killed in a fight with another labourer. The nature of the murdered man was violent and brutal. Due to the building's *yin* orientation and other negative factors, the dead worker's *residual energy form* was able to 'come through' into our client's office and attach itself to his *auric field*. The violent nature of the *entity* was the cause of our client's headaches, fits of bad temper and personality changes.

A ghost in an office unit

This type of occurrence is not as rare as people would like to believe. Priests of some religious sects deal with these phenomena by blessing the site, saying prayers for the dead and/or praying over the persons affected, which quite often solves the problem. Methods that adhere to metaphysical laws are my own preference, although, I will generally recommend whatever I consider appropriate for the circumstances and the belief systems of the persons involved.

In this case, I 'sealed the door' between the dimensions, and gave the client procedures for cleansing his *auric field*. I also changed the layout of his office and relocated the unit door and his desk.

CASE HISTORY #2 – THE LITTLE PEOPLE

This is a case of *earth elementals*, (also known as *gnomes, leprechauns, elves,* or *duendes*) that caused problems during the renovation of a house.

The owners of the house, which was in one of the city's smart subdivisions, decided to make some renovations. They hired an architect and a contractor. The contractor arrived with several workers, some of whom were from the provinces. As they were unable to commute to their homes, they were permitted to live in the house for the duration of the repair work. Folding beds were placed for them in the childrens' playroom, which was located in the basement at the rear section of the house.

Some days after the work began, the workers complained that they were not able to sleep because something or someone was jumping on their beds during the night. The owner and his family disregarded such talk but, two workers who claimed that they felt sick, walked off the job. The following night, the furniture and some of the children's toys in the playroom were moved around and their desks and stools were knocked over. In the morning the remaining workers packed their things and left the house – only the foreman stayed. He suggested that the cause of the incidents might be *duendes* and asked the owners of the house to call in a clairvoyant he knew. They agreed, and the clairvoyant was sent for.

After spending a night in the house, the clairvoyant declared that the *duendes* were angry, as one of them had been injured by a piece of lumber that was dropped by a worker. She advised the family to make an offering to the *duendes* so as to appease them – this was done. That night the house was peaceful. The next day more labourers were hired and the work continued.

A few days later, the toys and furniture were again moved around during the night. This time, one of the workers was hit by a falling tricycle. The following morning he quit, so did most of the other men. A friend of the family suggested that they call a *geomancer*.

When we arrived at the house, I took note of the orientation, the external factors and the internal placements. I then made a thorough inspection of the basement and the garden. After that, we returned to our office to study the findings and apply our charts to the house plan that had been drawn by my staff architect.

During our inspection of the house, I detected the odour of *duendes*. I noted in the plan where the odour was the strongest. I also took note of the day the work had begun.

FENG SHUI ANALYSIS:

Our investigations revealed that not only did the house had a *yin* orientation, but also that the work was started on an inappropriate day. In *feng shui* the day to begin repairing a house is very important. The *chi* of the day should be compatible with the *chi* of the owner and the lot, and, among other considerations, the day must not be 'broken' – a day is called broken when its *element* is 'opposed' to the *element* of the month.

When we drew up the *energy grid* of the house, we found that a negative star of the *annual cycle* had moved into a position that corresponded with the area where I had noticed the *duende* odour. The star formed a configuration that triggered the *yin* aspects of the basement section of the house. This, plus a badly placed rear entrance, had created an 'inter-dimensional door' through which the *duendes* were able to enter our human plane of existence; unfortunately this led to the injury of one of them. They sought to draw attention to their problem by throwing around the toys and jumping on the workers' beds.

RECOMMENDATIONS:

Our recommendation to the clients was to stop the work. We then gave them an appropriate date to begin again, and applied certain techniques to 'seal the door' between the dimensions.

We advised them to clean the garden area where I had smelled the *duendes* quite strongly, and not to allow the workers to urinate or throw their cigarette ends and rubbish there; the workers had been doing just that, right on the home ground of the *duendes*. We also gave them some procedures for making peace with the *duendes*. When all was done as we suggested, the work proceeded without further incident.

Toys scattered in the basement

Every culture has its folklore regarding *earth elementals*. In Ireland in particular, the 'little people' are often seen, and most Irishmen believe in their existence. Although some *elementals* are mischievous, they will usually only enter our dimension when they need to communicate something.

If you smell odd odours, or hear sounds of little footsteps, or if you feel that someone is jumping on your bed during the night, (a common habit of *duendes*) you should call a professional to deal with it.

Houses that have a negative orientation and an excess of *yin* factors, will not only attract *ghosts* and *elementals*, they will also lower the consciousness of susceptible occupants, leading them into crime, sloth, alcoholism, and other indulgences.

Note: *Do not be concerned if the forgoing aspects of feng shui do not jibe with your sensibilities or your belief system. Because, when stripped of the esoteric explanations, the analyses and recommendations stand firmly on the basic principle that good feng shui requires a balance of yin and yang energy; an excess of either one will lead to all manner of problems.*

Part Four

Home Buyers Guide

Feng Shui Tips for Property Buyers,
Real Estate Professionals
and You!

CHAPTER TWENTY EIGHT

FENG SHUI TIPS FOR PROPERTY BUYERS

Direction and Topography
Subdivisions and Housing Estates
Choosing a Lot or House
A Word About Chimney Stacks

Clients often come to us after they have bought a lot, to ask us to design their new home. Our design must provide for their specific needs, such as the number of bedrooms, bathrooms etc. It should be functional and beautiful, yet not violate any of the myriad rules of personalized *feng shui* – this is not an easy task. It is made even more difficult when the site of the intended house has *bad feng shui*. Occasionally the site is so bad, we can only suggest that the client sell it and purchase another. Subsequently, we assess new sites until a suitable one is found. With a little knowledge, such expensive mistakes can be avoided.

In professional *feng shui* analysis, we use an *energy grid* that we configure from an accurate orientation of the property, but we always factor-in the following rules of site analysis. These rules are an invaluable guide to those who intend to buy, build or lease a property.

DIRECTION AND TOPOGRAPHY:

Directional rule # 1. The North should have the highest ground:

The cold winds from the North should be blocked by high ground, tall trees, walls or structures.

Countries in the Southern hemisphere should reverse this rule to; *The South should have the highest ground..*

Directional rule # 2. The East should be lower than the West:

The lively *yang* energy of the morning sun, which emanates from the East, enhances the *feng shui* of a house. It should not be obstructed by high ground, tall buildings or tall dense trees.

The West emanates the *yin* energy of the setting sun, which should be filtered through trees or partially blocked by higher ground, walls, or structures; particularly in tropical countries where the heat of the afternoon sun is so strong that it is retained in the walls of the house. This not only induces lethargy, it also burdens the air-conditioning system.

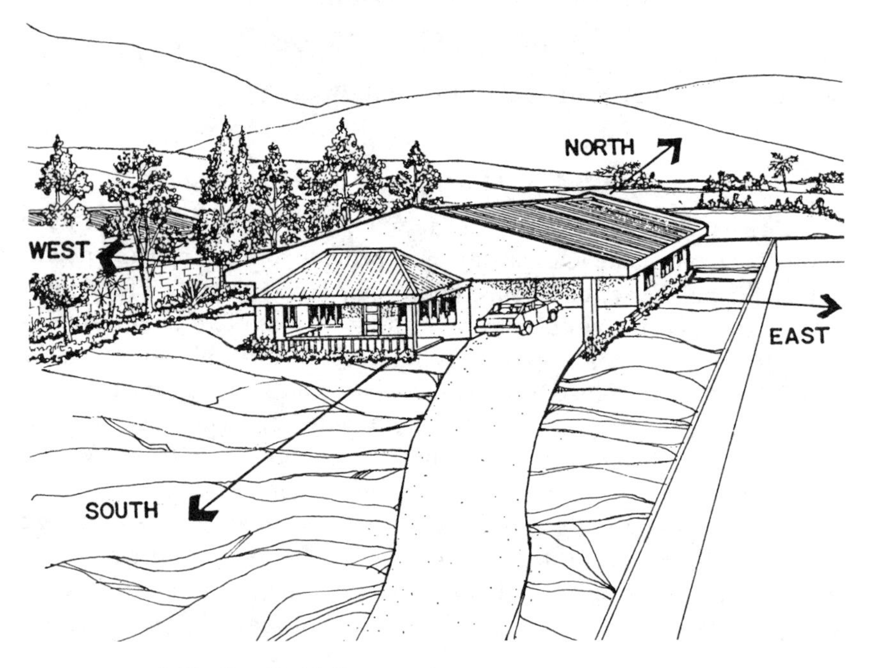

** North with high ground * East lower than West*

Topographical rule #1. The rear should be higher than the front:

The rear represents the future and the front represents the present. A lot or site that is higher at the rear means that you have the backing required by *good feng shui,* and that you will go up or be elevated in the future. It also indicates that your children will prosper.

If the lot goes down at the rear you can expect the opposite results. Not only that, everytime you enter the place your mind will register, "I am going down." And indeed you will, unless there are factors in your personal fortune that will help you to overcome this negative input.

Note: *Topographical rule #1 takes precedence over directional rule #1 (except in the cold climates of the Northern Hemisphere where the North winds must be blocked by higher ground.)*

Higher ground at the rear

Topographical rule #2. The left (dragon) side of the lot should be higher (and/or more active) than the right (tiger) side:

In *feng shui,* the left side is called the '*dragon,*' its energy is *yang* and positive. In order to draw good fortune into your lot and bring out the benefits of the *dragon chi*, there should be activity and movement on this side. The right side is called the '*tiger,*' its energy is *yin* and negative. In order not to activate the *tiger chi,* this side should be kept still or steady. (Left and right are taken when you are within the lot facing the street.)

Note: *Should topographical rule #2 conflict with directional rule #2, the directional rule will take precedence.*

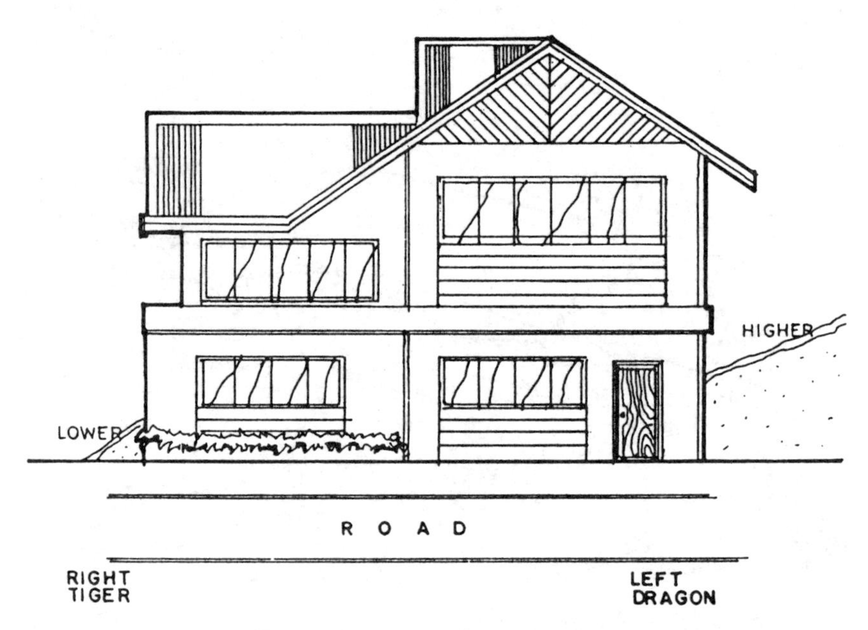

The dragon higher than the tiger

Topographical rule #3. The lot should not be on the lowest ground in the vicinity:

A very low location does not have good circulation of *chi,* consequently, business and family growth will stagnate.

Topographical rule #4. The lot should not be on the highest ground in the vicinity:

A lot on the highest point does not have any backing, and exposes the property to too much wind. When there is too much wind the *chi* cannot be contained, consequently, the health and wealth of the occupants will diminish.

Note: *Some topographical features of a site can be corrected by levelling the land, or by locating the main (most used) door to the side or even to the rear of the house.*

A house on the lowest ground in the vicinity

A house on the highest ground in the vicinity

SUBDIVISIONS AND HOUSING ESTATES

Subdivisions are mushrooming all over. How do you know which one to choose for your new home?

Most peoples' requirements differ according to their financial capacity, their health needs, proximity to their childrens' schools and other practical considerations. But once your choice has been narrowed down, the deciding factor should be the *feng shui*.

Subdivision planning involves many factors. The main concern of most developers is to maximize the usable land area in ratio to the infrastructure, i.e., saleable lots versus cost of roads, bridges, drainage,water and power systems, etc. Unfortunately, these plans are often made without considering the damage to the natural landscape.

When *geomancers* are consulted by urban planners, they work together with the project engineers to maintain the usable land to infrastructure ratio. In addition, they ensure that the entrances and exits are located and oriented so as to attract good *chi*, that the roads are laid out so as to provide the majority of the lots with a good orientation and shape, and that the power, water systems, and other utilities are located to enhance the feng shui of the site as well as being in accordance with practical engineering considerations. If you can find a subdivision that has been laid out with the aid of a *feng shui* consultant, so much the better. If not, then the following advice will be helpful in selecting a lot that will be beneficial to you and your family.

The general overview:

Visit the subdivision on several occaisions and in different weather condtions. Drive and walk around the to get the feel of the place. Sniff the air to test its freshness and take note of the wind velocity, which should be neither too still nor too windy. Check out the neighbouring areas, and the condition of the infrastructure, and on a rainy day take note of the drainage system. You should then get a subdivision plan and look for the following.

The shape of the subdivision: (applies only to sites under 20 hectares)
Does it look like a cross, or a letter 'H'?

These shapes are considered unfortunate whether for a subdivision, a lot or a building, because, large sections are missing and this creates an imbalance in the *chi-grid*.

Does the shape look like a chopper, knife or axe?

If so, do not buy a lot on the blade – the handle section has the '*controlling chi*' – see '*Feng Shui for High-Rise Living*' – *Chapter 29.*

Is the subdivision rambling with ill-defined borders?

If so, you will have to assess the positive and negative aspects of the neighbouring areas, as many of them will intrude into the subdivision space. Very irregular sites are problematic, not only for buyers, but also for developers.

There are many unfavourable shapes. When you lack professional advice it is safer to select a lot, within a subdivision that has a square or rectangular shape and clearly defined borders.

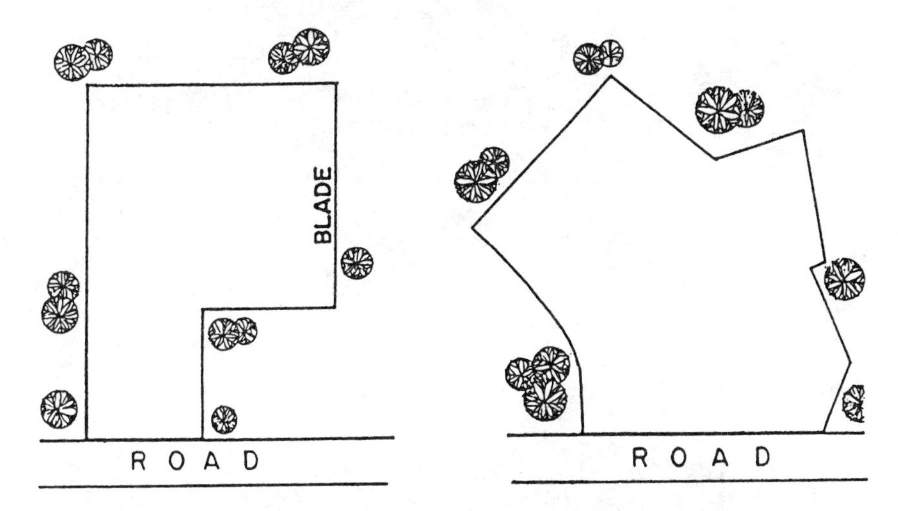

* *Chopper - do not buy on the blade* * *Irregular - problematic*

Topography:

The topography of a subdivision is another major consideration. Gently rolling hills are preferable for residential estates. This makes it easier to have lots with the classic ideal topography, '*higher ground at the rear and a clear view in front.*' It also indicates that the land has *dragon chi*. Flat land is often somewhat lifeless.

CHOOSING A LOT OR HOUSE

Orientation:

When *feng shui* is 'personalized' the orientation is chosen to match your year of birth. In lieu of this, the classic orientation is '*sited North facing South*'. Other orientations can also be suitable if the topographical features are favourable.

A subdivision with good topography

Shape:

Rule #1. The depth should be greater than the width:

Most Westerners prefer a lot or building with a wide frontage and do not look for depth. Asian buyers are not concerned with frontage, they look for a deep or long property. The proportion should not be exaggerated. The ideal is to have the width two-thirds of the depth.

The front of a lot or building is considered to be the present stage or condition. The rear is considered to be what you will attain, or the future condition. A deep property indicates that the occupants will have a long future in that place, or that they will stay there a long time. A shallow property means that their future will be short there and they will most likely not stay long.

Rule # 2. The rear should be equal to, or wider than the front:

If your property is as wide at the rear as at the front; it indicates stability. If it is wider at the rear than at the front; it means you will be able to expand in the future. When you enter your property and it widens as you penetrate, the psychological input is 'growth.' This can be the growth of your business or the growth of your family.

Note: *These rules apply, not only to residences, but also to commercial and industrial establishments.*

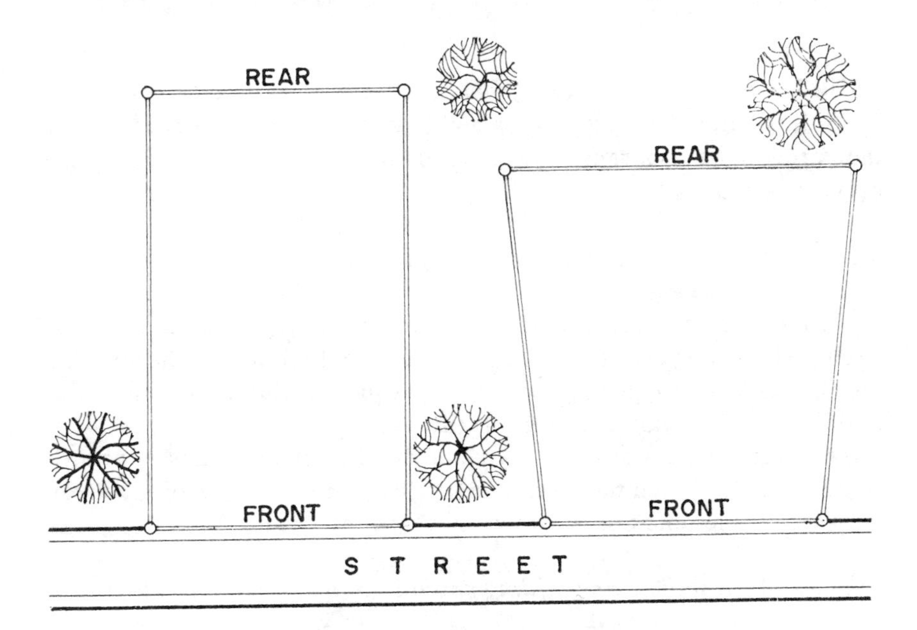

* *The depth greater than the width*
* *The rear wider than the front*

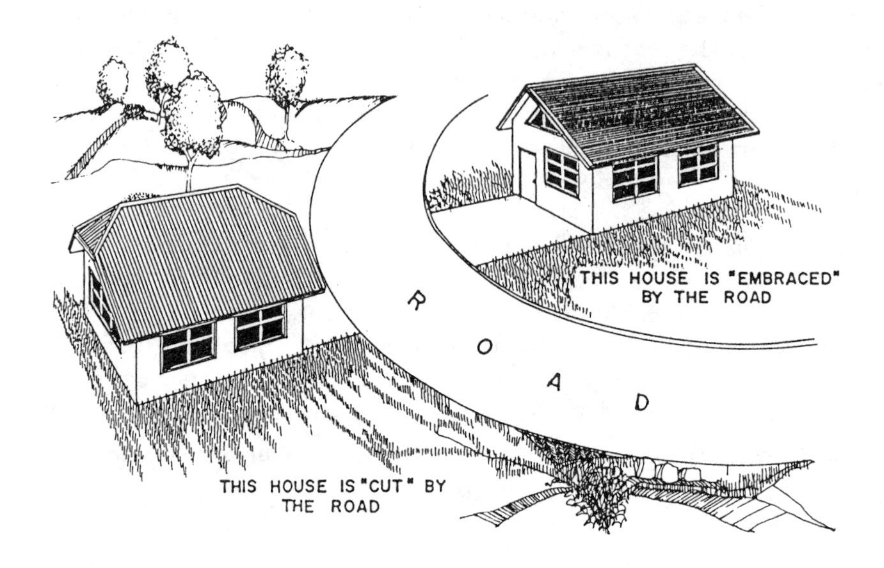

Rule #3. A lot, house or building should not be 'cut' by the curve of a road:

It is better for a property, whether it is residential, commercial or industrial, to be 'embraced' by the road rather than to be 'sliced' by the curve of a road.

Rule #4. A lot, house or building should not face an oncoming road or a dead end:

It is unfortunate for a lot to face or oppose the oncoming traffic of a road. The strong *chi* of the road is detrimental to the *chi* of the lot. This kind of '*chiong*' (opposing force) is sometimes useful for a commercial building, but it is not good for a residence.

Cures: for rules #3 and #4: (a) plant small trees or shrubs to absorb some of the *sha* from the road, and/or; (b) place a *ba-gua* or a convex mirror over the doors or windows that face the road.

Rule #5. A lot, house or building should not be sandwiched between tall structures:

If a lot is sandwiched between taller buildings, it will be pressured from both sides and the *chi* of the lot will be oppressed and constricted. If you rent or buy a house that is on this type of lot, you and your family will begin to feel the effects of the oppressive energy within ninety days of moving in. As time progresses, tempers will shorten, thinking will be

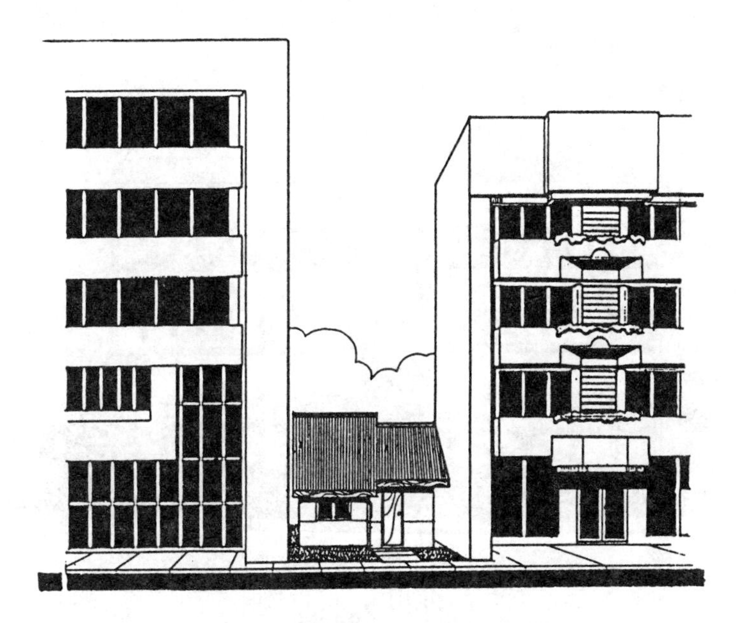

A house sandwiched between two tall buildings.

narrowed, business expansion will be difficult, and optimism and enthusiam will diminish.

Rule #6. *A lot, house or building should not face a taller building or higher ground:*

If you build your house on a lot that is facing a tall building, the *chi* will be blocked from entering your home, your view will be limited, and both physically and psychologically you will be 'confronted by obstacles' – see, *Chapter 7, page 55*
cures: For rule #5. Place a concave mirror on your roof to invert the image of the neighbouring buildings. And for #6. Hang a convex mirror over your door to diminish the oppressive *chi* of the facing building.

Rule #7. A lot, house or building should not face a narrow space between two buildings:

This configuration has a 'wind tunnel' effect. The *sha chi* of the wind tunnel will make the house prone to accidents and illnesses.
Cure: Place a *ba-gua* or a convex mirror facing the wind tunnel.

A house facing a wind tunnel

Rule #8. A lot, house or building should not have a creek or waterway at the rear:

A lot should have higher ground at the rear, this gives it support and backing. If there is flowing water at the rear, it connotes movement and a total lack of stability. Still water is also unstable and can often be stagnant and too *yin*. Only rarely can water at the rear be fortunate, this depends on the configuration of the *energy grid* of the lot.

Cure: A high wall, or a stand of trees at the rear of the lot will provide backing, and will block the view (and the *chi*) of the water.

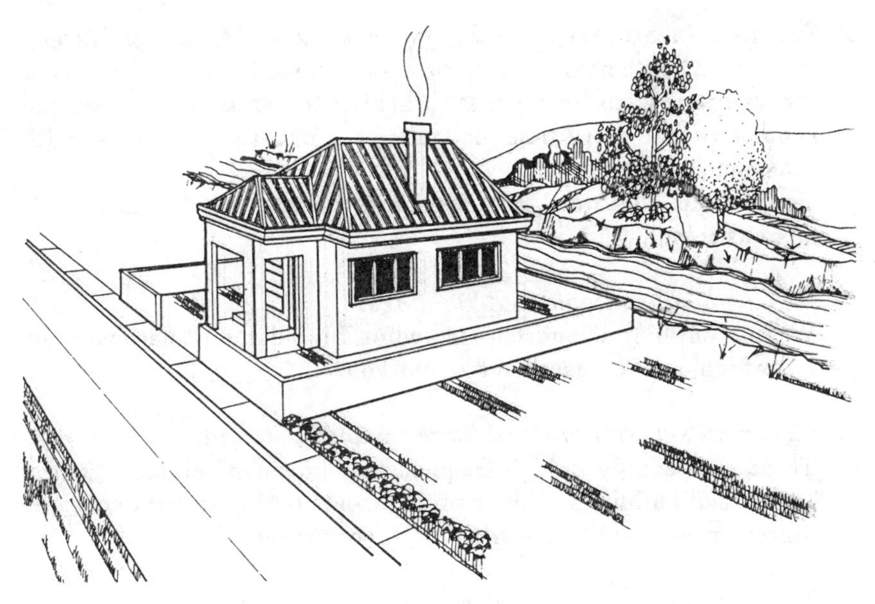

A lot with flowing water at the rear

Rule # 9. A lot, house or building should not face, overlook or be adjacent to any of the following:

a) *Graveyards, funeral parlours, churches or temples:*
All of the above deal with the world of the dead or of the spirit. The energy surrounding these places is *yin*. We belong to the world of the living or the physical world which is *yang*. A house that is built in close proximity to one of the foregoing establishments will suffer an imbalance in its *chi* which, in turn, will affect the equilibrium of the occupants. Places where people release emotional energy, such as grief for the dead or feelings of remorse, guilt or recrimination, will build up around them a field of heavily charged negative energy.

b) *Abattoirs and hospitals:*
Abattoirs are houses of slaughter. They emit a frequency of fear, pain and death. Hospitals emit a similar frequency of fear, pain and death. Although some joyous events (such as births) occur at hospitals, even these are somewhat eclipsed by the pain of labour.

c) *Fire stations; gas stations; industrial chimney stacks; garbage dumps:* Building a house near a fire station is not considered *good feng shui* for several reasons, one reason is that fire trucks are very noisy, and another is that every time the truck goes out it means disaster for someone, somewhere.
Gas stations, industrial chimney stacks and garbage dumps give off noxious fumes.

d) *Unoccupied or dilapidated buildings:*
When a building is unoccupied and/or dilapidated, it harbours *yin chi* which can be absorbed by your house.

e) *Electrical sub-stations and large t.v.and radio antennae:*
These emit energy in high frequencies which can permeate nearby houses and buildings. This is often a contributing factor to chronic illness or personality disorders of the occupants.

f) *Police stations, gambling dens, and houses of prostitution:*
These places, where people of confused persuasions gather, radiate energy that is dubious, to say the least.

Cures for rule #9 – items a-f: You can block negative views with blinds, curtains or plants. You can also place a *ba-gua* or a convex mirror over a door or a window that overlooks them. But, if there are more than two of the above items close to your house, it may be better to move out.

A WORD ABOUT CHIMNEY STACKS

Chimney stacks are not only abhorred for their noxious fumes, but in Asian countries and Asian communities in the West, they also have a cultural and psychological correspondence that is decidedly negative.

A view of two chimney stacks, which look like two sticks of burning incense, subtly registers 'death' on the mind of an Asian viewer because of the association with prayers for the dead.

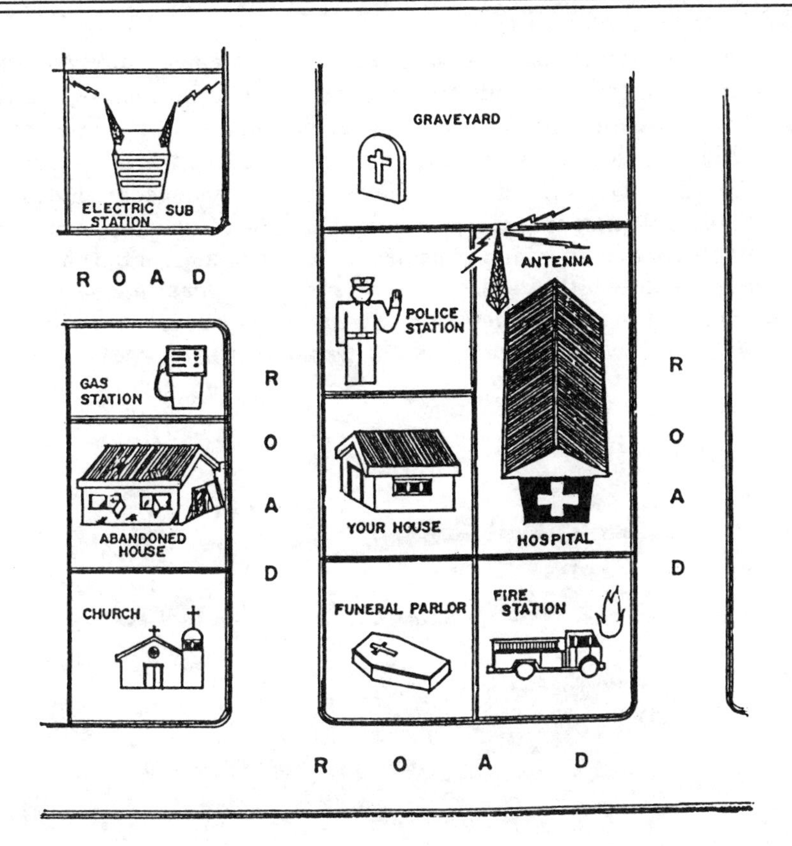

A house surrounded by negative aspects

Chinese and other Asian people are susceptible to this negative correspondence because, when prayers and offerings are made to recently deceased family members at temples and at ancestral altars, two sticks of incense are lit. One or three incense sticks are used for other rituals but, two are always used for the dead.

The next time you pass by a pair of chimney stacks, take time to really look at them. You will be surprized at their similarity to burning incense sticks. Even if you are not consciously aware of their correspondence with death but, you live in Asia or within or near an Asian community, your subconscious mind will be subtly influenced by the mass conciousness or *thought-field* of your surroundings.

The visual impact of constantly seeing two chimney stacks outside your window or fronting your door creates a slight uneasiness, which can induce a loss of concentration, miscalculations and/or wrong decision making. A view of one or three or more chimney stacks, although not favoured in *feng shui*, does not have a correspondence with death, hence, their influence is less virulent. But, a view of two has been held accountable for the downfall of business enterprises and for the physical injury or even the death of susceptible persons. *A susceptible person is one who has a predominance of yin aspects in his birthchart or who is in the throes of a bad fortune cycle or whose health is weak.*

A house facing two chimney stacks

CHAPTER TWENTY NINE

FENG SHUI FOR HIGH-RISE LIVING

Height and Shape
External and Internal Factors
Feng Shui Cures

This is the age of the condominium. For many people, living in a condominium is more economical, more convenient and can provide better protection against intruders than a house. In crowded cities where space is limited, high-rise living is quite often the only option.
Many factors should be considered when selecting a condominium unit. Whether it is for a home or an office, the most important consideration is the *feng shui,* as this provides the 'hidden plus' that assures the buyer of a sound investment and a healthy, positive home or work environment.

A building has good feng shui if;
a) it has been constructed to harmonize with the surrounding terrain;
b) its shape, height and orientation are compatible with each other;
c) its entrances have the location and exposure that attract good *chi* and
d) the internal components are well placed within its *energy grid.*

HEIGHT

If a high-rise building is considerably taller than other buildings in the area, it will protrude out of the *energy field* of the surroundings. It will also be over-exposed to wind, hence, it will not accumulate *chi.* If you really must buy a unit in such a building, avoid those on the uppermost floors.

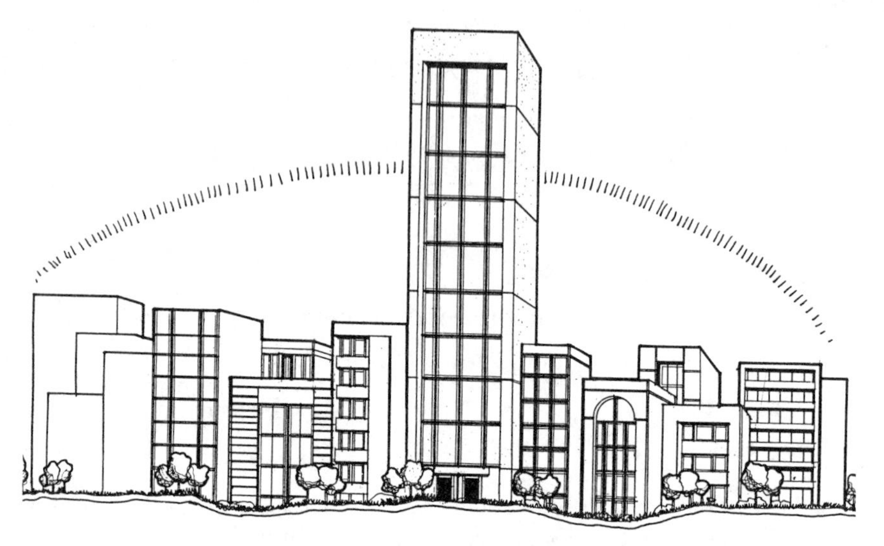

A tall building out of the city's energy field

A building oppressed by high structures

If a building is the lowest in a high-rise area, its *chi* will be oppressed, particularly those units on the lower floors.

Buildings that are more or less the same height as others in the vicinity, are neither oppressed, nor over-exposed. Units on the middle floors are the best choice.

SHAPE

Buildings come in many different shapes. From the point of view of *feng shui*, some are good and others are bad.

Good shapes for buildings are:
a) square
b) rectangular
c) square with a semi-circle in front
d) five connected squares or rectangles in a cluster
e) three connected wings at 120° to each other.

Note: *For shapes* (d) *and* (e) *to be considered 'good,' depends on the orientation of the building.*

Bad shapes for buildings are:
a) a cross
b) letter 'H'
c) triangular
d) hollow in the centre
e) irregular
f) circular (except for financial institutions)
g) letter 'T'
h) a chopper, knife or gun.

If a building is shaped like a chopper or a knife, do not buy or rent a unit on the 'blade.' Occupants of these units are prone to accidents and surgery.

Buildings shaped like a gun or a rifle often have violent incidents. The only acceptable units in chopper, knife, or gun-shaped buildings, are those located on the 'handle.'

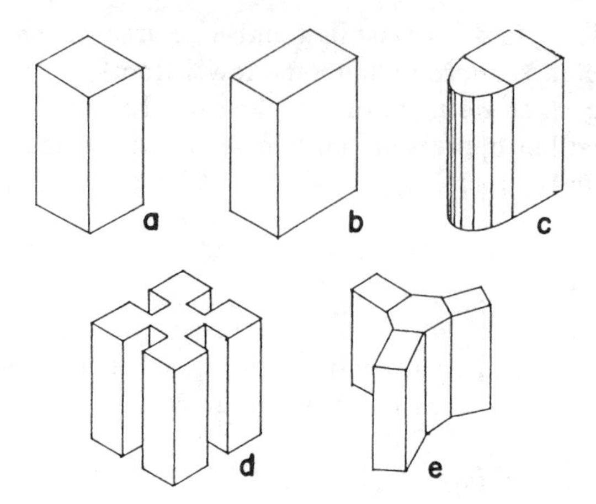

Good shapes for high-rise buildings

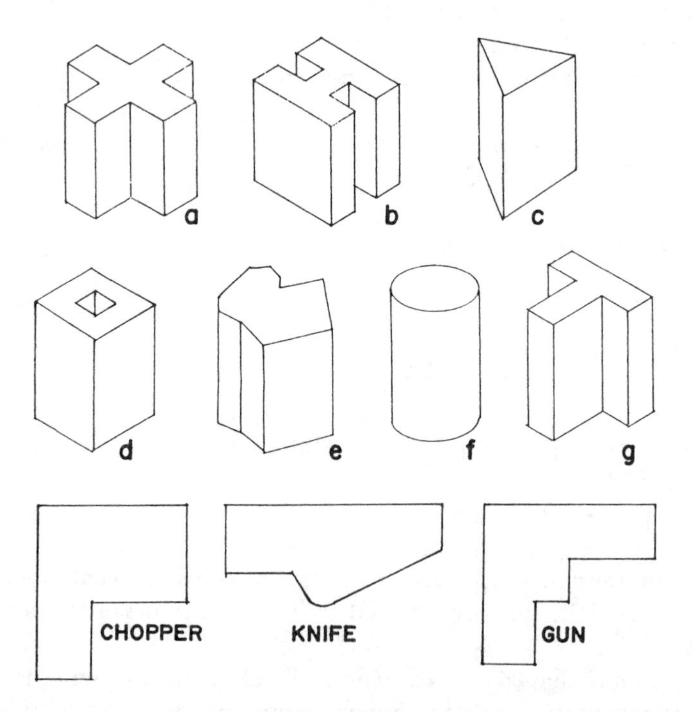

Bad shapes for high-rise buildings

Many *feng shui* defects in high-rise buildings can be corrected by the use of semi-circular balconies. These balconies can deflect or ward-off any '*arrows of chi*' or '*sha*' from the surroundings. *Arrows of chi* are emitted from the corners of neighbouring buildings, ridge lines of roofs, wind tunnels (narrow spaces between tall buildings) or from straight or linear features of the terrain. If they hit a curve, they bounce off and are neutralized. Curved balconies can also correct the sharp corners of a triangular building. When architects use curved balconies or rounded corners on the exteriors of buildings, knowingly or not, they are often enhancing the building's *feng shui*.

EXTERNAL FACTORS

Negative road configurations:

a) Elevated roads or railways running past a building can siphon-off *chi*.
b) The outer edge of a curve in the road or railway can 'cut' the building. A road or rail configuration, whether elevated or on ground level, must 'embrace' rather than 'slice' the building's energy field.
c) A building facing an oncoming road will be hit by the arrow-like *chi* of the road and the momentum of the approaching traffic.

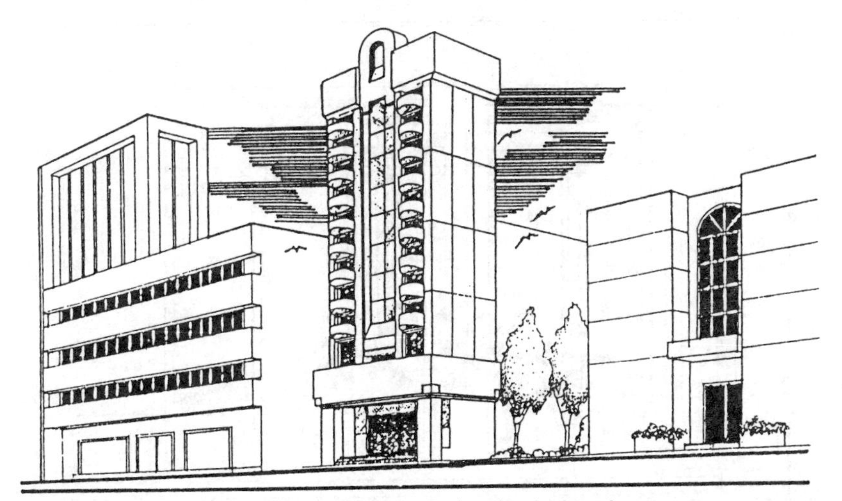

A building with semi-circular balconies

Sha from road and traffic configurations can be diffused by reflective glass cladding. In *feng shui* practice, glass cladding can also be applied to sections of a building to remedy any imbalance in its shape.

INTERNAL FACTORS

A car park within a building:

Basement car parks are suitable for high-rise buildings, but car parks above ground level are not good as they are usually directly below residential units. The movement and fumes of the cars below do not provide a stable base or good *chi* for a unit directly above.

Entrances:

a) A main lobby that has the front entrance aligned to the rear exit will not be able to accumulate *chi;* it will pass through the lobby without circulating within the building. This does not bode well for the occupants, particularly for those whose health or luck are declining. Occupants who are enjoying a good fortune cycle, and/or who have *good feng shui* in their individual units, may not be adversely affected. Sometimes the position of the elevators can offset this violation.

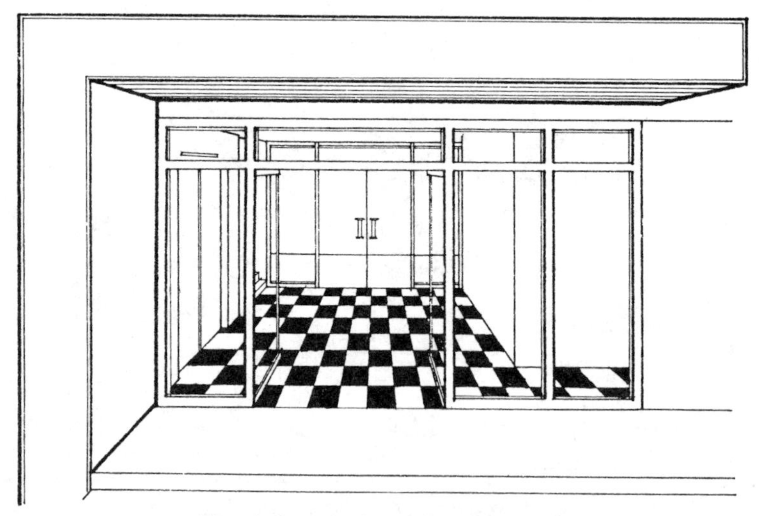

Front door facing the rear door

b) Another negative feature, is a staircase or an elevator door directly facing the main entrance.This can drain *chi* from the building.

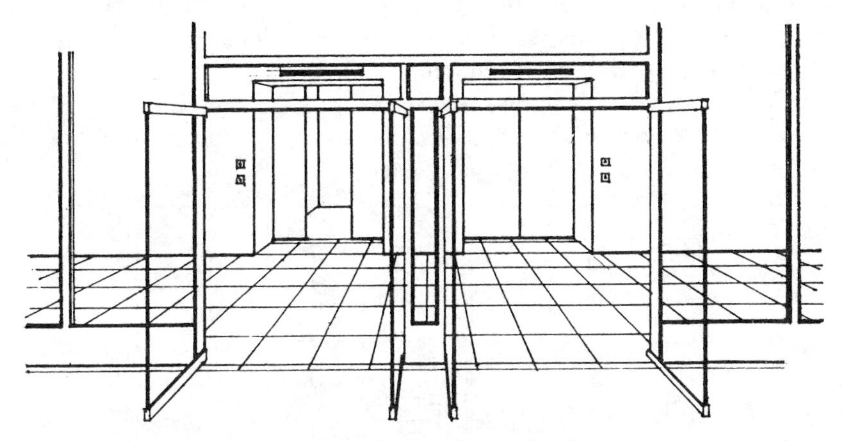

Elevators facing the main door

c) A unit door should not face a staircase. If the stairs go down from the door, the *chi* of the unit will be drained. If the stairs come down toward the door, strong *chi* will hit the unit.This is because of the natural tendency of *chi* to flow downward.

**Stairs coming down toward a door*　**Stairs going down from a door*

d) The doors of units should not directly or partially face each other across the hallway.

e) A unit door at the end of a corridor is not good as it will be hit by the corridor's compressed *chi* – the effect will be softened if the corridor widens in front of the door.

f) Corridors that are narrow, cluttered, dimly-lit and poorly ventilated are unfortunate as they do not convey good *chi* to the unit door.

** A cluttered corridor * Doors facing each other*
** The end door hit by the corridor chi*

YOUR FENG SHUI CURES:

1] If your unit door fully confronts the door of another unit; place a *ba-gua* over your door. If it partially confronts – place a plant outside your door, facing the confronting section.

2] If your unit door is at the end of a long corridor;
a) hang a windchime in the corridor or outside your door, and/or;
b) place a *ba-gua* or a convex mirror over your unit door, and/or;

c) place a screen, at least 1m (40") inside the door to deflect the strong *chi,* and/or;
d) fit an automatic closer on the door.

3] If the building's corridors have insufficient natural light and air; install a light on the ceiling in front of your door or on the wall above your door, and place live plants on either side of the door.

4] If there are stairs facing your unit door (whether they go up or down) you can apply cures #2c and #2d to prevent excessive *chi* flowing in or out of your unit.

5] Check the views from the windows of your unit. Any negative or doubtful view, based on the advice given in this book, should be corrected in any or all of the following ways.
a) Fit the window with vertical or horizontal venetian blinds and adjust the slats to block the view.
b) Place a *ba-gua* or a convex mirror above your window, facing the offending view. If it is difficult to reach the outside wall, you can tape the *ba-gua* directly onto your window, facing outward, but be sure the window is not used. A *ba-gua* should never be placed on anything that moves.
c) Install a plant box outside your window; this not only softens the oncoming *sha,* it is also decorative.

CHAPTER THIRTY

PLEASURE AND PROFIT FROM A HOLIDAY HOME

Sea-side Homes
Mountain Homes
Ranches or Farm Houses
Landscaping Cures

Owning a second home that can be used for weekends, vacations and/or retirement is gaining in popularity. In the long term, it is a better investment to buy a holiday home than to spend large amounts annually on hotels and resorts.

Another advantage is that your sports gear and vacation paraphernalia can be neatly stacked away in one of the rooms, which eliminates the hassle of packing and transporting it. You can arrive at your holiday home with only a tote bag, relaxed and unworried about forgotten items – now that's a great way to start a vacation!

If your holiday home is well-chosen, it can also provide you with profit from short-term rentals and, if your friends or relatives have houses in other resorts, you can share or exchange vacation sites with them.

Holiday homes can be located in the mountains, by the sea, or on the plains (such as the mini-ranches now popular in the U.S.) You should look for a resort that is not too distant or isolated from city amenities, such as; airports, bus terminals, hospitals, food supplies etc., then locate the area that has the '*dragon chi.*'

How to find the dragon chi:

This requires compass calculation, but since, in the broader sense of the word, a *dragon* represents positive energy, strength and vitality, then *dragon chi* can usually be found wherever there are dynamic new real estate developments, growth, and activity. In other words, it's better to buy a property in an area that is active and upcoming, rather than one that may have seen better days – Apply the following rules when selecting a holiday home.

SEA-SIDE HOMES

In the present *chi-cycle* apart from the classic orientation 'sited North facing South,' it is also *good feng shui* to have a house that is sited West, facing the sea in the East, or sited Northeast, facing the sea in the Southwest.

Do not buy a property that is located on a promontory, (a piece of land that juts out into the sea). This will be over-exposed to the elements of wind and water. Such a property will not be able to accumulate the *chi*.

Ideally, your resort home should be embraced by hills or higher ground and only the front should have wide exposure, lower ground, or a view of an expanse of water.

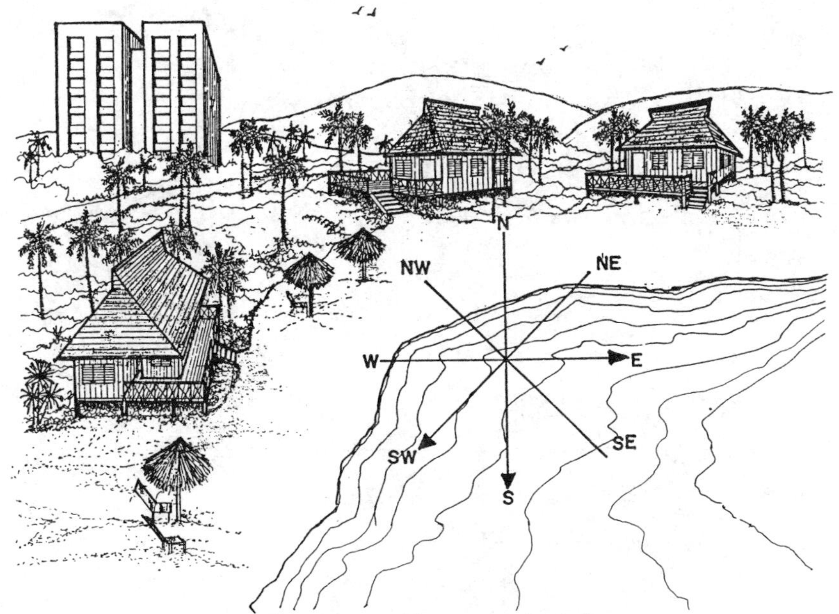

Beach houses with good orientations

MOUNTAIN HOMES

To have *good feng shui*, a mountain house should be nestled into the side of a well-formed hill that is not prone to landslide or erosion. It should have high ground at the rear and slightly less high ground at the sides. The front exposure should overlook lower ground, a lake, a river or a stream – the river or stream should not curve toward the house, but rather, embrace the frontage slightly.

Do not buy a house that is located on the edge of a cliff – this will incline the occupants to play the dangerous game of brinkmanship.

Avoid homes that are on the highest point of a mountain – these have no backing and are over-exposed to the elements.

Avoid also, houses that are under an over-hanging cliff – these predispose the occupants to accidents or danger.

A mountain home with good feng shui

A house on a promontory or a cliff

A house under a cliff

RANCH OR FARM HOUSES

Flat land rarely contains *dragon chi*. If you are looking for a farm or ranch retirement home, find a place with some hills and meandering streams. If you already own a piece of flat land, you can simulate good topographical features by using clever landscaping techniques.

FENG SHUI LANDSCAPING CURES:

a) A mound of earth covered in grass can represent a mountain.
b) Tall stands of trees can give a house backing; they can also block strong winds or excessive exposure to the sun.
c) An artificial creek, a fountain, a swimming pool, or even a bird bath can bring the *water element* into the landscape.

Feng shui landscaping

CHAPTER THIRTY ONE

YOUR FENG SHUI CHECKLISTS

Is Your City Yin or Yang?
Pre-purchase Cecklist
Hidden Hazard Checklist
Property History Checklist

IS YOUR CITY YIN OR YANG?

When you set out to buy a piece of real estate, whether it is for investment purposes, future development, industry or personal housing, you should first examine the *feng shui* aspects of your city. Most cities are either predominantly *yin* or predominantly *yang*.

In the Philippines, where this book was written, the city of Manila has good topographical features, i.e., mountain ranges 'backing' it and a good harbour in front. But, the mountains are in the East and block the invigorating *yang* east wind. Some areas of the city are below sea level which makes drainage difficult, and there is frequent flooding during the long rainy season. Consequently, Manila is predominantly *yin*.

Women generally cope quite well in a *yin* environment and many of Manila's women are prominent in banking, commerce and industry.

Men are adversely affected by an excess of *yin chi*. Some become lazy, and over-indulge in wine, women and song – which could be the reason why Manila's men are reknowned as romantic lovers! Interestingly, they are known to be industrious and disciplined when living in other countries.

Hong Kong has mainly *yang* energy, good circulation of wind, and good drainage. Visitors usually have more energy in Hong Kong than at home, and can shop for hours on end without tiring.

Men in Hong Kong play the dominant role in business, commerce and industry. While women, with some outstanding exceptions, occupy themselves in more traditionally feminine careers, e.g., secretary, minor executive, owner of a small business, or treasurer of the family business.

According to some *feng shui* manuals, the ideal energy balance of a site is two-fifths *yin* and three-fifths *yang*. Bearing in mind the *yin* or *yang* aspects of your urban environment, your next step is to select a property that will give you a predominance of *yang chi*.

If your city environment is excessively *yin*, you should look for a property with strong *yang* aspects, such as; higher ground in the North and/or the West; exposure to plenty of morning and early afternoon sunlight; an easterly breeze, and preferably not too much surface water in your surroundings.

Avoid living in a house that is too large for the number of occupants, as it will accumulate *yin chi* in the unused areas – You can enliven a large home, with lots of people and activity.

PRE-PURCHASE CHECKLIST

When you are about to buy a property, there are many hazards that unfortunately don't become apparent until after you have finalized the purchase. It takes a keen eye and the instinct of a detective to escape all the potential pitfalls of the property market, but with the aid of the following guidelines, you should be able to avoid many of them.

#1. Drainage:

One of the most common defects of a site is inadequate drainage. The best way to be sure that a property has either naturally good drainage, due to favourable topographical contours, or a good drainage system provided by the government or the property developer, is to inspect the site during or immediately after heavy rain.

Cities that use a lot of underground water, from individual or community deep wells, suffer from a constant lowering of the water table, which in turn causes the land level to sink. When you add to this, drains clogged by garbage or soil, you have the perfect conditions for urban floods. Too much water in or around your property, apart from restricting access, will create an atmosphere that is too *yin*.

Old or unused wells, ponds and open drains that have been carelessly filled or left to stagnate, exude damp, soggy, *yin* energy that can attract ***nature spirits***. Such properties are detrimental to humans and can be accident prone.

#2. Traffic Flow:

Another aspect that can affect the *feng shui* is traffic flow. The configuration of nearby roads, bridges, pathways and canals, can create *sha* or *arrows of chi* that may afflict the property.

Properties alongside or near a busy highway are are not only prone to excessive noise and pollution, but also to energy depletion. The heavy traffic of a highway or a main road is like a fast-flowing river; it carries the *chi* along with it, leaving nearby properties deprived of energy.

It may be that the city is planning, at some future date, to expand a major highway, or build some other infrastructure near or through your property. It is much better to find out now than later. Check with the appropriate government authority.

#3. Utilities:

Do not take for granted that clean and plentiful water, electricity, garbage collection and road maintenance will be available, regardless of the promises of the seller. Check with the utility companies and/or the developers, and be sure to inspect water tanks, transformers, generators and any other utility or facility that services the property.

Other Factors:

There are some hidden hazards that are usually overlooked, they should be thoroughly investigated before you sign on the dotted line. We are living in an age of increasing natural disasters, so hazards (a) and (b) should be prominent on your checklist.

HIDDEN HAZARD CHECKLIST

Avoid proximity to the following:

a) *A fault line*; you should be from fifty meters up to twenty kilometers away from a fault line, depending on the type of ground of your property, i.e., rock or soft soil.

b) *An active volcano*; or even one that is believed to be inactive – remember Mount Pinatubo.
c) *An electric generating plant or sub-station.*
d) *A warehouse that stores inflammable goods.*
e) *A funeral parlour or graveyard*; especially if the hearse has to pass in front of your property.
f) *A hospital or clinic*; especially if the ambulance passes in front of your house.
g) *All others listed under Rule #9 on page 223.*

Finally, you should investigate the history of the property.

PROPERTY HISTORY CHECKLIST

Ask the following questions:

a) Did any previous structure on the property burn down?
b) Did the site formerly house a facility for the sick, the insane, or the dead?
c) Was the property a former site of a church or a temple?
d) Did the previous occupant become bankrupt? – Buying a fore-closed property is not always a bargain!
e) Did the former occupants suffer an undue number of illnesses, accidents or deaths?
f) Are there any indications of *yin entities* occupying the house? – *refer to Chapter 32.*

Your *feng shui* checklist is now fairly comprehensive. Do not be too disturbed if the property you like has a few negative aspects. With the information given in this book, you should be able to avoid or correct most of the common violations of *good feng shui.*

Part Five

Other Dimensions of Feng Shui

CHAPTER THIRTY TWO

FENG SHUI FOR THE DEAD

Ching Ming – All Saint's Day, Chinese Style

There are two main branches of *feng shui;* one is for the living (*yang feng shui*) and one for the dead (*yin feng shui*). For Chinese people *yin feng shui* is extremely important, as those who have passed into the world of spirit can affect the fate of the living.

A family has a type of energy that is uniquely its own; it is passed down from the first ancestor to all the subsequent generations. The energy pattern of the ancestors' genes (you could call it the master blue-print) vibrates within all the direct descendants, linking them in a line of influence. While the family elders are alive, their actions affect the family members. When they die, the family will inherit their *karma.* It is therefore necessary to see that the deceased are at peace. Any debts they leave behind should be paid by the family, and gifts and donations to charity should be made in their names. This will help to ameliorate their *karmic debt* and improve the fortune of their descendants.

In order to give peace to the spirits of the dead, we should see that they are buried in a place that has benevolent *chi*. An ideal site will have higher ground at the rear, slightly less high at the sides and an unobstructed view in front. This will ensure a secure niche for the grave, good drainage, and protection from the wind and weather. Such a site is quite difficult to find, so it is often created by artful landscaping and the shape and design of the tomb.

The date of the burial should be chosen with great care; but perhaps the most important aspect of *yin feng shui* is calculating the orientation of the tomb and/or the memorial name plate (tombstone). When the *P'o* (earth-bound soul) of the ancestor enjoys the good vibrations that a well-placed grave can provide, these will be passed on to the living descendants who are 'tuned in' because of the corresponding energy pattern of their inherited genes.

If the dead are buried in the wrong place, at the wrong time and with a wrong orientation, another member of the family may die soon after – sometimes there are three deaths in a row.

Yin feng shui is not in popular practice today, due to the unavailability of good gravesites, but *geomancers* are often consulted to select an appropriate date for a burial.

CHING MING – ALL SAINTS' DAY, CHINESE STYLE

In the Christian tradition, the dead are honoured on All Saints' Day. The Chinese also have a special day for remembering their dead; it is called '*Ching Ming*' and is celebrated annually, on either the 5th or the 6th day of April. In places like; Hong Kong,Taiwan and Singapore, it is usually declared a public holiday so that everyone can visit their family gravesite. The rituals of *Ching Ming* are significant because they serve to cement family ties, and to impart a sense of unity and continuity to family members.

The preparations begin the night before. Some families spend the whole night cleaning and preparing the gravesite for the many people that will visit the next day. They light small fires and burn candles, sometimes they play mahjong to keep themselves awake.

On the day of *Ching Ming*, the head of the family lights incense and candles and offers food and drink to the Earth God. He then offers food and drink to his dead ancestors, usually their favourite dishes. The *chi* of the food is absorbed by the spirits of the dead. Paper money (which is especially printed for the offering) is then burned at a fire-pot, set to one side of the grave. The process of burning releases the *chi* of the paper money so it can penetrate into the spiritual world. This act of filial piety benefits both the dead and the living, because, by enriching the ancestor in the spiritual world, the descendants expect to gain merit and wealth in the physical world. Everything is a matter of give and take, and time and space are no barriers to the process.

Another interesting custom is the pasting of small pieces of white paper all around the grave. All the relatives and visitors to the gravesite paste up a few pieces of this paper and light two candles and two sticks of incense. A grave with many candles, incense and pieces of white paper gives 'face' to the dead ancestor.

Any newly-married male member of the family should bring his wife to the grave so she may pay her respects to her husband's ancestors. For a Chinese, the most important consideration is the continuity of the family line. It is a son's duty to marry and produce progeny. Some families place egg shells around the grave as a symbol of their willingness to propagate the tribe.

When a family is rich and has a large mausoleum, they entertain many visitors and offer the guests quite lavish food and drinks. Filial piety is the motive for all this display; it also serves to improve the family's social standing in the community. Overall, serving one's ancestors can have quite a few fringe benefits.

Not all Chinese families keep up the rituals of *Ching Ming*. Many have adopted All Saint's Day instead. Whatever date and ritual is followed, both *Ching Ming* and All Saint's Day are opportunities for the living to remember the dead and renew family ties.

Offerings at the grave site

CHAPTER THIRTY THREE

FENG SHUI FOR SPECIAL OCCASIONS

Party Feng Shui
Cheers and Good Chi at Christmas Time
Welcoming the New Year

PARTY FENG SHUI

At the suggestion of the host of a t.v. talk show on which I guested, I have compiled a few tips for party givers.

How can *feng shui* help you to become the 'Host with the Most'? Let me count the ways;

1. *The entrance should draw in the chi:*
   The front gate and the main entrance to the house should be brightly lit, to attract and welcome the guests and draw in the *chi*.

2. *Choose the right colours*:
   Colour schemes should be chosen for their harmony, based on the *five elements*. Colours are rays of light in different frequencies.

   The compatible colour frequencies are:
   a) *red* with *green* and/or with *yellow* – but not *green* and *yellow* without *red*
   b) *yellow* with *red* and/or with *white* – but not *red* and *white* without *yellow*.

c) *white* with *yellow* and/or with *blue* – but not *yellow* and *blue* without *white.*

d) *blue* with *white* and/or with *green* – but not *white* and *green* without *blue*

e) *green* with *blue* and/or with *red* – but not *blue* and *red* without *green.*

See Chapter 2 for the productive cycle of the elements and their corresponding colours.

3. *Create the right chi-flow:*
   Place your tables and seating arrangements to allow traffic to flow toward the focal points of your party. If you are focusing on the food, the aisles between the tables should gently curve toward the buffet. If entertainment is provided, the aisles should direct the guests and their attention toward the entertainment area. The same applies to parties with dancing. Highlight the focal points of your party with special lighting. This will draw the *chi* and the guests to those areas. Traffic flow of the guests, waiters and others should be planned to avoid collisions. Nothing can spoil a party faster than spilt drinks and ruined clothes.

4. *Match your party to your guests:*
   Match the party to the energy of your guests, for instance: If your guests are under thirty, the features of your party should be *yang*, to match their energy. *Yang* features are bright, colourful, or strobe lighting, loud music, and a barbecue for supper.
   For sophisticated guests, subtle lighting, soft music and fine food would be compatible with their *chi*. Having one aspect 'out of sync' is unsettling for the guests and ruinous to the ambiance.

5. *Invite helpful guests:*
   Another secret of a successful party is to have two or more helpful guests. Helpful guests are those delightful people who enliven the party with their enthusiasm, good conversation, and their willingness to begin the dancing or to be first at the buffet table.

6. *Crystal chi – that 'something extra' for the perfect party:*
   If you have pieces of quartz crystals, place a few small ones under the sofa cushions. This may have some interesting effects on your shy guests, and can mellow out the boisterous ones. You can also put crystals in the drinking water to 'tonify' it. Place large chunks of rock crystals around the house and in the garden to uplift the *chi*– your guests will dance all night. If you are giving a swimming party, place a few chunks of rock crystal in the pool to charge the water with 'crystal energy.' This also turns the pool into a beauty bath.

7. *A formal dinner:*
   In the Chinese tradition, at a formal dinner, you do not seat your guests under a beam or with their backs to a door. The main guest should be seated at the dining table, facing the dining room door and to the left of the host. In the Western tradition, the main guest is seated to the right of the host. In Hong Kong, when we entertain, we are sometimes able to have both a Chinese and a European 'guest of honour' without either one being aware that the other also has this rank. This ploy is often used at diplomatic parties where 'face' must be given to both sides.

From a *geomancer's* point of view, the most important service we can offer is to select the right date for the party. This will depend on what type of celebration it is. There are different days that are appropriate for different occasions. In all cases, the horoscopes of the host and the celebrant have to be calculated and the almanac consulted.

A wedding date is the most difficult to select, as so many aspects need to be considered. Traditionally, it is not unusual for the couple to wait two years or more for a suitable day. To be wed on an auspicious day, is to start married life on the right wavelength.

Whatever the occaision, once you have done everything possible to ensure that your party will be a success, relax and enjoy it. A relaxed and happy host sets the tone for a truly enchanted evening – Happy Hosting!

A garden party – with good feng shui

CHEERS AND GOOD CHI AT CHRISTMAS TIME

Feng shui principles, when correctly applied, can enhance any event in our lives, especially our Christmas celebrations. The correct placement of the dining table, the Christmas tree and other decorations can create an atmosphere of harmony and love that is so important at family gatherings.

The quality of energy that is created within a home depends, for the most part, on the orientation of the house as well as the layout of the inner components. Within any given space there are different qualities or frequencies of energy, these are calculated from the *moving star grid* and are called '*the five chi,*' namely; '*killing chi,*' '*living chi,*' '*peak chi,*' '*depleting chi,*' and '*dead chi.*'

Geomancers of the *Moving Star School* chart the *chi*, then place the components of your house so as to take advantage of the positive energy zones and neutralize the negative zones. This is best left to the professionals, but you can apply some simple rules of the *form school of feng shui* to enhance your Christmas cheer.

How to place your tree:

The Christmas tree is a symbol of the season and a great joy to the children. If your tree is well-placed, it will increase the happiness of the occasion by distributing (through its lights) the good *chi* of its location.

Recommended placements are:

a) Along the front wall of the room; (front means where the door is)
b) Along the left wall of the room.

Not recommended placements are:

a) Along the rear wall of the room.
b) Along the right wall.
c) In the centre of the room.
d) Directly facing a door.

Note: *Take left and right when standing in the centre of the room facing the door; if there are two doors, face the one that more directly leads to the front of the house.*

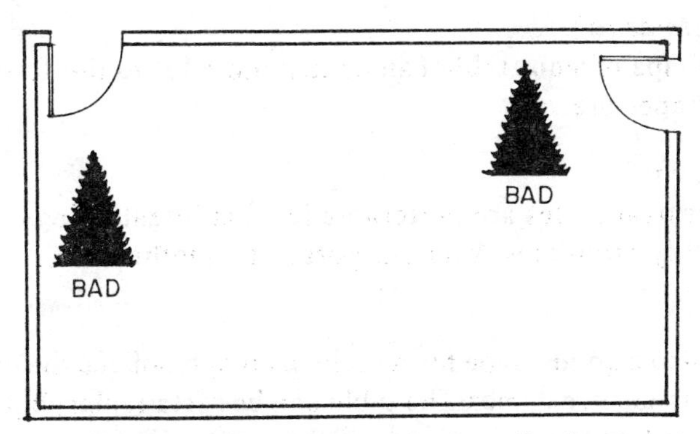

A door should not directly face the tree

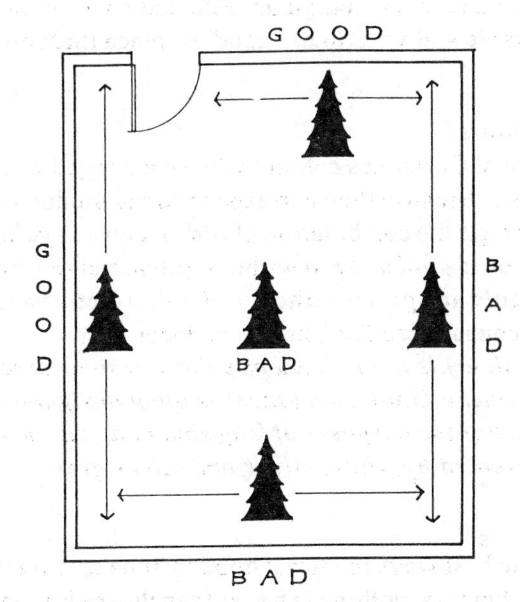

Good and bad tree placements

Trees with blinking lights:

Blinking lights activate the energy of the area in which they are located. If the blinking lights on your tree frequently burst, they could be in the *killing chi* zone of your house. If you find yourself running out of energy and/or money, your tree lights could be blinking away in the zone of *depleting chi*. When in doubt, use steady lights on your tree.

Your Christmas table:

The shape of your table can contribute a lot to the festive mood. The best shapes are:

Round or oval:

Round or oval tables are preferable for family gatherings, as the energy smoothly circulates from one person to another.

Square:

This is also a good shape for a table, as it symbolizes the earth, from which all sustenance comes.The table can be rectangular, but the width should not be less than two-thirds of the length. Christmas candles can be placed on a square or a rectangular table, but not on a round one. If you have a round table and want to use candles, place them on side tables or on the buffet.

Christmas colours:

The traditional Christmas colours when used together are productive and lucky; this is because they correspond to the productive cycle of the *five elements*; e.g., the combination of ***red, green*** and ***gold*** is productive and lucky; so too is ***gold*** and ***red*** without ***green,*** and ***red*** and ***green*** without ***gold;*** but ***gold*** and ***green*** without ***red*** is destructive and unfortunate. ***Blue*** is not recommended for Christmas decor.

Note: ***Gold (colour) is interpreted as yellow, which corresponds to the earth element. Gold (substance) is often designated to the metal element. For the purposes of feng shui analysis the metal element is represented by white, silver and silver grey.***

Outdoor lighting:

One of the best ways to attract good fortune is to light the entrance of your house. For this, nothing is better than the traditional five-pointed Christmas star, which not only enlivens the *chi,* but also deflects negative energy away from the door. The star lantern should be lit all night, so that darkness is never over your door during the festive season.

Don't place blinking lights on the trees in your garden, as most trees have *indwelling spirits,* particularly fruit trees and large, old trees; linking lights can arouse these entities. Non-blinking lights are beautiful and do not disturb the tranquility of the garden.

A star lantern over the door

A happy Christmas scene

In the final analysis, your love is the greatest gift that you can share with your family and friends. The love and sharing of Christmas can be extended throughout the year, if you have *good feng shui* in your home.

WELCOMING THE NEW YEAR

Pros and cons of firecrackers:

On New Year's Eve it is customary to ward off unwelcome spirits, and herald the incoming year with fire crackers and lots of noise. You can use the judas belt type of crackers, which are loud enough to do the job. You can also add excitment to the festivities with brilliant rockets and sparklers, but do avoid firecrackers that are extremely loud.

Loud noises shatter the *energy field* of the house and disturb the *garden spirits*. Shock waves from loud firecrackers harm the *energy bodies* of young children, old folk and house pets. Unborn children react violently to loud sounds, so pregnant women should avoid the noise (and the pollution) of fireworks.

Chinese New Year customs that start the year right:

There are some other delightful Chinese New Year customs that I would like to share with you. These are based on the belief, that how you act and feel on the first day, will affect your luck for the remainder of the year. Follow the advice below and start the year feeling great!

a) Do not enter the New Year in debt. This refers to personal not corporate debt. Not only money, but kindness should be repaid in kind.

b) Resolve all quarrels and misunderstandings before the New Year, so that family and friends can renew their ties with peace in their hearts.

c) Thoroughly clean your house and office and discard old, worn out or broken objects.

d) Have lots of good food in the house, such as; dishes of golden fruit, chocolate coins wrapped in gold foil, and other sweet and preferably round goodies.

e) Have as much cash on hand as safety permits. This imparts a feeling of wealth – it is a bad omen to run out of money during the New Year.

f) Wear new clothes in cheerful colours on New Year's Day.

Welcoming Chinese New Year

g) Cumquat and plum blossom trees (if available) should decorate the entrance hall or living room. These are symbols of wealth, endurance and renewal.

h) Do all the major cooking the day before, so that on New Year's Day you don't have to use a sharp knife or a chopper.

i) Give extra money and food to those who have served you during the year. In Hong Kong, little red envelopes containing 'lucky money' *(lai see)* is given, not only to those who have served or aided us, but also to all the young or unmarried people who wish us '*Kung Hei Fat Choi*' (Happy New Year).

j) On this special day do no menial work, relax and enjoy being with your family and friends.

k) Think positive thoughts, do not speak negative words, and do not scold the children.

All these wonderful customs create a feeling of goodwill and happiness. It is a way of preparing ourselves physically and psychologically for whatever the New Year will bring. If fortune comes, we have made space in our lives to receive it. If problems arise, we will be in good condition to cope with them.

CHAPTER THIRTY FOUR

WHAT'S IN A NAME

How Your Name Affects Your Fate
Numerology and Name Analysis
Numbers and their Meanings

HOW YOUR NAME AFFECTS YOUR FATE

It occasionally happens that the feng shui of a place is very good, yet the occupants suffer misfortune, ill health, and other calamities. In this situation, the *geomancer* has to probe deeper to find the cause of the problem.The following true story happened in Hong Kong; it gives an example of the importance of name vibrations.

A certain Mr.Choy arrived from China to start a new life in Hong Kong. He had very little money, but he was able to find a job and rent a room from a widow who owned a house in the district of Sham Shui Po.

Mr.Choy was a large man and very energetic, his face looked something like a goldfish, with large lips and protruding eyes. Since he was a child he had been likened to a 'big lively fish,' in fact, this had become his nickname.

'Big Lively Fish' soon became very friendly with the widow and, because he showed a natural capacity and energy for business, she entrusted to him her savings.They opened an import/export company and it flourished. Every year the business improved and they became wealthier.

In the tenth year of their partnership they decided to move to the more fashionable district of Tsim Sha Tsui. They called in a *geomancer*, who found a suitable house for them and, on an appropiate day, the prosperous couple moved in.

After a few months in their new home the business started to suffer setbacks, and 'Big Lively Fish' lost some of his liveliness – he developed breathing problems and obscure illnesses, but his doctors could not find anything wrong with him. Several *geomancers* were called to look at the house, but none of them could find anything wrong with the *feng shui.* In the meantime, life was being drained from the 'Big Fish' and the business began to deteriorate. Finally, they heard of a *geomancer* who was a master of metaphysical arts.They invited him to look at their house.

The old man inspected the house and the immediate vicinity, he found nothing wrong until he came to a picture on the wall. "Big Fish" he said, "look at this picture, it's a desert scene; your name is 'Fish' and a fish needs water. Not only that, when you lived in Sham Shui Po you prospered, as Sham Shui means 'deep water.' Now you have moved to Tsim Sha Tsui which means 'sharp sand.' Can a fish prosper in sand? You must move back to your former area."

Big Lively Fish (who was no longer lively) did just that. He and his partner returned to their old house, which they had maintained as a warehouse. After a few months his health and business improved.

'Big Lively Fish'

The principle behind this story is an important one. The sound and/or meaning of your name can either be harmonious or discordant with other names. If it is discordant with the name of the area where you live, there can be a negative effect. Even members of the same family, whose names are discordant with each other, will have some mutual antipathy. That is why, when we analyze a name, we first examine its meaning, then we look for possible hidden meanings or negative inferences.

We all react emotionally to many of the words we hear. These reactions can range from the hardly noticeable to the dramatically violent. Even words that sound similar to our 'trigger words' can induce either a positive or a negative conditioned response. Our reactions to people's names can influence our perception of them, for example; when we hear the name 'Stella Winters' it elicits a feeling of distance (Stella) and coldness (Winters). Stella Winters may get a cool reaction from people simply because of their conditioned response to her name. This in turn will incline her to withdraw from them, hence, poor Stella may not have many friends.

NUMEROLOGY AND NAME ANALYSIS

In both Eastern and Western numerology, the numerical value of a name is analyzed, based on the significance and correspondences of the numbers involved. The correspondences are; *elements*, planetary influences, colours, etc.

For western names, I use Chaldean numerology. Every letter of the alphabet has a sound frequency that corresponds to a number. The name vibrations of persons, places, or business corporations will be the sum total of all the numbers allocated to the individual letters of the name. Consonants and vowels have different significance in name analysis.

If there is any discordance within a name, or with a name and a birthdate, or between names of spouses or business partners, or between owners of a business and the corporate name, adjustments can be made in the spelling and pronunciation to neutralize the discordant factor.

In Chinese numerology, the strokes in the Chinese characters are counted and the numbers evaluated according to their correspondences and meaning, here too, the hidden meanings and the sounds are studied.

Selecting a name for a new baby is quite a complicated procedure, among other things, the generation name and other family data must be considered.

NUMBERS AND THEIR MEANINGS

In Hong Kong and other Chinese cities or communities, numbers that sound similar to words denoting wealth or fortune are sought after because of their positive psychological effect. Numbers that sound like words suggesting illness, death or misfortune are carefully avoided.

Lucky and Unlucky Numbers:

The Cantonese population of Hong Kong believe strongly in the significance of numbers and are willing to support their belief with a great deal of money. Every year, the government of Hong Kong holds a public auction of car plate numbers, the proceeds of which are donated to the community chest or other charities. It is not unusual for a Taipan to pay HK$1,000,000 or more for a lucky plate number.

The number 8 is probably the most popular in the world. In some Western schools of numerology, it represents wealth and position. In Chinese, it sounds like the word for prosperity. Addresses, car plates, telephone and bank account numbers with 8's in them are eagerly sought after. Number 8 is undoubtedly suitable for those with an entrepreneural personality and high aspirations, although it can sometimes lead to disaster if ability does not match ambition.

The number 4 is the least popular as it sounds almost exactly like the word 'death.' This holds true for all the major Chinese dialects, i.e., Cantonese, Mandarin, and Fookienese. People avoid addresses with the number 4 in them. Cars with plate numbers having more than one 4 are said to be accident prone. A hospital room on the 4th floor does not augur well for the recovery of the patient.

Combinations of numbers:

Numbers combined in a 'going up' sequence are considered good. Those combinations that are 'going down' are considered unfortunate. For instance, it is easier to find a tenant for an apartment numbered 123 than for an apartment numbered 321.

The following are some meanings of number combinations, based mainly on the Cantonese and Fookienese dialects:

Numbers that are considered lucky:

168 or 68 – considered to be a very lucky combination. It sounds like 'luck all the way'

66 – sounds like 'to gain something'

88 – sounds like 'double wealth'

67 – sounds like 'get a wife'

57 – this number has a special meaning for men as it sounds like 'afternoon wife' (mistress)

37 – this sounds like 'three wives' – which could be too much even for a super macho.

Numbers to be avoided:

333 – emphasizes the negative

35 – sounds like 'bad for me'

45 – sounds like 'I will die' – this would be a disastrous number for a hospital room

55 – could be interpreted as a 'missed opportunity'

48 – sounds like 'dead father'

49 – sounds like 'dead dog' – this could indicate that there is no chance for improvement.

Geomancers also study hand and face reading which, combined with other forms of fortune analysis, they use as an aid to understanding the personality and fortune of their clients. They then tailor the *feng shui* to overcome many of the forseen problems.

CHAPTER THIRTY FIVE

NATURAL OR MAN-MADE DISASTERS

THE CASE FOR FENG SHUI

Consciousness Precedes Events
Can Feng Shui Overcome Negative Events?

Can *feng shui* protect us from natural and man-made calamities? This question is often asked by people who have suffered physically or mentally from such events. All calamities have both metaphysical and scientific explanations:

Tectonic plates move and an earthquake happens – but why here and why now? A volcano erupts because of pyroplastic build-up – but why now? A typhoon strikes in a place outside the typhoon belt – Why? Science explains the 'how,' metaphysics explains the 'why.'

CONSCIOUSNESS PRECEDES EVENTS

Have you ever wondered why disasters happen in a series? – first one, then another, then another. Look at Bangladesh or the Philippines. In the Philippines, a major earthquake in the North was followed by a disastrous typhoon in the South, drought in several regions, then a major volcanic eruption, followed by severe flooding, lahar flows and more...

It is truly said that '*consciousness precedes events*.' The mass consciousness creates an atmosphere or vibratory rate that precipitates a disaster. This can be natural or man-made, such as; political violence, civil war, escalation of criminal activities, etc.

If the majority of people in a country or state are thinking negatively about their government and their living conditions, and if they harbour attitudes of discontent, violence and pain, the frequency of their mass mind will attract disasters that are violent and painful. Once the disaster has occurred, the people will start worrying about a possible second disaster. That worry or thought concentration again creates a vibratory rate that invites another calamity. Now, the fear and negative thinking become more powerful as the imagination of the public projects images of more possible calamities – and they will continue to manifest untill the mass mind says "Enough!" and the people are ready to take remedial action.

CAN FENG SHUI OVERCOME NEGATIVE EVENTS?

Nothing happens by chance. What appears to be an accident or a spontaneous event is actually a link in a long chain of causes and effects emanating from the past, and moving toward the future. The causes are our thoughts, actions, and reactions to people and our environment. The effects are the events in our lives.

If we upgrade our thoughts, actions and reactions, we can produce more positive events in our lives. One way to do this is to live and work in an environment that has the balanced and harmonious energy that can uplift our spirits, improve our mental attitudes and elevate our consciousness. When we live and work in the environment of good *feng shui* positive thinking comes easily and leads to good intentions and good deeds which, in turn, creates good *karma.*

Although the *wheel of karma,* once set in motion, continues to turn, the effects will be felt only on the same plane (energy level) as the cause. If we have elevated ourselves to a higher mental and spiritual plane, we will be able to transcend or transmute much of our negative *karma.*

Does this mean that if the government and residents of a city plan their environment to have the harmonious energy of good *feng shui*, the collective effect will not only make the city more happy, healthy and prosperous, but also less prone to man-made and natural disasters? "Yes indeed!"

A word of warning:

It is truly said that 'a little knowledge is a dangerous thing.' *Feng shui* is not an easy subject to master. A practitioner has to be well-versed in its many aspects before attempting to design or adjust another person's environment. Just as *feng shui* can be used in a positive manner, it can also be used destructively to cause the downfall of enemies or to enrich criminal elements. Those who misuse these arts will be certain to reap heavy *karmic repercussions.*

Glossary

Arrows of Chi: Sharp arrow-like energy
Astral Form: – see, *energy body*
Astral Realms: A plane of existence, on a more subtle frequency than our physical world.
Ba-gua (Latter-day): Also called *'later heaven ba-gua',* is used in analyzing the *feng shui* of a site. It has the trigrams in a different sequence to the *primordial ba-gua.*
Ba-gua (Primordial): Also called *'early heaven ba-gua':* A figure comprised of eight trigrams. These trigrams have many correspondences including the eight major directions of the compass, the changing seasons, and the movements of the sun and moon. The *primordial ba-gua* is usually seen over the entrances of houses and buildings where the harmonious energy of its design neutralizes or deflects inauspicious energy.
Chakra: An energy centre or vortex of the subtle body. *Heart chakra:* located near the physical heart; among other functions, it influences the capacity for love. *Sex chakra:* located near the genitals; it influences physical stamina and sex drive.
Chi: Intrinsic energy; cosmic breath; life force; *prana;* subtle currents of energy.
Ching Ming: An annual Chinese festival to honour the dead.
Chiong: A confrontational force.
Devil's Back Door: A term used to describe the direct Southwest, which emanates malefic energy to lesser degree than the Northeast.
Devil's Gate: A term used to describe the direct Northeast, which is said to generate malefic energy.
Duende: Gnome, elf or nature spirit related to the earth element.
Elementals: Nature spirits
Elements: A term describing the five types of energy that pervade all matter. Each *element* has a *yin* and a *yang* aspect; these combined, are called *'the ten heavenly stems.'*
Energy Body: Also called *'subtle body.'* There are several major frequencies in which energy manifests. The ones refered to in this text are the *etheric* and the *astral.*
Energy-grid: A method of *feng shui* analysis based on precise bearings.
Feng Shui: Literally translated as 'wind and water' is a methodology for assessing the qualities of a site or building and its effects on the occupants.
Four Pillars of Fate: Also called *'eight characters.'* A method of fortune analysis that is based on combinations of the *ten heavenly stems* and the *twelve earthly branches.* One stem and one branch each being assigned to the year, month, day and hour of birth.

Geomancer: A practitioner of Chinese *feng shui,* or of the *geomancy* practiced in the West.
Gua: A term used in *feng shui* to describe segments of the compass.
Horoscopic Signs: The twelve animal signs of the Chinese horoscope, also called *'the twelve earthly branches.'* Each sign covers one year of a twelve-year cycle.
Horoscopic Zones: 15° segments of the compass that correspond to the *twelve earthly branches* (horoscopic signs)
I-Ching: The Chinese classic 'Book of Changes,' comprising 64 hexagrams derived from combinations of the 8 trigrams of the *ba-gua.* It is used in fortune analysis and in advanced methods of *feng shui analysis.*
Karma: Basically, the law of cause and effect.
Karmic Effects: The events and circumstances produced by thoughts and actions.
Lai See: Money given in red envelopes, mainly on Chinese New Year.
Moving Star: A method of *feng shui analysis* using time cycles, and energy grids based on the orientation of a site.
Moving Star - Shien Kong Style: An advanced formula of the *moving star* method of *feng shui* analysis, used mainly by Hong Kong *geomancers.*
P'o: The Earth-bound (lower) soul.
Prana: *Life force, intrinsic energy, chi.*
Sha: Negative or sharp penetrating energy.
Tael: A measure of gold, slightly over one ounce, which is still used in China and Hong Kong.
Three Harmonies: A method of *feng shui* analysis that stresses the compatibilities between certain *earthly branches* (horoscopic signs)
Three Yuen: A method of *feng shui* analysis that includes aspects of the *I-Ching* and the principles of Earth, Heaven and Man.
Tong Shu: Also called the *tong sing*: The Chinese almanac.
Ten Heavenly Stems: The *yin* and *yang* aspects of the *five elements*
Twelve Earthly Branches: – see, *horoscopic signs.*
Tzu Wei: A popular system of Chinese astrology.
Yin and Yang: The law of polarity. The two poles are represented by; *yin,* which is magnetic, negative, dark and female, and *yang,* which is electric, positive, light and male.

Index

Index

BETTER LIVING FENG SHUI SERVICES, Inc.
P.O. box 9249, MSC Mailing Center, 1231 Makati, Metro Manila, Philippines.
tel: 812-4743 & 813-4703 fax: (63-2) 8934793
e-mail: fengshui@surfshop.net.ph